D1562774

Modelling
Complex
Projects

Modelling Complex Projects

Terry Williams

JOHN WILEY & SONS, LTD

Other Wiley Editorial Offices

John Wiley & Sons, Inc., 605 Third Avenue,
New York, NY 10158-0012, USA

WILEY-VCH Verlag GmbH, Pappelallee 3,
D-69469 Weinheim, Germany

John Wiley & Sons Australia, Ltd., 33 Park Road, Milton,
Queensland 4064, Australia

John Wiley & Sons (Asia) Pte, Ltd., 2 Clementi Loop #02-01,
Jin Xing Distripark, Singapore 129809

John Wiley & Sons (Canada), Ltd., 22 Worcester Road,
Rexdale, Ontario M9W 1L1, Canada

British Library Cataloguing in Publication Data

A catalogue record for this book is available from the British Library

ISBN 0-471-89945-3

Typeset in 11/13pt Baskerville MT by Footnote Graphics, Warminster, Wiltshire.
Printed and bound in Great Britain by T. J. International Ltd, Padstow, Cornwall.

This book is printed on acid-free paper responsibly manufactured from sustainable
forestry, in which at least two trees are planted for each one used for paper production.

Contents

1 This book

Introduction to the book and the author

This book is about how to model the behaviour of complex projects. It isn't about how to manage projects—although you'll be expected to know the basics of project management—and reading this won't make you into a better project manager. This book is written for analysts and workers in project management who find themselves needing to model how a project behaves. This could be at any point in the project life-cycle—from feasibility studies before the project proper begins (when the modeller might be helping to advise and inform senior management about project strategies and risks) to project post-mortems after the project is completed (when the modeller might be helping a project team understand what happened in the project to learn lessons for the next project, or might be involved in preparing legal claims) and, of course, all points in between. The modeller can be fulfilling any of a number of roles: independent auditor, advisor to a project manager, part of a project support office, expert witness for a legal claim, consultant to a project client, and so on.

The book doesn't offer one particular point of view or technique. It collects together techniques that have been found useful by the author in his practice as a project modeller over the past 15 years. So perhaps a brief introduction to that experience would be useful here. The author is an operational researcher ("OR"-er) at heart, starting his career with a few years' lecturing in OR. He then moved to work in OR in an engineering and naval consultancy. There he quickly became interested in modelling some of the big defence projects, particularly looking at their risk before the projects began, and developing prototype project risk analysis computer tools. This field of work was given added emphasis at the time as there were political moves to pass risk from government to private industry—so, for example, industry had to be sure that it was not taking on too much risk, while government had to be satisfied that it wasn't being charged too much in terms of risk premium for having risk taken away from it. But the work was at that point given a particular incentive by the mandating of formal project risk analysis and management by the Ministry of Defence (MoD)'s Chief Scientific Adviser (CSA, in MoD jargon—he has a crucial role on MoD's Equipment Acquisition Committee). This was largely a consequence of the Nimrod project, a story which is well told by Humphries (1989), then Assistant CSA. But as well as pre-project risk analysis, the author was also involved in mid-project reviews, then, when the consultancy was taken over by a major defence contractor, acted as risk manager on major multi-company defence contracts. After nine years with this company, the author rejoined Strathclyde University's internationally known Department of Management Science, to research and carry out independent consultancy in project modelling and risk analysis (and also in his spare time to look after an MSc class in OR!). There he immediately got involved in the other end of project modelling: post-project claims for litigation. His first project was the building of the wagons for *Le Shuttle* in the Channel Tunnel (described in more detail in the list of projects below): a project which had significantly overspent for reasons which were at that point not particularly clear, and difficult to prove were the fault of the project client. A team led by Professor Colin Eden, with Dr Fran Ackermann (both well-known in eliciting information from groups and analysing the structure of causality to gain understanding of the dynamics in "messy" situations) and the author, built up models and evaluated the extent to which the overspend and time overrun was due to "disruption and delay" caused by the project client. This supported a large claim to this project client. This work has led to work on other disruption and delay claims by the same team (later joined by Susan Howick), and some of these will be referred to in this book. It also led to research and teaching within the manufacturer to learn lessons from the project. Carrying out project post-mortems is a very good source of knowledge and experience to help carry out risk analysis and risk monitoring—it is surprising how often, in practice, risk analysis is carried out by "risk analysts" while post-mortems are carried out by claims consultants, with little communication between them, instead of each being informed by the other.

Coming back to this book, as an introduction we'll look at why the book has been written, and why the subject is becoming of increasing importance; then the structure of the book will be briefly described and, finally, you will find out what you need to know about already to be able to read this book.

Why is there a need for this book?

In the next chapter, we'll describe what we mean by a "project" for the purposes of this book. Taking for now the common usage of the word, projects have always been important in the development of the environment in which the human race lives. This is true in two common senses of the word "project"–construction projects with a tangible output (the Pyramids; Stonehenge; the Great Wall of China) and projects which bring about a change in the organisation of society (the biblical bringing the Israelites out of Egypt, claimed by Martin Barnes as the first recorded major project; Columbus' setting out and discovering America). While it is true that society has always tried to improve incrementally the way it operates and produces goods, projects have through history formed the major stepping stones for step-changes. This continues to be true today, and indeed projects are becoming more important to industrial life. The preface to Turner (1993) extrapolates from statements by British Telecom to suggest that the annual spend on projects in the UK would be around £250mn.

A whole field of endeavour has therefore arisen to try to manage projects better. "Project management" had its origins in the chemical industry as far back as the 1930s, but really became well-defined and developed in the 1950s: the key point at which it became a discipline in its own right was in the Atlas and Polaris programmes. Gradually, methods were formulated and codified. Professional societies were developed: the US Society became the Project Management Institute (PMI); European nations' national societies joined in a society initially called "Internet" then later (as something else with this name became widespread!) this was renamed the International Project Management Association (IPMA). Degree courses (generally at Masters level) are offered at many universities around the world. PMI also has a widely recognised accreditation scheme, and many IPMA member societies have their own accreditation schemes.

But the nature of projects has been changing in recent years. One change has seen the continued rise of extremely large projects. While we have already mentioned a few giant projects that occurred before the mid-twentieth century, and of course many other major construction projects can be included, such projects are becoming more common. Kharbanda and Pinto (1996), for example, list over 40 projects underway in the mid-1990s in India, China and south-east Asia alone, each forecast to cost over $1bn. These are mainly construction projects, but engineering projects are also becoming larger in some industries as the investment needed to develop new products increases—the break-even point of an aircraft development programme is generally held to be at least 300 units, and the development cost of a new model can approach the sales equivalent of the order of 100 units. But, along with their size, it is generally held that the complexity of projects is also increasing: "Construction projects are invariably complex and since World War II have become progressively more so" (Baccarini 1996). What complexity is, and why it is increasing, is explored in more detail in Chapter 4. But it is worth noting two compounding causes for projects increasing in complexity (from Williams 1995c). The first is that products being developed today are increasingly complex themselves, which leads to more complex projects. The second is that projects have tended to become more time-constrained, and the ability to deliver a project quickly is becoming an increasingly important element in winning a bid; and furthermore, there is an increasing emphasis on tight contracts, using prime contractorship to pass time-risk on to the contractor, frequently with heavy liquidated damages for lateness. Chapter 4 will look further into how this compounds increasing project complexity, and Chapters 8 and 9 will look at how to understand and model this compounding.

The last four decades of project management are characterised according to Laufer *et al.* (1996) by an evolution of models appropriate to changing dominant project characteristics: they characterise the 1960s by scheduling (control), for simple, certain projects; the 1970s by teamwork (integration) and the 1980s for reducing uncertainty (flexibility), both for complex, uncertain projects, and the 1990s by simultaneity (dynamism) for complex, uncertain and quick projects. These latter are precisely the challenges we will face in this book, and it is the increase in such projects that has given rise to the need for models to support the projects, and has led to a need for this book.

> One aspect of the future is obvious: all new undertakings will be accomplished in an increasingly complex technical, economic, political and social environment. Thus project management must learn to deal with a much broader range of issues, requirements and problems in directing their projects to successful conclusions. Certainly, project management in every field will be called upon to address complexities and risks beyond anything experienced in the past (Tuman, 1986).

So how successful have projects been in the past? If we have been successful at bringing projects in, then perhaps new methods aren't needed. Some anecdotal evidence is available: for example, Cleland and King (1988b) cite half a dozen American examples, including Forbes magazine's comments on the US nuclear power programme, and the well-known case of the $8bn Trans-Alaskan Pipeline, of which the State of Alaska claimed that an $1.6bn spend was "imprudent". This evidence is not sufficient to draw firm conclusions. However, there has been a certain amount of work collecting data on historical project out-turns, beginning with work such as Marshall and Meckling (1959), who collected data to try to predict over-runs. Let us look first at four studies done in the late 1980s.

- The key text in summarising the historical evidence, at least up to 1987, is Morris and Hough (1987). They list 33 references containing data-bases of project out-turns, and the reader is strongly recommended to read the beginning of this book to study the conclusions drawn. Morris and Hough's preface to their list of databases states that:

> Curiously, despite the enormous attention project management and analysis have received over the years, the track record of projects is fundamentally poor, particularly for the larger and more difficult ones. Overruns are common. Many projects appear as failures . . . particularly in the public view. Projects are often completed late or over budget, do not perform in the way expected, involve severe strain on participating institutions, or are cancelled prior to their completion after the expenditure of considerable sums of money.

In summarising their database, they state that, "There are hardly any reports showing underruns. . . . In all the other cases, representing some 3500 projects drawn from all over the world in several different indus-tries, overruns are the norm, being typically between 40 and 200 per cent, although greater percentage overruns are found in a number of groupings, particularly certain defence projects and in the US nuclear industry." (This last figure relates to cost overruns.)

It should be noted, however, that Morris and Hough also give a number of caveats to their cost overruns which are worth considering, as we will need to bear these in mind when we look at our example projects in the next section. First, some of the "overruns" relate to customer-requested changes. Some of these are simply increased order quantities (indicating a successful rather than an unsuccessful project). Regulatory changes, such as in the US nuclear industry, causing "a substantial proportion of the cost growth in this industry", are also included in this category. However, this is perhaps too simplistic—for semi-public or mixed private/public projects, which increasingly make up mega-projects, regulation changes are possibly the major risk, and will feature in the discussion of systemic effects in Chapers 8 and 9. The second most important caveat is the treatment of escalation. Many government projects specifically exclude any allowance for inflation in the tender price, and escalate payments in accordance with some accepted index;

an example quoted in Morris and Hough is that the "Central Electricity Generating Board (CEGB) discounts all costs back to the project's budget base dates. This makes comparison of overruns on UK nuclear power plants with those experienced by the US nuclear plants, for example, almost impossible to make accurately—US plant costs include not only inflation but generally the finance charges for funds used during construction". Third, the treatment of contingencies differs from datum to datum: quoting again, "The Apollo programme, for example, came in at $21 billion, only $1 billion over its original estimate. Few know that the initial estimate included $8 billion of contingencies . . . Very few public projects have even semiformal contingency budgets". Finally, of course, cost- and time- out-turns are not the only measures of project success, a subject which will be considered further in Chapter 2.

- A major study carried out since Morris and Hough is Merrow (1988). This is an analysis carried out with RAND on a database of 52 projects, all worth over $500mn. Analysis showed that many projects met their time-target—the average slippage was 17%—but there was a clear overrun on cost—the average overspend was 88%, although the caveats made by Morris and Hough must be made here, since it is not clear what the original budgets contained for the projects. The main problem causing overrun was again found to be regulatory problems, and we will revisit this question of regulatory problems later in the book, in particular, in the naval ship life extension example in Chapters 7–9.

- One database quoted by Morris and Hough that is perhaps worth mentioning, as it has in the past been an important source of world data, is the World Bank Tenth Annual review of project performance audit results (World Bank 1985). The results show a gradual decline over time in performance, with cost overruns shown up to 560%, cost often being contained at the expense of scope (although their overrun figure includes inflation (see discussion above) and the effects of the oil crisis); time overruns average 61%.

- In the UK, one of the key clients for large and complex projects is the Ministry of Defence (MoD). The MoD's key auditors on expenditure are the National Audit Office, whose report on the control and management of the development of major equipments (National Audit Office 1986) examined 12 projects, and found real increases of almost £1bn (91%) after the project staff requirement was approved. In the US, a survey of 246 US army programmes by Arbogast and Womer (1988) showed cost overruns of −21% to +437% (mean 15%) and time overruns of −8 to +74 weeks (mean 7 weeks).

Studies done in the 1990s have generally found similar results, although with less easily quoted statistics. Most collections have been to study particular aspects of overruns (e.g. Chan and Kumaraswamy, (1997), which analyses varying causes of overruns in construction projects). The inescapable conclusion is that our history over the past few decades of managing projects is not particularly good, and many of the example projects described in the next section will show this.

Furthermore, this book will outline why the changes in project characteristics described above imply that classical ways of analysing projects within the canon of project management, which are based on breaking down a project into its consituent parts, are becoming less appropriate for modern projects. This book explains where the use of modelling can help to estimate, monitor, control and analyse projects, and thus help their successful implementation—for any project, but especially for today's large, complex, uncertain and fast projects.

The structure of this book

The title of this book is *Modelling Complex Projects*; so the book begins with three chapters that take each of these three words and deconstruct them.

- Chapter 2 discusses what a *project* is, and the type of projects we will be discussing here, giving references and thumbnail sketches for the case studies.
- Then Chapter 3 discusses what we mean by *modelling*: Why do we model? What is modelling? How does modelling work in practice? How can we validate our models?
- Chapter 4 moves on to the adjective *complex*, and discusses what constitutes project complexity, and what it is that makes a project complex.

While these might appear at first glance to be simply introductory flannel, they do highlight many of the issues that form the book's *raison d'être*—the reasons behind the inadequacies of classical project management decomposition techniques for complex projects, the types of modelling we will be using, and why, and so on.

The heart of the book concentrates on the models, using the dimensions of complexity outlined in Chapter 4.

- Chapters 5–6 look at individual and discrete probabilistic effects within projects, and the use of simulation to understand how these affect projects. This adds the complexity effects of uncertainty into the models. Chapters 5–6 deal mainly with identifiable physical events; however, there are many "softer" elements that have a major—often crucial—impact on projects. Chapter 7 looks at modelling these effects, including perceptual issues and the role of information flows.
- The effects generated by the elements on Chapters 5–7 are systemic, and can set up portfolio effects, dynamics and feedbacks. Chapter 8 considers these, and discusses both qualitative and quantitative ways of modelling.
- A natural way of modelling the systemic effects of Chapter 8 is by a method known as *System Dynamics* (SD). Chapter 9 looks at how SD can be used to model these effects, and how it demonstrates the compounding of effects so commonly seen in projects (sometimes referred to as "2 + 2 = 5"). Again, questions of data collection and validation are discussed, since it is important that these methods are seen in the context of their use in practice. Chapters 8–9 include the complexity effects defined in Chapter 2 as *structural complexity*.
- We have now looked at probabilistic methods, which analyse the operational level of the project, and at deterministic methods which analyse a project's systemic effects at a more strategic level. Chapter 10 looks into a variety of hybrid and mixed methods to bring together the benefits of these methods, and suggests this as a way forward.

To complete the book, Chapter 11 looks at the role of the modeller. After introducing different roles within project management, the chapter looks at where and how modelling should be used at the start of a project (for example, during estimation and risk analysis), during the execution of a project (monitoring and replanning) and after a project has ended (carrying out post-mortem analysis and claims preparation). It looks briefly at the role of models in programmes of projects, and at where a modeller fits in to the project management team.

Chapter 12 ends the book.

What do I need to know before I read this book?

Since this is a book about modelling projects, it's not surprising that some basic knowledge will be assumed of two areas: projects and modelling.

As far as projects are concerned, you will need to be aware of two areas. First, you will need to be aware of how projects work in general. This would ideally be by personal experience if you really want to relate to the problems this book is trying to address—it is only by personal experience that you can relate to the feel of project life: the suspension of everyday life for a year or two, the working away from home, the gearing of effort to a single temporary end. Failing this, however, Turner (1995) gives a good description of the commercial environment in which projects are undertaken. In particular, you will need to understand the following:

- The idea of *project life-cycles* and *project phases*. Terms used differ between engineering, construction and IT projects, but typically a project might consist of: proposals being formulated and feasibility established in a "feasibility" phase; task identification, initial estimates and plans, and sometimes initial design drawn up in a "definition" or "project definition" (PD) phase; the work carried out in an "execution" or "design and initial production" phase; then (depending on the context) perhaps a "full production" phase, or a "commission" phase; then close-out. In addition, we shall discuss moves towards concurrency (some overlapping of the phases, in particular the design and manufacture phases, to shorten the project duration—see Syan and Menon 1994).
- The idea of the *legal contract as the basis of the project*. Most of the projects discussed (although not all) were carried out for a client or owner (who initiates the project, specifies the requirement, supplies the finance, and owns the final product) by a contractor (who controls the resources to carry out the project, and who executes the project). You should be familiar with the ideas of contract clauses (ideas such as "Force Majeure" might be helpful, too).
- Still in the area of the contract, you should be aware of *penalty clauses* and *liquidated damages* (the costs a contractor must pay if he does not meet all of the project requirements, in particular the due date). You should be aware of the issues behind different contract payment types, such as "Cost Plus", or more properly Cost Plus Percentage Fee, and Cost Plus Fixed Fee; at the other end of the spectrum Firm Fixed Price; and typical positions between the two, such as Cost Plus Incentive Fee, where there is a percentage fee payable, which can vary within set upper and lower limits in accordance with a formula tied to allowable actual costs (with a sharing formula by which costs are shared between the two parties). (For more information, see In't Veld and Peeters 1989).
- *Typical management structures* generated to manage projects, in particular

the idea of *matrix management*. Functional organisational structures (which divide the people in a company into groups of similar specialisation) have problems when faced with large projects. They cannot cope with the dynamic changes and complexities; they do not allow the clear line of authority from a project manager that is a prerequisite for good project management; and they cannot cope with industries where design, procurement and manufacture overlap in time. Therefore, the matrix organisation was developed in the 1980s (see Cleland (1984)'s handbook), where workers have a responsibility both to their functional superior and to the project manager(s). Surveys (such as Larson and Gobelli 1989 and Gray *et al.* 1990) have shown this to be a superior management structure for multi-project-oriented companies, although the mid-1990s has seen a move towards flatter structures, and the impact this will have on project management is not yet clear.

As well as being aware of how projects work in general, you will be expected to understand the basic tools and techniques of project management. A summary of all of these elements from a US viewpoint is given in the Project Management Institute's *Project Management Book of Knowledge*, or "PMBOK". A good project management textbook will describe the basics. There are lots of good textbooks: Lock (1994) is a good overall handbook; Cleland and King provide an excellent handbook for engineering projects; the American Management Association also have their own handbook (Dinsmore 1993); and my favourite, and a book which has become a recognised classic, is Turner (1993), which describes management by projects in a generic way. Many of these techniques are based on the idea of decomposing the project into its constituent parts in an orderly, structured way. You should be familiar with:

- How the scope of work is defined, decomposed and controlled, in particular the ideas of *specifications*, the *Work Breakdown Structure (WBS)* and *configuration control*.
- How time is defined, decomposed and controlled, in particular the ideas of network scheduling (the use of activity-on-the-node and activity-on-the-arrow networks, also called Critical Path Method, or CPM, and developed into the Project Evaluation and Review Technique, or PERT) and the use of *Gantt charts*.
- How costs are defined, decomposed and controlled, in particular the ideas of *cost-breakdown structures* (more advanced readers will be aware of how estimates are built up from the cost-control cube, which relates the WBS, Organisational Breakdown Structure and Cost Breakdown

Structure, as in *C/SCSC*) and *earned-value analysis* (analysing budgeted, committed, incurred and forecast costs).

- How *project estimates* are drawn up: Turner, (1995), for example, lists methods including step-counting, exponential and parametric methods, elemental, empirical and bill-of-quantity methods and (for the IT industry) analogy, top-down and bottom-up, COCOMO-type (COn-structive COst MOdel) models, and function-point analysis.

Finally, you will need some basic mathematical modelling skills—the books referenced in Chapter 3 give some useful background here. You will need to be familiar with using equations to represent real situations, basic probability and the use of simulation; and later chapters will introduce the technique of System Dynamics, for which references will be given. But you won't really need any ideas more advanced than the idea of statistical "correlation". Key here, though, is a sympathy with the idea of building a mathematical or analytical model of a real situation and interrogating the model to learn about the real world.

Conclusion

No more needs to be said, other than I trust that you will join me on this journey. I have found that the modelling of projects both gives me excitement and makes a real contribution to the projects in which I've been involved—I hope you do too!

2 Projects

What is a project?

Most of the standard textbooks on project management begin by agonising over this question, and we don't want to labour the issues in this book. But so that we know what we're talking about, we should try to define what we mean by a "project" for the purposes of this book—and also what types of project we'll be dealing with, as projects come in all shapes and sizes. In this chapter, we'll make four points about what a project is, and discuss project objectives, give a brief reminder of the basic project management techniques, then describe the projects that will come up as examples in the book.

First, a typical definition is as stated (for example) by Buchanan and Boddy (1992): "A project is a unique venture with a beginning and an end, conducted by people to meet established goals with parameters of cost, schedule and quality." This captures most of the essential qualities of a project, and most definitions refer to this combination of uniqueness, defined objectives, limited time-cycle and three-fold constraints (cost, time, quality).

In trying to capture the essence of what it means to work in a project-oriented environment, most authors contrast this environment with one that is operations-oriented. In particular, Turner (1993), in his classic, *The Handbook of Project-based Management*, concludes that the difference between these environments is that projects are unique undertakings, which implies that they:

- are one-off, not repetitive;
- are time-limited;
- bring about revolutionary (as opposed to evolutionary) improvements; and
- therefore create a state of disequilibrium, so the project manager must disrupt the status quo (as opposed to balancing conflicting requirements to maintain equilibrium);

- use transient or novel teams of people;
- to some extent always start without precedent;
- are goal-oriented;
- are risky, because a project starts from limited experience.

Those readers who have worked in a project environment will relate to most, or maybe all, of these points.

Second, we need to say that this book will only be concerned with individual projects, not with programmes of projects. A whole field of study has developed over recent years in programme management; Geoff Reiss, an expert in the field, gives four common definitions of a programme, namely:

- a collection of many projects within the one organisation, using common resources but with no common objective;
- a mega-project (such as a space project);
- many projects being carried out by an organisation for one client;
- a collection of many projects within an organisation, which are specifically designed to change the organisation itself.

(Extracted from Williams 1997a).

It is only the second of these definitions that can be considered a project within the meaning of this present book: the other three categories are not individual projects and, indeed, often have quite different characteristics from a "project".

Third, we'll be dealing with large or complex projects—but both of the adjectives "large" and "complex" are rather difficult to define. If a definition of "large" is needed, some authors try to put a lower limit on cash value to define a "large" or "mega" project: Merrow (1988), for example, defines mega-projects as those worth $1bn or over (in 1988 terms) and "big projects" as those worth $0.5–1bn, although there are clear problems with this (for example, a project with a great deal of manpower might be much "larger" in organisational terms than one with very few workers but which is very expensive in materials). And what "project complexity" means is an even more difficult question to answer than what a "large project " is: we'll discuss this in detail in Chapter 4. Morris and Hough (1987) somewhat tautologously define major projects as "those which are particularly demanding either because of their size, complexity, schedule urgency or demand on existing resources or know-how." One characteristic of a major project it is perhaps worth noting is the risk involved: Fraser (1984) says that "normal" projects have the characteristics (among others) that "risk assessment can follow well established procedures as all risks are visible", "there are no catastrophic risks", "the scale of individual risks is small compared with the size of the parties involved and therefore there is no completion problem", but that "none of these characteristics is true of the largest projects": "in general, beyond a certain size, the risks of projects increase exponentially and this can either be appreciated at the beginning or discovered at the end."

Certainly, we'll be dealing with projects large and complex enough that a project manager cannot understand them simply by using his brain and the standard project management tools alone (those mentioned in Chapter 1, including ideas such as Work Breakdown Structures and PERT/CPM). In the section "Projects referred to in this book" below, we'll look briefly at around 20 projects discussed in this book, which will give an idea of the sort of size and complexity of project we'll be concentrating on.

Finally, projects come in a variety of domains. Lock (1994) defines "three broad categories of projects . . . each with its own characteristics and demands upon project management methods":

1. Manufacturing projects.
2. Civil engineering, construction, petrochemical, mining and other projects requiring external organisation.
3. Management projects: this would include management of change, R&D (research and development) projects and IT (information technology) systems projects.

We will be looking at projects with a tangible "product" or output, which come in the first two categories above, such as (1) designing and building wagons for a train, or (2) designing and developing a metro system. IT systems projects, which have an identifiable output but one which is not tangible, will be discussed (and a few case studies investigated), and most of the techniques discussed here are applicable to them (although we'll need to remember that IT systems projects have their own very specific characteristics). We won't discuss projects in (3) which don't have a tangible output, although many of the techniques may still be applicable.

What are project objectives?

We're going to build models in order to evaluate what is *going to* happen (or what *is* happening, or to understand *what has* happened) to our project. This means that we will be looking at various conditions and their effects on the project *outcome*. We need to consider first, then, what we mean by project "outcome". What will we be measuring? What aspects of the project outcome are we interested in? This is a question not only for modellers, but also for management. It is a fundamental tenet of project management that the objectives of a project must be defined (Knoepfel 1990), and the project managed towards achieving those objectives (Turner *et al*. 1988). The first step in any risk management (as defined in the *PRAM Guide*, Simon, Hillson and Newland 1997) is to "define the project", and the first words of the section describing this step are "Any project to which PRAM [Project Risk Analysis and Management] is to be applied should have well defined objectives". So what are these project objectives, by which project "success" and "failure" are judged, and how can we measure them in our models?

Steiner, in his book *Top Management Planning*, defined a project as "an organisation of people dedicated to a specific purpose or objective. Projects generally involve large, expensive, unique or high-risk undertaking which have to be completed by a certain date, for a certain amount of money, within some expected level of performance". These three criteria of success—meeting cost, schedule and performance targets—have become widely used as the standard success criteria, and are generally deemed to catch the essential task of the project manager. Barnes (1988) (with particular reference to construction projects) states that "the client's objectives are *always* [my emphasis] a combination of the objectives for performance of the completed scheme, for achieving this performance within a named cost or budgetary limit and for getting the project into use by a target date".

The three criteria also catch the essential trade-offs that the project manager must make: working toward achieving one of the objectives is usually detrimental to the other two. Kohrs and Welngarten (1986) report seeing a sign: "Good! Fast! Cheap! Pick any two"—it is often the case that two of the objectives can be achieved easily if it were assumed that the third criterion was of no interest at all: a project can be completed well and quickly given an infinite sum of money, or the project could easily be completed quickly, cheaply and very shoddily (and so on).

But the three criteria of success are carefully written above *not* simply as "on time, on budget and on spec" but as "meeting cost, schedule and performance targets". These targets are not simple one-dimensional measures. Instead,

- We want to know whether we have achieved interim milestones and the final project completion date;
- We want to know not only whether the overall project cost is within budget, but also the cash-flow (Turner 1995), often the unit cost of the

final product, and frequently (with schemes such as Build-Operate-Transfer) the Life-Cycle-Cost of the final product.

- We will also in general have a whole series of performance targets to meet, some of which will be more important that others, some of which will be more easily achieved than others; some will be essential for client acceptance, some will have liquidated damages attached, and so on.

However, many authors feel that defining success is not as easy as even this modified three-fold criterion suggests. Indeed, the Project Management Institute in USA dedicated a whole conference to the definition and measurement of success (Project Management Institute 1986). De Wit (1986), for example, discusses two elements:

1. Priorities of project objectives will change between project phases. At its most simplistic, Avots (1984) suggests that schedule is most important early in the project, while during the project cost becomes most important, and after the project, only technical performance is remembered. Certainly a jaundiced view of projects sees a great deal of activity around the project network in the planning stage, then during the project, cost control becomes a much more dominating feature so that no one can spend more than his section of the project's budget—but long after a project is complete, we remember the physical outcome, not the project performance (everyone admires Concorde—but how many now remember the overruns or overspends?).
2. There are often a lot of stakeholders with different objectives seeking success. Salapatas and Sawle (1986) define success to have been achieved only when three groups perceive success: the client (from the viewpoint of performance, budget and reputation), the builder [or contractor] (from the viewpoint of profitability, reputation, client and public satisfaction) and the public (from the viewpoint of environment, reliability, cost, and perhaps safety). Baker *et al.* (1988) require satisfaction from the parent [sponsor], the client, the users/clientele and the project team itself in order to say the project has been "successful".

A third element encountered in fields such as information systems (IS) is that often the project objectives themselves change during the project as alternatives are shown to be more supportive of the overall organisation's strategic objectives. Willcocks and Margetts (1993) study a number of such projects, and conclude that we need "to extend the assessment of risk by focussing on broader possible desirable outcomes than those most often encountered, that is, limited assessments of risk against 'in time, within budget, to acceptable standards' type criteria." This is of course particularly so when those objectives are initially ill-defined—one of the elements of the definition of the complex project, as we shall discuss in Chapter 4.

And of course there are much wider issues than the three criteria listed above. Morris (1989), for example, includes the technical and commercial definition of a project, and the consideration of strategic and external factors.

In conclusion, then, we must therefore be careful at the start of our modelling to:

- define the project objectives
- understand the breadth of the definition of these objectives
- recognise the possibility of these objectives changing during the project
- establish measures of achievement of the objectives
- identify the relative importance of the objectives, both subjective and in terms of penalties for shortfalls, (and recognise the possibility of changes during the project)
- evaluate trade-offs between the objectives.

Basic project management techniques

We said in Chapter 1 that we need background knowledge of the basic project management tools, including how to define, decompose and control the scope of work, the timescale of the project, the cost, and the risk involved. We will summarise briefly the first three of these here—the last will be left until Chapter 5, as we need to discuss issues of uncertainty and probability first. But the key to all of these techniques is the ability to decompose the project in a structured way, into manageable sub-sections which together encompass all the content of the project. This idea has been the key to the success of project management—but paradoxically also, as we shall see in Chapters 8 onwards, a significant hindrance to the effective modelling of complex projects.

Managing scope

The key to managing scope is the *Work Breakdown Structure (WBS)*. This breaks down the work of a project into a hierarchical structure of elements, in order to manage and control the scope. This allows good definition of the

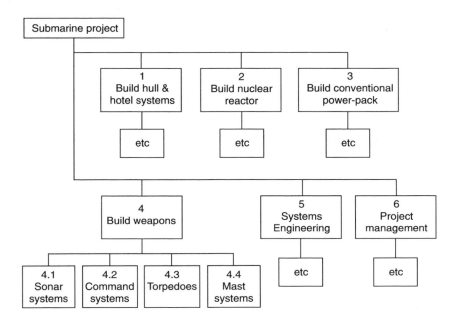

Figure 2.1—A typical Work Breakdown Structure

work, and allows discrete, coherent packages of work to be estimated and then delegated. A typical example might be Figure 2.1, which shows the WBS for the construction of a nuclear submarine.

The hierarchical structure of the WBS facilitates the hierarchical division of responsibility within the project. In fact, responsibility is often defined simply by the WBS, although it is better to use the ideas of the cost-control cube in C/SCSC, discussed below.

The second key technique for managing scope is the *Milestone Plan* (Turner 1993). Indeed, Goal-Directed Project Management treats this as the key technique for project management with (Andersen et al 1987). As well as defining the work packages—in parallel with or even before defining the work packages—the deliverables or milestones must be defined. As well as giving a tool for managing the project at a strategic level, this ensures that the focus of management is not on carrying out the work but on achieving the purposes of the project. A very brief milestone plan for the above submarine project might look something like Figure 2.2.

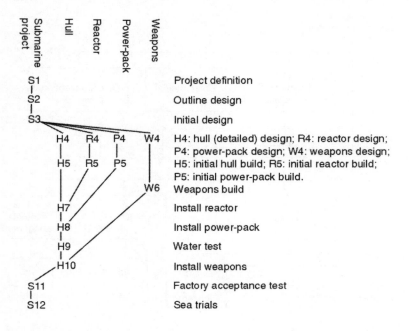

Figure 2.2—A milestone plan

Managing cost

When cost estimates are drawn up, it is common to use a breakdown structure not unlike the WBS, a *Cost Breakdown Structure (CBS)*. Where the organisational structure of the project is also broken down using an *Organisational Breakdown Structure (OBS)* this gives a three-dimensional matrix (WBS x OBS x CBS) known as the cost-control cube, as shown in Figure 2.3.

Here, each cost item can be assigned to a cell of the cube, and thus given a place in each of the three breakdown categories, allowing aggregation to any level in any of the three dimensions. This is the basis of the US DoD methodology known as C/SCSC (or C/SPEC) (discussed further in Farld and Karshenas 1986).

The cost breakdown, as well as providing an initial estimate of project cost, can also be used to track spend against time and progress, assuming that activities have been scheduled into a base time-plan, a topic we'll come to shortly. This tracking uses the ideas of *Earned Value Analysis* in which, at any point in time, a certain amount of each WBS item has been performed, at a certain cost. Then,

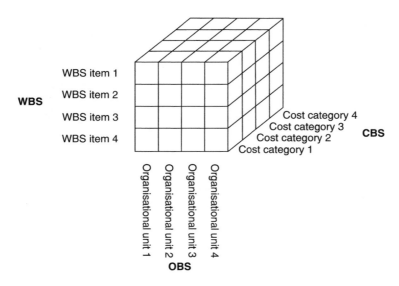

Figure 2.3—Cost-control cube

- the total Budgeted Cost for the Work actually Performed so far is denoted by BCWP;
- similarly, the total Actual Cost for the Work actually Performed so far is denoted by ACWP.

The cost variance is then BCWP − ACWP, and this is sometimes scaled up to give an expected cost to completion (e.g., and at its most trivial, TotalBudget × ACWP/BCWP). When you also compare the work done against the planned schedule,

- the Budgeted Cost for the Work Scheduled (to date) is denoted by BCWS.

This then gives us the schedule slippage, as BCWP − BCWS. Perhaps more usefully, it allows Earned Value progress curves to be drawn to plot the course of the project, as shown in Figure 2.4. In this project, by the end of September it was forecast that we would have spent around 69% of the project budget, whereas we have actually spent around 77%. However, it can be seen that the performance of this project has gradually decayed, and in fact BCWP is 63% of the original budget (that is, work is costing 122% of what was budgeted), and a comparison of the BCWP and BCWS lines shows that we are almost one month behind schedule (in this global, cost-oriented, view).

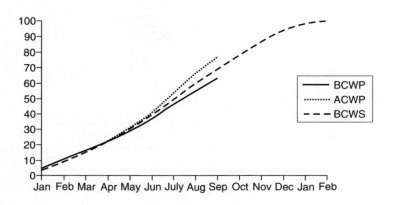

Figure 2.4—An Earned Value Curve

Managing time

It is assumed that the reader is familiar with the concepts of project networks, both activity-on-the-node and activity-on-the arrow networks; this is also called Critical Path Method (CPM), which was then developed into the Project Evaluation and Review Technique (PERT) in 1958 for the US Polaris programme (reported in Malcolm *et al.* 1959). Activity-on-the-node networks represent activities as arrows between nodes, which denote points in time (dotted lines denote "dummies" which have no concrete equivalent but are necessary to represent the logical precedence require-ments) (Figure 2.5).

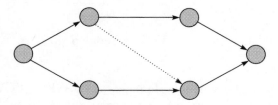

Figure 2.5—Activity-on-the-arrow

Activity-on-the-node networks use nodes to represent activities, while lines between them denote logical relationships. These are more flexible, as they can denote, as well as start-start relationships, start-start, end-end and start-end relationships, and summary and hammock (Lockyer and Gordon 1991) activities can be easily incorporated (Figure 2.6).

These networks can be analysed very easily to find (ignoring any

Figure 2.6—Activity-on-the-node

resource constraints) the minimum duration for the project, and thence the critical path. When resources are taken into consideration, there are well-known heuristics for resource smoothing and levelling. Such calculations are detailed in any basic project management textbook, such as Lockyer and Gordon. There are very sophisticated algorithms for dealing with resource smoothing and levelling, including the effects of incorporating uncertainty in the calculations; these are very specific and in the author's experience rarely used in practice; these methods and their extensions will not therefore be discussed in this book.

A structured approach

Obviously, these techniques should not be used in isolation. Or, at least, this seems obvious, although in practice it seems that sometimes the techniques are started off and run for their own sake, reminiscent of a Kafkaesque bureaucracy. In fact, as we said at the start of this section, the key is to be goal-directed, to work towards the purpose of the project. Modern project management best practice is epitomised by Turner (1993), who describes managing project scope, cost and time as well as organisation and quality through three levels (integrative—where the project is integrated into the business and its environment—strategic, and tactical), merging the techniques together as described in his book. We will return to this in Chapter 11.

Projects referred to in this book

The discussions in the book will refer to a number of real-life projects. Some will be studied in detail, as models used can be described fully; others will only be touched upon as examples of situations where models could be used. Some can be discussed in detail, as they are in the public domain, while some are confidential so can only be referred to tangentially. But to help you keep track of which project is being discussed, and to study these projects further, this section gives a thumbnail sketch of each project and some references.

There are a number of good books available which can act as source material for the stories behind major projects. Probably the best-known of these, and the ground-breaker in the field, is *The Anatomy of Major Projects* by Morris and Hough (1987). This describes the results of a long and intensive study into eight projects by the Major Projects Association at Templeton College, Oxford, UK, and the lessons that can be learned about the management of major projects. A second book, perhaps slightly more accessible to the lay reader, is *What Made Gertie Gallop* by Kharbanda and Pinto (1996). This describes 13 well-known projects (one of which is the Tacoma Narrow Suspension Bridge, the dramatic collapse of which in 1940 was captured on film—the violent movements of the bridge caused it to be dubbed "Galloping Gertie", hence the book's title). This book again takes each project in turn and extracts a series of "how not to" rules for successfully managing projects.

Of the projects described in these two books which will be referred to here, are the following four.

Concorde is described by Morris and Hough and, much more briefly, by Kharbanda and Pinto. The story of Concorde is well known. It was a joint venture between the British Aircraft Corporation (BAC) and Sud Aviation in France, supported by the two governments. The first estimate for the development of the plane, in 1959, was below £100mn, and this was later re-evaluated in 1962 to £150–170mn. The original agreement, in 1962, was for a seven-year project (to the achievement of the Airworthiness Certificate), based on an initial budgeted cost for development of £135mn. An initial production run of 100 planes was envisaged. The course of the project saw the election of a new UK government facing a large balance of payments deficit, which led to largely unsuccessful attempts to scale down the project. A number of technical difficulties were met and overcome, and the first flights eventually took place in 1969; the Airworthiness Certificate was finally achieved in 1975. Only nine planes in all were sold. By 1979, when the plane was in regular service, the development cost had grown to over £1.1bn, seven times the 1962 estimate; almost half of this increase was due to inflation, with a further 10% of the increase due to exchange devaluation; however, over 40% of the increase was due to design changes, underestimation and delays.

The Channel Tunnel is described by Kharbanda and Pinto, but with further useful information in a third book, *Beyond 2000: a Source Book for*

Major Projects, from the Major Projects Association at Oxford University (Major Projects Association, 1992). The Channel Tunnel project is one of the largest civil engineering projects of the past 10 years. The project was carried out by the private sector, with a concession agreement with the two governments concerned, and strict control exercised by the governmental safety authority specially set up for the project (which will be important when we discuss the Channel Tunnel Shuttle Wagons sub-project below). Three tunnels were dug between the UK and France, one service tunnel and two carrying a variety of rolling stock: high-speed passenger trains, goods trains and *Le Shuttle* which transported vehicles from one end of the tunnel to the other. The contractors, TML, a consortium of five French and five UK construction companies, not only had to dig the tunnels, but also design and construct the rail infrastructure, two major terminals and the locomotives and wagons. The initial estimate of project cost in 1987 was £4.8bn (of which, £2bn was administration costs and interest charges), with completion in 1992. In fact, the tunnel costs eventually reached £10bn, saddling the owners, Eurotunnel, with large debt repayments. Furthermore, the Tunnel did not open until late 1994, bringing considerable delay to the inflow of revenue. The combination of these factors initially put the overall long-term viability of the project in some doubt.

The Sydney Opera House is again described by Kharbanda and Pinto and is similarly well-known. The design for the Opera House was an ambitious and innovative, but unproven and very preliminary, design chosen from a global competition attracting 200 entries. The first official government estimate in 1958 put the cost at less than Aus$10mn. However, there were problems with realising the design in practice, and this led to increasing rancour between the architect and the engineers involved. The building was not inaugurated until 1973, and finally cost over Aus$100mn.

The *Calcutta Metro* is also described by Kharbanda and Pinto. This took 23 years to construct, at a cost of around US$5bn (although little happened in the first six years due to funding constraints). There were significant technical and logistical difficulties, including earth removal, the effects on nearby buildings and utilities, flooding, traffic diversion and so on. It is debatable whether the resulting line will cover its losses, but it has enabled a journey which previously took an hour in the overcrowded city to be completed in a quarter of that time.

A fourth source book for case studies of large projects is the Project Management Institute (PMI)'s *Project Management Casebook*, edited by Cleland *et al.* (1998). This book consists of a series of articles and symposia papers drawn from PMI's literature, each of which describe a project with particular lessons for project managers, and the editors help the learning process along by supplying a few questions at the end of each case to guide the reader's thinking into the right areas. Among the projects described, the following two will be referred to later.

In late 1993, Sydney, Australia, was awarded the right to host the *2000 Olympic Games*. There were a number of facilities to construct (mostly as part of a major redevelopment programme in Sydney), and infrastructure development went on locally in parallel to support the Games. These were the responsibility of the government, while a body set up by legislation, SOCOG (Sydney Organizing Committee for the Olympic Games), was responsible for the organisation of the events, with a budget of almost Aus\$2bn. Clearly this was a strictly time-limited project, with no overrun permissable into the period of the Games.

Kuwait Oil Field Reconstruction: Kuwait was liberated in early 1991 following the Gulf War, but damage had been caused to 750 oil wells, 26 gathering/production centres, two marine export facilities, a great deal of crude oil storage tankage, three refineries, and communications. Clearly, rebuilding these facilities, in an execution timescale of around 27 months, was a major operation, particularly as the original design material had been destroyed during the war. Around five million man-hours were required for engineering, project management and construction management, half a million tons of material was imported, and over 50 million hours of field labour used.

Chapter 1 discussed work done by the author, mainly as part of a team led by Professor Colin Eden and with Dr Fran Ackermann, building models to support delay and disruption litigation claims in major projects. Four of these claims will be mentioned in the book.

The Shuttle Wagons. As discussed above, a major claim concerned the shuttle wagons for the Channel Tunnel, discussed in detail in Williams *et al.* (1995 and 1995b) and Ackermann *et al.* (1997). Eurotunnel had contracted a consortium TML to build the Channel Tunnel, and TML had sub-contracted a consortium of rolling-stock manufacturers ESCW (to anglicise, the EuroShuttle Wagon Consortium) to build the shuttle wagons, which were constructed in plants in Canada, France and Belgium (roughly 100 single-decker wagons and 100 double-decker wagons). A number of aspects of the design, construction and operation of the Channel Tunnel required approval from the Intergovernmental Commission (IGC), a body of British and French civil servants (see Major Projects Association 1992). Design changes required by the IGC caused delays, and work had to proceed prior to gaining IGC approval, with subsequent changes and rework when IGC decisions turned out not to be favourable. In addition, the manufacturers claimed, there were significant delays in the client approving design documentation and requests for "gold-plating". This all led to a major overspend (according to Major Projects Association (1992), the cost of the total rolling stock—which included not only the shuttle wagons but also locomotives and HGV-carrying wagons—rose from £245mn to £583mn between 1987 and 1990). It also caused a significant delay in delivery, despite the manufacturer's efforts to accelerate the project. Although this all seems clear now, the reasoning behind the situation appeared much more "messy" at the time, and the analyst team was brought in first to determine the reasons for the delay and disruption caused to the project, and demonstrate causality and, second, to quantify it with an auditable model to form the basis for a legal claim.

Naval ship life extension. This was a much smaller piece of work: to carry out a high-level study and provide an initial estimate of delay and disruption and an indication of its causality, as described in Williams (1997c). The project was the life extension of an old naval support ship, involving the insertion of an additional mid-section and a complete refit. A design office was subcontracted for design services, and the work on the basic drawings was scheduled to take place over nine months in 1994/5. The contract required compliance with the regulations in force at the date of signature; however, in October 1994, 92 SOLAS (Safety Of Life At Sea) new safety regulations were ratified (Payne 1994), and shortly afterwards the Ministry of Defence decided that this ship would be subject to those regulations. These changes, coming mid-design, with the ship in dry dock (so any timescale slippage was very expensive) caused the basic design work to rise to roughly three times the man-hours that had been budgeted.

Construction project X. A project which at the time of writing is still the subject of litigation was a major construction project, with a timescale dictated by governmental environmental regulations, built under a fixed-price Equipment Procurement and Construction contract. It was the contention of the contractors that the clients had interfered with and delayed the design process, required numerous additions to the scope of work, and required a lot of studies beyond the requirement of the contract, and this had pushed the total spend up by some 40%. Particular problems here were, first, that the construction was delayed so that work had to be done in winter in an extremely cold environment; second, the acceleration caused overcrowding on the site and, third, there was considerable re-design as construction either failed commissioning or was changed by the client very late in the design process. Again, the role of the analysts was to prepare a litigation case ready for court, acting under a firm of lawyers.

Engineering project Y. A fourth claim, on which the author spent only a little time, looked at a project making large parts for the aerospace industry. The client made two important changes very late in the design process, the first changing the material out of which the parts (for half of the contract) were to be made, the second changing the aerodynamic lines of the parts very slightly—which caused the parts now to be left- or right-handed. As well as delay and disruption in design, both here and in the shuttle wagons claim, the understanding of manufacturing learning curves became relevant. Again, design and manufacture costs ended up much higher than originally forecast.

A number of projects whose details can be found in the public domain will also be mentioned in the course of this book, including the following four:

Montreal Olympics 1976 and *Los Angeles Olympics 1984.* As well as discussing the Sydney Olympics, some of the issues that arose in the preparations for two previous Olympics will be mentioned. The story of the construction of the facilities for the 1976 Montreal Olympics is not unlike that of the Sydney Opera House, with construction beset by problems, particularly associated with constructing a difficult roof-design. Neil (1986) begins his summary thus: "The main stadium was by far the largest and most costly structure. Estimated by Montreal's mayor to cost $40 million in 1970, out of a total estimated complex cost of $120 million, the main stadium eventually cost in excess of $836 million and the total price exceeded $1.5 billion." Construction continued until the very beginning of the games.

The Los Angeles games, by contrast, had few construction problems, as many existing facilities were used, and large venues requiring construction, such as a swimming pool and a velodrome, were built well in advance. The Games were the first to be organised by a private body and financed entirely by private money. The Games made a profit of $225mn, and opened on time (and it was claimed that they were viewed by more than two billion people worldwide). The period from start of bidding in 1977 to the Games itself (1984) represents a large and complex project that is therefore worthy of study. (Details in the public domain can be found, for example, in Amateur Athletic Federation of Los Angeles 1985).

The *London Ambulance Service* despatch automation project had very well-publicised problems. The requirements-definition phase of the project began in late 1990 for a system consisting of computer-aided despatch, a computer-map display, and an Automatic Vehicle Location System. Implementation was required in January 1992, and there was a budget of £1.5mn. There were considerable problems during the development—in particular, use of an inexperienced software contractor who had bid well below other bidders. A partial implementation was eventually carried out, which was partially successful. However, when the system went fully live in

October 1992, response times started to slow, then a week later the system locked up completely, and fallback to the standby system did not work—both of these problems were later found to be due to very minor programming errors (but of course they had major impacts). Full details of the post-mortem of the project are given in HMSO (1993).

KDCOM project. This was another IT project, which will be of interest in this book not so much for the project itself but because new modelling methods were used during the project. The project was to develop a Command and Control Fire Control System for the Korean Destroyer, undertaken by a UK prime contractor and several subcontractors in Europe and Korea. Analysis of the project, and the new techniques, was done by Alexander Rodrigues, and it is described in Rodrigues and Williams (1998).

As well as these projects, two other sets of projects will be referred to:

- Abdel-Hamid and Madnick (1991) describe a number of cases in their book *Software Project Dynamics*, in particular a NASA project called DE-A.
- A number of projects will be mentioned from the author's experience in the defence domain, but will not be named, nor will identifiable details be given.

Conclusion

So these are the types of projects we'll be looking at in this book. One or two of the examples above are projects we'll use simply to illustrate ideas. Most, though, fall within the definition of the target of this book—the "complex" project. So let's have a look in the next chapter at what we mean by "complex".

3   Modelling

We said that this book is about *how to model complex projects*. Chapter 2 looked at what was meant by *projects*. Chapter 4 will go on to discuss what it is about a project that means we can call it *complex*. Before we go on to model complex projects, we need to think about what is meant by to *model*. There are obviously various meanings of the word "model", and we need to define which meaning of the word we're using in this book. It is then important to discuss what we're actually doing when we model, and ensure that we've addressed the fundamental generic questions about models, before we go on to try modelling our specific interest—the behaviour of projects.

So this chapter starts by looking at what we want to model—what outputs are we interested in when we model? Then the chapter looks at what we mean by "a model", and "modelling", then considers why we model at all, rather than taking some other approach. The final two sections consider some of the issues involved in modelling in practice, such as, How does the process work? How do we go about validating our models (that is, ensuring that the model is a good representation of reality)?

What is a model?

This book is about constructing models to study the behaviour of projects—but what is a model? There are clearly a number of different meanings. As a young boy I was interested in two types of model: one type was made of plastic and came in the shape of fighter aircraft (made by Airfix) and the other type was made of human flesh and appeared on the television or in the pages of glossy magazines such as *TV Times*! Well, this second type of "model" has quite a different meaning than in this book. The first type of "model"—physical models such as a child's toy car or an architect's model of a planned building—has the same meaning as our use of the word, but this type of model and our type of model have a number of differences. Physical models represent physical reality using physical materials, such as clay or balsa wood. In this book we're interested in what could be called "management science" models, a term which would encompass any model of human or operational systems, whether of the "hard" quantitative type or the "softer" qualitative type. The materials we are going to use are concepts and mathematics. And the models are going to have certain attributes that define them to be "models"—it is these attributes that this section seeks to explore and define. At an intuitive level, modellers know what a model is—but it is surprisingly difficult to come up with an all-encompassing definition that tells us the essence of being "a model", that is suitable for all types of management science models. However, as the issue is so central to our book, we shall try to define what we mean in this section.

A good start is always the dictionary. The Collins English Dictionary (1986) tells us that a model is "a simplified representation or description of a system or complex entity, especially one designed to facilitate calculations and predictions." This definition tells us lots of things:

- a model *represents* or *describes* something real;
- a model *simplifies* that real entity;
- the production of a model has a *purpose*, generally to make some sort of calculation or predict how the entity will behave.

The first two points are our starting point: our models take something in the "real world", simplify it and attempt to represent or describe it. Now the term "the real world" needs some further consideration, as does the word "simplify", but let's look first at the idea of "representing" or "describing" the world. Can anything that represents or describes the "real" world be termed a model? (Well, perhaps it can in the colloquial sense of the word "model", but what about in our more specialised sense of the word?) We are all familiar with one popular form of representing the real world: a painting or photograph. Does this constitute a model? Intuitively, management scientists would think that it doesn't, but why not? The answer to this question actually lies in the third point—the purpose of the model. A painting represents a single, static representation of reality which, having been created, is not changeable. As a contrast, we want to *manipulate* a model to tell us something useful, such as to explore alternative realities or to explain why the differences between these realities occur. This is because a model not only defines parts or conceptual elements of a whole, it must also define the *relationships* between the concepts.

Since we wish to manipulate these definitions, they must be *formal*, *theoretically based* definitions of reality that can be manipulated. This means that the "language" of the model will need to be as consistent, unambiguous and precise as possible. This often means using some form of mathematics rather than the English language, which tends to be inconsistent, ambiguous and imprecise. But here we are not limiting ourselves to mathematical models, and indeed many of our quantitative, mathematical models will be developed from qualitative models expressed in "English" terms—but in formalised formats so that the concepts are made as consistent, unambiguous and precise as we can make them, and the relationship structures (for example, causal relationships) between these concepts is expressed.

We must have a vision for the scope of modelling. Those who see simple equations as the only sort of "model" will have a very jaundiced view of what modelling can do for them. For example, Jobling (1994), discussing probabilistic risk modelling, gives only a heavily qualified acceptance to the technique, claiming that many risks cannot be credibly modelled using probabilistic techniques; the impact of identified risks cannot always be predicted; those risks that can be modelled are those that can be quantified . . . in a limited number of applications where data is available. But this is to limit the application of our models much too severely—in fact, it hardly seems worth starting to model. In contrast, I believe that modelling can be used—indeed *must* be used—to represent the whole breadth of reality as we see it (subject to all the caveats below, such as about requisiteness) and, although one technique may be more useful than another, modelling must be available to model any aspect of a project.

So let us say that we have an explicit representation of "the real world"—what is this "real world"? Traditional operational research at its most simplistic viewed the world as an absolute reality, which the modeller sought to represent. However, in practice the modeller gains much of his knowledge about the reality he is seeking to model through human actors who will each have their own world-views or *Weltanschauung*. In particular, knowledge comes through those humans who represent the "client", that person or body who has requisitioned the model, who understands the system and who will be the recipient either of the model or of the results of an analysis of the model. When we reach the latter sections in this chapter, we'll explore this issue further, but we must recognise that this means that often we are modelling our subjects' *perceptions* of the real world rather than the reality itself.

The second bullet point above said that a model is a *simplified* representation of reality. This is a fact of life—we cannot reproduce reality exactly in a finite period of time. But it is not a disadvantage of modelling, but indeed one of its most powerful advantages: that we seek to abstract the key elements of reality to provide us with the information we need. This enables us to analyse the model and come to some simplified conclusions about the real world which would be impossible to reach if we had to deal with all the richness, complexity and detail of the real world. Although not a model in our sense of the word, think of the London Underground map, an example taken from Pidd (1996): this is a simplified view of reality, since in reality stations are not spread neatly around, nor are the lines straight. Nor, for that matter, are the railway lines actually single lines in gaudy colours. But the map provides its readers with the information they need in order to travel on the Underground. Indeed, a precise map of the tube lines with all the detail of crossing-points, branch lines and differing depths, with all the lines coloured accurately (i.e. all a similar metallic colour!) would be totally useless for the purpose. So now we come to our third bullet point: the degree of simplification that we impose on reality to produce our representation depends on the purpose for which we are building the model. In the latter sections of this chapter, we'll look at this question in more detail.

So if the *purpose* of the modelling is so important, for what sort of "purposes" might we be modelling? We'll look at this question for our particular domain of modelling projects in the next section, but in general, Pidd (1996) says that two key purposes of management science modelling are: *decision-making* and *control*. Our models will be built with the explicit purpose of helping a decision-maker to make a better decision, or helping a manager control a system more effectively. However, this is inadequate and we should add a third category of purposes for our work in this book: to *understand* a system better. Although some would argue that management science exists to make active interventions, in our particular case the post-mortem analysis of projects is key both to claims analysis and to enabling managers to learn from projects in order that they make better decisions in the next project. And while this might be true of projects in general, in complex projects this is particularly true: Simon's rule (1982) that in complex systems, "given the properties of the parts . . . it is not a trivial matter to infer the properties of the whole" reflects that complexity, to help us to understand the properties and behaviour of the overall project.

Let's summarise all of the above:

> A model represents or describes perceptions of a real system, simplified, using a formal, theoretically based language of concepts and their relationships (that enables manipulation of these entities), in order to facilitate management, control, or understanding of that system.

This is a model: there are lots of other important things that constitute a *good* model: coherence and added value, for example. These don't belong in the definition of a general word like "model", as you could have an incoherent model, or a useless model, but that does not disqualify them as models! But it's worthwhile looking briefly at these aspects of a good model. These aspects will also come up later in this chapter. Among other features, a good model should:

- be empirically based: informed by data that is objective—we want our model to stand up to scrutiny and inform us about the reality with which we have to deal;
- be theoretically sound: agreeing with the body of knowledge of management science, or perhaps more particularly embedded within a sub-body of this knowledge;
- be coherent: the elements of the model should not contradict each other, but should fit together in a self-sustaining edifice, facilitating coherent, consistent decisions;
- be simplified to a requisite degree: reality needs to be simplified to such an extent that it can be modelled and analysed; however, the model has to be of "requisite variety" (Ashby 1956)—a concept originating in cybernetics that says that there must be sufficient variety within the model to represent reality *for the purposes of the model*; there is a trade-off here which will be discussed further in the section below on validation;
- address the complexity of the system, which we define properly in Chapter 4, otherwise the system will behave in ways not predicted by our model;
- add value: it should help to understand the phenomena that we are studying, otherwise the model does not practically help us!
- impact decisions: we have already said that we build models in order to facilitate management, control or understanding of a system: this implies that a good model will influence these management decisions, and the decision-makers will need to be involved in the design and building of the model.

These are all aspects that will come up during the next few chapters. But first we need to convince ourselves of the value of modelling by considering why we model, and what we are trying to achieve.

Why do we model?

Why should we model—in practice, rather than in theory? What benefits do models bring? I would guess that many readers are already convinced of

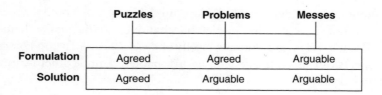

Figure 3.1—Types of modelling situations. Pidd, M. (1996) *Tools for Thinking: Modelling in Management,* John Wiley & Sons Ltd, Chichester. Reproduced by permission of John Wiley & Sons Ltd. All rights reserved.

the value of models, otherwise they would not be reading this book! Perhaps, like me, you have always been convinced that models of reality could contribute to our understanding of, and management of, that reality. But we need to have a good understanding of the role of models in order to translate that understanding into concrete contribution. That means we must also understand *when* modelling is applicable.

As will be clear from our definition of what a model is, there is one key principle: *There is no point in modelling unless it affects decision-making.*

According to our definition of a model, this could be by directly affecting decision-making (in terms of management or control of the system), or by increasing, say, understanding, dialogue or learning. This key principle of implementation must guide when we model and how we build our models: the types of decisions that will be affected provides reasons for building the model, and thus determines how those models should be built.

Having said that, models are not required for every type of situation—I decide each morning what to wear, but I don't require or even want a model to help me decide. It has become commonplace in management science to categorise different types of situations in which understanding is needed or decisions required (and such a categorisation will guide the structure of this book). This is typified by Pidd (1996)'s figure shown in Figure 3.1, which leans heavily on Ackoff's pioneering work (1974, 1979). In this, the top axis is taken to be three points on a spectrum:

At the left-hand end of the spectrum is "puzzles". Here, there is no ambiguity about the formulation of what needs to be solved; the issues and options are clear, and the answer is unarguably the correct one. These require logical thought, and are not always easy to solve, but are not the domain in which we want to model. The nature of the real world is such that puzzles can only be hypothetical—in reality, issues and options are never perfectly clear. But as clarity decreases while we move along to the right-hand end of Pidd's spectrum, there is a range of real-life situations. In the mid-point of the spectrum come what Pidd simply calls "problems", epitomised by the well-defined management science or operational research (OR) problems tackled since the 1960s. Here the formulation of the problem is usually pretty well agreed, but there are a variety of approaches to solving it. Pidd takes a seemingly straightforward question, "how many depots do we need in order to provide daily replenishment of stock in all our supermarkets?" and then goes on to show how even this apparently innocuous and unambiguous question can itself be questioned, and various aspects explored: experience shows that two analysts will rarely have the same approach, although many approaches may tend towards similar answers. In our domain of modelling projects, Chapters 5–7 will cover a variety of problems. However, as OR has proved adept at tackling a range of problems, it was faced with the requirement to tackle the many situations in which there is a lot of ambiguity, no agreement about the issues, or about concept relationships, or about what is going on, or whether a solution exists at all—these situations were termed "messes" by Ackoff (1974, 1979). In such situations, a modeller cannot move straight in with his toolbox of mathematical tools and start modelling—the mess must first be defined and structured and made amenable to analysis. Since this is the situation in so many of our projects ("it all went wrong—why?", or, "it's all going wrong—what should we do?"), Chapters 8–10 will tackle messes in projects and try to make them amenable to modelling.

Given that we have a problem or a mess that can be modelled, why should we model—what advantages does it bring and, in particular in the domain we're interested in, what advantages does it bring the project management team? To start with, Schultz and Sullivan (1972) describe four advantages that will arise *during* the building of the model:

1. *Confrontation*: rather than allowing vague generalities to be aired, these generalities will be faced and tested to ensure they are believable—it's surprising how often assumptions are made within the project team, but never actually tested.
2. *Explication*: rather than using imprecise general statements, assumptions must be made explicit in order to build a model; thus the process of building a model requires the analyst to define explicitly what his assumptions are.
3. *Involvement*: the process of building highlights gaps in knowledge, and motivates the modeller to try to fill in those gaps (otherwise his model has holes in it). Often, therefore, in the process of modelling the analyst will uncover truths that management ought to have known and are helped by being made aware of—the modeller will get a reputation for investigation, even though that is not his primary role. This is simply

because the activity of systemically building the model has defined those areas which required filling in, or has uncovered elements of data which do not triangulate (an important idea that we'll discuss later), prompting just the right line of questioning or just the apposite investigation.

4. *Dialogue*: again, the activity of building the model requires the analyst to work with people from the range of the disciplines involved in the project, which can initiate dialogue and lead to an improvement in communication within the project.

And these four also imply a fifth:

5. *Learning throughout the modelling process*: the process of continuous conceptualisation, quantification, experimentation and application means that the modeller will learn about the system and be able to apply that learning to the real system.

These are all advantages gained *during the process of building the model*—that is, the process of building the model helps the analyst (and, through the analyst, project management) to understand the project better. But once the model is built, the classic benefits of the model are gained:

- First of all, and crucially, the model can show how inputs combine—for example, it can demonstrate the cumulative and compounding effect. We have already discussed Simon's definition of complexity, that in a complex project "it is not a trivial matter to infer the properties of the whole [from the parts]." In a complex project, how the individual influences combine is not obvious, and a model enables us to understand this combination. For example, while we understand (to take the Channel Tunnel Shuttle example) that design-approval delays will affect the project, and that design "gold-plating" will also affect the project, how these two compound each other cannot be intuitively understood—a model is needed. This example will be looked at in more detail in Chapter 10.
- Then the model enables scenario analysis and "what-if" studies. Having a model enables all sorts of analyses that would not be possible by experimenting with the real system. To quote one of the great figures in modelling socio-technical systems, Jay Forrester said that "in the model system, unlike real systems, the effect of changing one fact can be observed while all other factors are held unchanged. Such experimentation will yield new insights into the characteristics of the system that the model represents. By using a model of a complex system, more can be

learned about internal interactions than would ever be possible through manipulation of the real system" (1961).

- Finally, having a project-wide model helps project management to visualise the whole project, or to understand how the project *as a whole entity* behaves.

And as the model informs project management:

- The model helps management to prepare the project plan, allocate contingency, and make the necessary pre-project planning.
- Furthermore, the model is auditable, and having a model makes the planning process auditable; this means that the project management's "back is covered" as they can point to the model to support their decisions, and project review teams, or senior management, can understand why decisions have been taken and the assumptions underlying those decisions. The transparent model can even be used (later) to prepare auditable claims against the client where necessary.

Finally,

- Effective use of a model enables senior management and project management teams to learn from experience. When a project has gone wrong, the reasons for this are usually not clear, or how the problem-triggers combined to cause the project disaster is not fully understood. A post-mortem model has been found to be a powerful tool in understanding why and how projects fail. This will be explored more fully in later sections.

Of course, such modelling is not without its dangers. Some that have been claimed are as follows, and it is worth bearing these dangers in mind as we seek to apply our models to real projects with real project management.

- First, there is the danger of the "black box" syndrome. It is vital to keep project management involved in the process of model-building. Once they become disconnected from the process, they will become uninterested in the results, and unconvinced of the validity of the inputs, the assumptions or the results. Project management buy-in is an essential part of the model-building process and the *sine qua non* of making the model effective in influencing management.
- At the other extreme, there is the danger of over-reliance on the model—this is the syndrome popularly known as "Garbage In, Gospel

Out"—seeing the numbers come from a good-looking computer model (and in colour, too!) gives them a validity way beyond that justified by their assumptions. It is essential that the modeller is honest in his assessment of the strength of his model, so that management can give appropriate weight to its conclusions.

- Finally, there are the dangers of "Do It Yourself" modelling—"a fool with a tool is still a fool". We recognise that the ambition to see models on managers' desks is a noble ambition, and one which should be encouraged. But we must recognise that DIY modelling does have its dangers, particularly in this field where intuition and seat-of-the-pants thinking are not always good guides. Chapter 12 will discuss in some detail the role of the modelling specialist in project management teams.

Modelling in practice

So far we've been fairly philosophical, and it is worth making some practical points about modelling before we look at models of specific projects. We'll look first of all at the two parties involved, the modeller and the person who has commissioned the model (i.e. the "client" as far as the consultant is concerned, but this is *not* necessarily the "client" of the project!), which means also looking very briefly at the process gone through during the modelling. Then we'll cover three types of problem that occur in every modelling exercise: data problems, the trade-off between accuracy and simplicity, and validation issues, which form a section on their own (see below).

The parties and the process

Who the modeller is, and how he models, play a crucial role in the modelling process. Different modellers or teams will arrive at different models and, even using the same models, modellers can arrive at different predictions (Rouse 1982). Hence, for example, the great "ORSA missile debate", in which OR (operational research) analysts advised each of the two opposing sides in the US national debate on nuclear deterrent policy in 1969; the spectacle of OR analysts opposing each other but each claiming OR models in their defence led to the ORSA (OR Society of America) developing their "Guidelines" for the practice of OR. This story is told in Churchman and Wagner (1972) and Machol (1982). Thus we need to consider the process by which these modellers model, and in particular the relationships between the client and the modeller during the modelling process.

We have said that the client—modeller relationship is critical to the success of any modelling exercise. This means that the consultant who takes a contract and hides in a room, coming out at the end with a model, to a fanfare of trumpets, may well satisfy the terms of a contract, and may occasionally satisfy the client. But generally he will be faced with a complete absence of client buy-in, and a consequent lack of model credibility. The consultant who develops a rapport with his client will be the one whose model is accepted and gets the follow-on contracts. The first commercial contract I ever had was to build a simulation model (not of a project)—I developed such a rapport with the client that developments and follow-on contracts followed, to a value of around 20 times the original contract.

If this situation is crucial when the modeller is taking a well-defined situation and modelling it, it is even more so when the client objectives, data and the relationships within the data are only vaguely understood. In this, the "complex" situation, the modeller must journey together with the client to look further into the problem facing them. The modeller in this situation is acting as a *problem-finisher* rather than a *problem-solver*, to use Eden's language. Eden's work offers a way of working for analysts that is "different from the focus of Checkland (1981) on design (as exemplified by seeking to discover the 'root definition') . . . Similarly, it is different from the focus of Ackoff (1974) on 'redesigning the future' which is oriented to solution/end-point rather than process" (Eden 1987); "Problem-finishing as a description of working on a problem directs attention to the 'management of meaning' and thus the role of the consultant intervening in the act of deliberation (Eden 1987)." As the modeller explores the real situation with the client, they discover meaning and develop understanding together in a cyclical process: the modeller and client together consider the situation, out of which important issues and solutions emerge, which are modelled, enabling more informed reconsideration to take place (having a better understanding of the issues and about how outputs from the complex situation result from the inputs), which enables refinement or recasting of the model, and so on.

This process will be explored in more depth in the section on project staffing in Chapter 7 but even at this point it should be noted that this process is unlike the clean, well-defined process offered by some writers. Gass (1987, 1990), for example, has a 13-stage process covering initiation, feasibility, formulation, data, design, verification, validation, training/education, installation, implementation, maintenance/update: a good checklist for delivering the computer implementation of a well-defined, entirely specified model, but much too neat for the practical intervention in a complex "mess". "Model building," says Pidd (1996), "may feel like muddling through."

Practical issues: data

Three practical issues need to be discussed before we can start to investigate specific models. First of these is validation, which is significant enough to be treated in a separate section (see below).

The second issue is the status and meaning of data we use to populate our models (Pidd (1996, Chapter 4) gives a useful discussion). We have already said that we are often modelling not the *objective* world but our client's *perceptions* of the world. We rely on our clients for data, and if that data is filtered before it gets to the client, or if the client takes underlying data and interprets it or overlays additional understanding, then we must seek to understand these processes in order to understand the degree of validity of the data. There is an epistemological issue here about the existence (or not) of an objective real world that we can try to measure and understand. We will not take the line of denying any objective reality, but we must understand what our data represents. Where data purports to represent a particular parameter, we must ensure that this is indeed what is being measured. For example, project-control data concerning the completeness of each activity often gives misleading results (many activities being "90% complete" and staying so for a long time). Figures of customer demand taken from a company's database will often actually be customer deliveries (so ignoring instances where customers ordered different items, or didn't bother ordering from that particular company at all). But more subtle misrepresentations can occur where what is being measured is not the same as what is thought of as being measured—we must define carefully what is being measured, and what it signifies about the real objective world. And, of course, any data collected is only a sample, and then only from a particular moment in time.

The discussion a few paragraphs above about the process through which models are built is very similar to Eden and Huxham's (1996) "action research", and some of their "15 characteristics of action research" apply here. "A high degree of systematic method and orderliness is required in reflecting about, and holding on to, the research data and the emergent theoretical outcomes of each episode or cycle of involvement in the organisation". "The processes of exploration of the data—rather than collection of the data—. . . must either be replicable or, at least, capable of being explained to others." And, critically, "the opportunities for triangulation that do not offer themselves with other methods should be exploited fully and reported"; triangulation (cross-checking data with other sources and other types of sources) is, of course, vital as a means of validating our data, but our research methods must allow triangulation to provide cyclical data collection, where points at which data do not triangulate provide a dialectical opportunity for exploration and developing the modeller's and client's understanding.

Practical issues: accuracy versus simplicity

The third practical issue involved is how complex or how simple should a model be? There are two key balancing principles generally accepted in modelling. The first is known as "Occam's razor". There are various forms of this principle, which dates back to the fourteenth century. Essentially, it expresses the idea that if a few entities or reasons are sufficient to explain a phenomenon, this is a preferable explanation to one using many entities or reasons. (The statistical idea of "parsimony" is similar.) Now the decision about whether an element of a model is necessary to explain the phenomenon being modelled is often not easy, and will depend on many issues, including the purpose of the model, the intended closeness with which the model must replicate actuality, and so on. But the general application of Occam's razor to our analysis and modelling will lead us to using the simplest models appropriate to our task. The error which Occam's razor tries to prevent us making is that of needlessly overcomplicated models: if we fail to define our system tightly enough (thus try to model the whole world around our project), or include every possible interaction, whether or not it is significant, we lay ourselves open to many problems: unnecessary work, possible emergence of false or misleading results, unrobust models, accusations of "fiddling". Morgan and Henrion (1990, Chapter 11) give some useful examples of problems which have arisen due to overcomplex models being constructed and (mis)used. All of this, however, must be balanced by the second principle.

"Requisite variety": this idea, from Ashby (1956), derives from the world of cybernetics. A model must be able to represent the features in the system that the modeller is interested in, thus must have sufficient variety. Thus again requisite variety is not an intrinsic feature of the phenomenon being modelled; rather, it is a function of the phenomenon when considered with the purpose of the model, and so on. The error which we must try to avoid here, of course, is of oversimplistic models. A model of a complex project which does *not* have requisite variety, in other words does not represent sufficient features of the project, will not display the essential Simon features of a complex project (as will be defined in Chapter 4): where the whole acts in a way beyond simple combination of the parts. Our models must represent sufficient variety in their elements to replicate the complexity of our project.

It must be emphasised that the judgement of simplicity versus complexity requires consideration of the purpose of the model, which will also imply the desired degree of replication of actuality. To take one of our examples, a model which seeks to demonstrate the idea that client-approval delays and contract changes compound in a "2 + 2 = 5" type of rule might need a fairly small model which does not purport to replicate what actually happened in a project, but does supply an explanation. However, when we built the model for the shuttle wagons claim we needed to be careful to ensure that the model gave at least a reasonable representation of actuality, so that we could show that those particular client-approval delays and those particular contract changes actually compounded in that particular way.

Pidd (1996) offers two further guidelines to underline these major principles:

- "Think complicated, model simple": simple models should spring from, be embedded within, and be supplemented by, rigorous and critical thinking.
- "Start small and add": models should ideally be developed incrementally, starting simply then adding complications as they are required; any modeller with even limited experience will have witnessed an attempt to build a complex model in one "big bang", which almost invariably ends in either an ill-suited and unrobust model, or simply complete failure.

Validation

The final practical issue we will look at in this chapter is validation; in other words, checking that the model is a good representation of reality. As well as being critical to achieving a useful model, it is often at this point that the credibility problem occurs with models—if someone doesn't think your model represents the actuality they can observe, they won't be interested in either using your model or in any results from that model.

Yin (1994) offers four types of validation. These relate to his concept of research by "Case Study" so are not immediately relevant for our purposes, but adapting three types gives us the basic types of validation for the elements that make up a project model. They are:

- *construct validity*. Looking at the individual elements or concepts in the model, are we really using the correct operational measures for the concepts we claim to be measuring? Obviously, if we intended to measure, say, the proportion of the design work carried out so far on the design phase of a project, but in fact we neglect to take into account design rework following changes (say following test failures), then we'll get incorrect results.
- *internal validity*. Turning from the individual elements or concepts in the model to the relationships between them, are these relationships true and correctly specified? Again, clearly if we posit, say, an incorrect relationship between product changes and the degradation of the manufacturing learning curve, our model will again give incorrect results.
- *reliability*. As in all management science studies, could the procedures for establishing the above two factors—identifying the concepts, measuring them, establishing and quantifying the relationships between them—be repeated by another analyst, and get the same results?

(Since I know you'll want to ask, Yin's fourth type is *external validity*—establishing the domain to which the model's results can be generalised. We don't need this now, for validating models, but we will mention it later on when we consider whether a model can be used generically for "projects" or only for the specific project for which it was developed.)

These are the ideas we'll use to validate the *elements* of our model. But once we've combined these elements into a whole model—and remember, we're interested in "complex" projects where the behaviour of the whole doesn't follow obviously from the elements—we now need to validate the whole model.

Wahlstrom (1994), at a slightly trivial level, says that validating a model presents us with a dilemma. If we compare predictions with actual system performance, and there is a good match, then we are happy to accept the model; but even then there are two problems. First, there is always the possibility that the model gives good predictions for old sets of values of parameters (which were used to formulate the model) but bad predictions for new sets of parameters values. Second, if the model generates only accepted results then there is often little information in the results, and they provide little value; on the other hand, if the results are very different from what is expected, they will not be believed. Wahlstrom goes on to suggest that "a model . . . should therefore generate only mild surprises, which can be believed or at least supported with common sense reasoning from the model assumptions."

In Chapter 9, we'll be considering a particular method of modelling, called *System Dynamics*. Workers in this area have studied the problems of validation in some detail, and we'll be looking at their work further in Chapter 9. But their work is based on the ideas of Forrester and Senge (1980), who set out a list of "Confidence Tests", with the idea that as a model passes these tests we gain confidence in its validity. These tests consist of "tests of model structure", "tests of model behaviour", and "tests of policy implications", and it is the second of these sets from which we want to draw a test to look at the validity of models. The key test within this set is:

- *Behaviour reproduction*: how well does the behaviour of the model match behaviour that can be observed in the real system?

Subsidiary to this come four particular aspects of checking that the model behaves similarly to the real system:

- *Symptom generation*: where the building of the model has been motivated by particular problems or difficulties within a project, the model should reproduce the symptoms of the problem—otherwise it will not be much use in the diagnosis or assessment of proposed corrective actions.
- *Behaviour characteristics*: the model should reproduce typical character-istics of the real system behaviour.
- *Behaviour prediction*: the model should predict patterns of behaviour in the future which appear to be qualitatively reasonable.
- *Surprise tests for behaviour anomaly*: if a model generates behaviour which is unexpected, surprising or different from what has been experienced to date within the real system, then the causes of this behaviour should be traced, and if possible the real system checked to see whether it could also produce this type of behaviour under these conditions.

Finally, if the model is run under a variety of conditions two further technical tests can be carried out:

- *Extreme-value testing*: this is when the model is run under extreme con-ditions, to check that the behaviour is sensible and consistent with what is considered would actually occur in the real system.

- *Sensitivity tests*: this is where the sensitive parameters in the model are identified, and the tester considers whether the real system would be similiarly sensitive.

This will give us a set of ideas that we can use to increase our confidence in the validity of our models.

Conclusion

We've said that we're going to use models to look at the effect of various events and effects on projects. We have characterised a model as representing or describing perceptions of a real system, simplified, using a formal, theoretically based language of concepts and causal relationships (which enables the manipulation of these entities). We've said that a *good* model should also be empirically based, theoretically sound, coherent, should add value and impact decisions. Building a model in a "messy" situation will bring many benefits through the actual process of model-building. Then once the model is built, it will give an auditable, transparent process to facilitate management, control and understanding of the project. Finally, we've looked at various aspects of validation, how to trade off simplification, and the need to model requisite variety. So let's start modelling projects!

Acknowledgements

Thanks are due to the Department of Management Science at Strathclyde Business School, Glasgow, Scotland, for help and guidance in formulating the definitions in the section, What is a model?

4   What is a complex project?

Introduction

While many project managers use the term "a *complex* project", there is no clear definition about what is meant. There is a general acceptance, however, that it means something more than simply a "big" project. Sietsman (1994), for example, defines types of projects in a cube diagram, classifying projects on the axes of size, uncertainty and complexity—so he clearly thought that these three are different aspects. We'll return to the matter of uncertainty later in this chapter—but for now, let us consider the differences between complexity and size. Let's consider as an example the Kuwait Oil Field Reconstruction project: the statistics quoted in Chapter 2—repairing 750 oil wells, 26 gathering/production centres, two marine export facilities, tankage, three refineries and so on—clearly show that this was a very big project; but was it complex?

We need to understand what complexity is if we are to model and manage complexity. This book will often contend that it is a failure to comprehend and thus deal with the complexity either of the product or of the project that leads to problems. This is true as we model the project throughout its phases, but perhaps the most obvious examples are where complexity has been underestimated at the start of the project. In the London Ambulance Service despatch-automation project, the software development bid from the suppliers, at £35 000, was considerably lower than any other bid; with hindsight, it could be seen that this was because the suppliers greatly underestimated the complexity of the product they would be required to produce—but we'll look at this example later to show that it could have been predicted that producing the software would be a complex sub-project separate from the complexity of the product.

We don't want to restrict ourselves unduly in this book, so this chapter isn't going to try to give a definitive definition of complexity; instead, we'll try to explore a number of the aspects within the idea of project complexity—we'll aim to be inclusive rather than exclusive. We'll consider whether these aspects can be operationalised, and give some reasons why project complexity might be considered to be increasing. Finally, we'll see in what areas this implies new methods are needed. Many of the ideas in this chapter are taken from Williams 1997b, 1999c.

Why are complex projects different from other projects? Simon (1982) gets to the heart of what complexity is: a complex system is essentially "one made up of a large number of parts that interact in a non-simple way. In such systems the whole is more than the sum of the parts, not in an ultimate, metaphysical sense but in the important pragmatic sense that, given the properties of the parts and the laws of interaction, it is not a trivial matter to infer the properties of the whole." This highlights the paradox pointed out in Chapter 2—that while traditional project management techniques (which decompose a project in a structured way into manageable sub-sections, which together encompass all of the content of the project), have proved very successful, they hinder the effective modelling of complex projects, whose behaviour is beyond the sum of their parts and whose reaction to changes in inputs is difficult for the human mind to predict.

A good review of project complexity was published recently by Baccarini (1996), and this provides a useful starting point for this discussion. He stressed the importance of the concept of complexity to the project manager, and its role in the strategic management of projects. He also states, as a given, referencing Morris and Hough (1987), that "complex projects demand an exceptional level of management, and that the application of conventional systems developed for ordinary projects have been found to be inappropriate for complex projects"—so we are justified in looking at our project management methods and considering whether they are adequate for such projects.

What is complexity? Structural complexity

Let's start with Baccarini (1996)'s definition. He proposes a definition of project complexity as "consisting of many varied interrelated parts". This he operationalises in terms of *differentiation*—the number of varied elements —and *interdependency*—the degree of inter-relatedness (or connectivity) between these elements. These measures are to be applied in respect to various project dimensions, and he discusses two of them:

1. In terms of organisational complexity, "differentiation" would mean the number of hierarchical levels, number of formal organisational

units, division of tasks, number of specialisations etc; "interdependency" would be the degree of operational interdependencies between organisational elements.
2. In terms of technological complexity, "differentiation" would mean the number and diversity of inputs, outputs, tasks or specialities; "interdependency" would be the interdependencies between tasks, teams, technologies or inputs.

This clearly defines an important element of project complexity, perhaps the element which we think of most often when we consider a "complex" project: complexity is concerned with the underlying structure of the project. In this book, we'll call this *structural complexity*.

For projects such as design-and-manufacture, or design-and-build, the first major source of *project* (structural) complexity is *product* (structural) complexity, where the product is the physical deliverable (the product being designed and manufactured, or the building being built, etc.). A project to develop a more complex product must normally be a complex (in this sense) project, but it is useful to distinguish the cause and effect of product type of complexity first. Product (structural) complexity, in the Baccarini sense, is the number of sub-systems of a product and their inter-relationships (where an inter-relationship can mean, for example, that changes in the design to one sub-system produce cross-impacts and affect the design of the other system). When modelling or analysing a project that is producing such a product, measures of complexity can be propounded in order to quantify these inter-relationships. As an example, take the shuttle wagons project. Here, the system (i.e. the product) was divided into around 50 sub-systems, and a "cross-impact matrix" P developed, giving the probability p_{ij} that a change in sub-system i would affect sub-system j. From this could be defined, for example,

- sequential (product) complexity: the likely length of a sequence of interactions (i.e. if sub-system i affects sub-system j, which affects sub-system k, this is a length of 3);
- feedback (product) complexity (the probability that a change in system i eventually affects system i).

Having measured product complexity, such measures can then be used to investigate aspects of project complexity. For example, if you want to evaluate the effect of a client change on a project, it is very important to think about how many changes to other systems are likely to be required, or how many systems hitherto considered as "frozen" will need to be redesigned ("unfrozen"). The cost- and time impacts of such changes, as we shall see, increase markedly as these cross-impact effects increase—and these, of course, are functions of the measures of product complexity outlined above.

Clearly, merely counting interdependencies within the project structure is not sufficient; the nature of those interdependencies is also important (as Baccarini also points out). One of the best-known papers in this area, Thompson (1967), looked at interdependencies and identified three types:

- *pooled*, in which each element gives a discrete contribution to the project, each element proceeding irrespective of the other elements (Figure 4.1);
- *sequential*, where one element's output becomes another's input (Figure 4.2);
- *reciprocal*, where each element's output becomes inputs for other elements, so the actions of each must be modified to the actions of others (Figure 4.3).

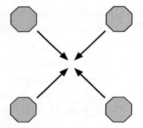

Figure 4.1—Pooled interdependency

Figure 4.2—Sequential dependency

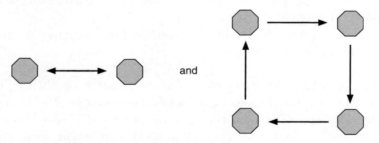

Figure 4.3—Reciprocal dependency

It is this last type of interdependency that intensifies complexity. In particular, reciprocal interdependencies will produce the type of feedback effects that we will discuss in later chapters. To take the shuttle wagons project as an example again, this type of interdependencies meant that client comments caused work to return to the designer, which caused changes to other elements which themselves returned to be reworked. Such effects, of course, run counter to the assumptions of the first-generation project management tools such as PERT, which assume steady progress through a project.

These reciprocal effects can be seen in the case of a set of designers designing a product subject to a cross-impact matrix as described above. But less easily modelled reciprocal interdependencies occur, for example, when there are functional aspects affected by, and affecting, many activities (e.g. the weight of the product, electromagnetic interactions, safety issues—in any of these, a significant occurrence in one activity can have major effects across all of a project), or when events occur that affect many project elements (e.g. loss of a prototype, change in regulations—the possible list is endless). Clearly, the more complex the type of interdependency, the greater the added complexity. Again, one factor causing an increase in reciprocal interdependencies is the rise in concurrent engineering to enable increased parallelism; discussed in Chapters 8 and 9.

These are the key aspects of structural complexity, concerned with the multiplicity of project elements, that will mean we have to model our projects carefully in this book. However, there are two other aspects of structural complexity we also need to take into account.

The first of these is to do with the objectives of our project. As we saw in Chapter 3, virtually all projects are by definition multi-objective, with conflicting goals (either objectives which must be met—finish by 31 December 1999—or parameters to optimise—at minimum cost). This adds (structural) complexity, since the effects of activities on all goals have to be assessed, and trade-offs have to consider the balancing effects of other activities.

The second point is that virtually all projects have complexity within the stakeholders. Many projects have a multiplicity of stakeholders, not only the obvious—client, project manager(s) and project team—but also owner, champion, the public, sometimes public bodies, and so on. Many larger projects have complexity even within the client. This will add complexity in a similar manner to the multiplicity of goals. A good example of this latter type of structural complexity is seen in the Channel Tunnel project. The description in the Major Projects Association book (1992) shows the complex interactions well. At the top level, there are interactions between the Eurotunnel Concessionaire, the French and British governments, the

ESCW ◀──▶ TML ◀──▶ Euro tunnel ◀──▶ IGC

Figure 4.4—Shuttle organisation relationships

InterGovernmental Commission and the *Maître d'Oeuvre* (an independent overviewing organisation). But Eurotunnel also had to interact with the financiers (a syndicate of international banks), and with the users (essentially the two national rail companies, British Rail and SNCF) and, of course, finally with the contractors, TML. But even within Eurotunnel, there was a web of subsidiary companies, with French and British companies reproduced symmetrically (so that 49% of Eurotunnel Services Ltd was owned by France Manche Link and 51% by Channel Tunnel Group Ltd, which were themselves owned by Eurotunnel SA and Eurotunnel Ltd respectively). Also, the contractors consisted of two joint ventures, one of five British companies and one of five French companies. For some purposes, this complexity does not need to impinge on the analyses and thus does not need to be comprehended by the models. But consider the problems of the shuttle wagons project: we said in Chapter 2 rather simplistically that creeping improvements in safety required by the IGC caused major headaches for the contractor (we'll discuss this further in Chapter 9)—but of course the requirements of IGC were contractually communicated to the Shuttle subcontractors ESCW by the route we've identified above (see Figure 4.4), so this complexity caused delays and late changes to the requirements—in a project where just these problems became a major issue.

While the Channel Tunnel organisation is perhaps unusually complex, this interacting of heterogenous stakeholders is not unusual, even when the outside observer might expect a more unified decision-making structure. To take a typical example, in the Sydney 2000 Olympics, while the State government's coordination authority SOCOG was responsible for constructing new sporting facilities, refurbishing existing facilities and organising the events, the responsibility for infrastructure construction lay with the government, overseen by the Olympic Coordination Authority. The International Olympic Committee were also obviously intimately involved, and the City Council and Australian Olympic Committee were also interested parties. Hetland and Fevang (1997) discuss complexity further and identify implications for contracting mechanisms (such as the use of alliances etc.).

What is complexity? Uncertainty

But there's more to project complexity than just the complexity of the structure. Let's look further into what has been found to cause problems of complexity in projects. One interesting paper is by Jones and Deckro (1993) who discuss the social psychology of conflict within project management; they define "technical complexity" as a three-fold concept: the variety of tasks, the degree of interdependencies within these tasks, and "the instability of the assumptions upon which the tasks are based". The first two of these, of course, are the same as Baccarini's two aspects, which we have termed structural complexity. The third, however, is one example of *uncertainty*, which brings a further element to the idea of complexity—although we can perhaps widen the scope beyond Jones and Deckro's example.

(It should be said here that I believe that uncertainty adds to the complexity of a project, therefore it can be viewed as a constituent dimension of project complexity. There is a body of thought that views uncertainty and complexity as two separate concepts—we've already talked about Sietsman's cube of project types, and some of Baccarini's references also discuss this. Indeed, the discussion of Shenhar and Dvir's paper below appears to strengthen this view. However, this view can be equated to our contention that uncertainty and structural complexity are separate concepts, while, together, they produce the overall "difficulty" and "messiness" of a complex project, and it is this last idea which we are calling overall project "complexity". Most previous definitions of "complexity" simply report structural complexity, while we are seeking to define complexity in this overarching sense.)

The idea of uncertainty within projects is discussed in a well-known paper by Turner and Cochrane (1993). They classify projects by two parameters: how well-defined the goals are, and how well-defined are the methods of achieving those goals—a classification arrived at by a number of authors. They then identify four distinct types of project, depending on whether the goals are well- or ill-defined, and whether the methods are well- or ill-defined, and suggest different management and project start-up methods for the four types. We can see these two types of uncertainty as two dimensions of added complexity to projects.

Dealing with the second dimension first, uncertainty in the *methods* needed to carry out a project will add complexity to the project. Turner and Cochrane point out that, if methods are uncertain, the fundamental building blocks of project management will not be known: the WBS, the tasks required to complete the job and their sequence, the Organisational Breakdown Structure, etc.; and even when they are planned, the plan will be subject to change. Clearly, then, some of the characteristics of structural complexity will occur here: as the team structures the work and refines the methods, there will be considerable interdependencies between project sub-teams and, as methods are tried and replanned, feedback loops will naturally occur, and so on.

Uncertainty in methods is frequently considered to be related to complexity. For example, Shenhar and Dvir (1995) undertook a field study to distinguish good management styles and practices for different types of projects (for engineering projects). They classified projects by two parameters: system scope (assemblies, systems arrays—one component of our idea of structural complexity) and "technological uncertainty" (the newness of the technology to be used—i.e. the uncertainty in the methods).

We should note here that "uncertainty" is being used in the broad sense, including both those elements which are stochastic or resulting from probabilities (so-called aleatoric uncertainty, as in reliability calculations) but also those resulting from a lack of knowledge (epistemic uncertainties—these two types of uncertainty are described in Williams 1994). It is in fact the latter that cause problems in project complexity. Clearly, a project where a body of knowledge exists (e.g. building an aeroplane) is less complex than a state-of-the-art project where there is no experience. When Concorde was built, according to Kharbanda and Pinto, the plane had to be built to deal with the temperatures generated at high speeds (at Mach 3 and $-55°C$ outside, the aircraft skin will rise to $345°C$), to ensure there was no instability, which would at that speed cause the aircraft to flip and disintegrate within seconds, and so on. There were significant unknowns relating to the best methods for dealing with these problems.

But while uncertainty in the methods used brings about one element of added complexity, even when the methods are known, another—and frequently more important—dimension of added complexity comes about when there is uncertainty in the *goals*. Turner and Cochrane discuss software development projects as typical of projects whose methods are known but whose goals are uncertain, since users' requirements are difficult to specify, and are often changed when initial prototypes are seen; software development projects are for this reason renowned for continual changes in requirements and specifications. The essential difficulty with such projects is that the requirements are not frozen, and uncertainty or changes in some requirements will mean that interfacing elements also need to change, and again we have cross-impacts, rework, feedback loops—an increase in the features of structural complexity. Another good example is the shuttle wagons project: as we hinted in the thumbnail sketch of the project (and we'll discuss in detail in Chapter 9), a significant problem was the insistence of the Intergovernmental Commission (IGC) on design changes through-out the design of the wagons—so "freezing" and "unfreezing" of sub-system designs formed a central part of the claim model. Many such occur-rences in practice find themselves put under the heading of "delay and disruption". Wozniek's "clarity of scope definition" (1993) is similar to Goals Uncertainty.

Further to this, a key element of the added complexity brought about by the changes or modifications that result from uncertainty in goals is that these changes often cause two separate increases in complexity:

- not only does the action of making the changes increase the project (structural) complexity;
- but also the individual changes themselves often combine to increase the product complexity, and thus the project complexity.

For example, continually adding elements will cause disruption to the project (the first point above), but it will also eventually mean that it is extremely difficult to put in any more cableways, or fit all the elements into a constrained space, or work out how to fit in the pipework (the second point). In evaluating such a project, then, not only does the product com-plexity have to be taken into account, but so does the increase in product complexity throughout the life of the project. For the shuttle wagons, for example, the underside of the wagon got increasingly complex as bigger batteries and more equipment was required to be added to a limited space, and designing each undercar change became more and more difficult as the project progressed. (And, of course, we'll be explaining in later chapters that the effect on the project of many changes is more than the sum of the effects of each change individually—the $2 + 2 = 5$ rule.)

Although we can define these uncertainty measures qualitatively, and consider whether we "feel' they are increasing, both measures are difficult to operationalise into quantifiable parameters. The vagueness of the goals might be measurable by how long it would take to establish whether the goals were satisfied; changes in goals could perhaps be measured in terms of contract changes, but these might be difficult. It is not obvious how uncertainty in methods could be operationalised, beyond vague terms such as "newness of technology". Fortunately, we do not need to operationalise the measures for the purposes of this book, but you should be aware of the issue.

What is complexity? Summary

The conclusion of the above is that overall project complexity can be characterised by two dimensions, each of which have two sub-dimensions, shown in Figure 4.5.

The two sub-dimensions of structural complexity lead to a complex system in which the whole is more than the sum of the parts. In these systems, as in Simon's definition (1982), it is very difficult to intuitively infer the behaviour of the system from the behaviour of the sub-elements. In fact, Forrester, inventor of System Dynamics, said that such systems are likely to exhibit counter-intuitive behaviour; and we shall look at some counter-intuitive results (such as Cooper's well-known "$2000 hour" effect; see Cooper (1994)) in Chapter 9. We have developed abilities in comprehending and managing such systems when they are reasonably known and deterministic. However, when uncertainties arise, either in the goals or the methods, they cause perturbations and dynamics to be set up within the structurally complex systems, causing complex dynamic behaviour. Uncertainty in goals (say), on its own might not cause complexity—but add uncertainty in goals to, say, a product development project which is already structurally complex, and changes and perturbations cause cross-impacts, feedback, dynamics effects and behaviour much too complex for simple intuitive understanding—in fact, we need models to comprehend what is happening (or what might happen, or what has happened, depending on at which stage the modeller is working)!

Let us now return to the example of the Kuwait Oil Field Reconstruction project that was mentioned in the first paragraph of this chapter.

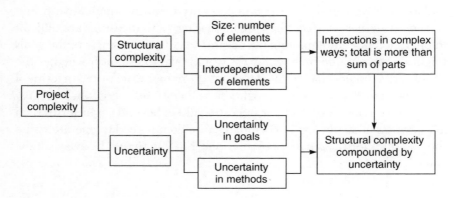

Figure 4.5—Dimensions of project complexity

It is clearly a big project—indeed, it was a massive operation undertaken at high speed in a sophisticated, coordinated way. But is it complex, in the sense used in this chapter? It has many structural elements (so, being a big project, on our first sub-dimension it scores high). But it is not apparent that these elements have a great deal of inter-relation. Rather, it appears as a programme of many coordinated projects. Furthermore, the project specification appears fairly constant, and, although there was considerable upgrading of what had been there before, the methods were well-defined before the start of the project (although working in an area that until recently had been a war zone clearly implies some Methods Uncertainty). So this is a project whose complexity, while considerable, does not match its size.

On the other hand, what about the London Ambulance Service despatch-automation project—a much smaller project? In fact, how about its software development, by comparison with the Kuwait project an insignificantly tiny sub-project? You will recall from the beginning of the chapter that the suppliers had put in a very low bid, and we said that, with hindsight, they could be seen to have greatly underestimated the complexity of the software product. But software production was one element within a complex project with a number of interacting parts, and it needed to interface with (say) the radio interface system, and a computerised gazetteer, adding to the structural project complexity. Furthermore, we've already noted how software production projects are renowned for their uncertainty in goals, since specifications change throughout projects, and changes were made here too, particularly as the delays compounded and eventually led to a requirement for a partial system implementation, adding to the overall project complexity. So this tiny project had a complexity significantly greater than its size would suggest.

Increasing complexity

It appears to be an accepted fact in the project management world that the "complexity" of projects is increasing. Baccarini's review begins with the statement, "Construction projects are invariably complex and since World War II have become progressively more so." It also seems to be an accepted fact—without a lot of evidence—that this increasing complexity is part of the cause of projects going wrong: Helbrough (1995) states that "increased complexity of projects and the project environment have meant that despite improved methods, many projects still fail to meet expectations"; Dalcher (1993) says that "contemporary project management practice is characterised by: late delivery, exceeded budgets, reduced functionality and questioned quality. As the complexity and scale of attempted projects increases, the ability to bring these projects to a successful completion dramatically decreases."

Williams (1995c) points to two compounding causes for projects increasing in (structural) complexity. The first derives from the relationship between product complexity and project complexity, discussed above. As new products are developed which extend, or improve upon, previous generations of product, those products become more (structurally) complex, because of extra functionality, or reductions in physical size, or closer intra-connectivity, and so on. This means that the projects developing those products appear to increase in structural complexity, with a larger number of project elements and a greater degree of inter-element connectivity. It should perhaps be said that this view is supported by anecdotal evidence only: without a clear definition of complexity, I don't know of any quantitative evidence collected to investigate this. Furthermore, this view is based on design-and-manufacture and software projects, and it is not clear whether this also applies to, say, the civil engineering domain.

The second cause concerns the length of projects. Projects have become more time-constrained (Clarke 1994), and the ability to deliver a project quickly is becoming an increasingly important element in winning a bid. There is an increasing desire to reduce times to market. Products become obsolete so quickly that manufacturers have very small windows of opportunity: Kharbanda and Pinto (1996) compare the case of the "IBM System 360 . . . which continued as a viable product for nearly a decade" with the situation today where "year-old PCs quickly become passé". But this need to develop products faster and better than the competition does not simply apply in electronics;it is true across the whole develop-and-manufacture domain.

Not only are projects increasingly time-constrained, there is an increasing emphasis on tight contracts, using prime contractorship to pass time risk on to the contractor, frequently with heavy liquidated damages for lateness. We've already mentioned, for example, in the main Channel Tunnel project, that the completion date was key: the overspend on its own was bad enough, but the tunnel also opened late, missing the early years of its revenue stream and throwing the financial calculations into disarray— so much so that Kharbanda and Pinto (1996), towards the end of their description, claim that "the Chunnel will continue to be a financial drain well into the future, obviating its usefulness".

Why is this increased compression of projects important? Barnes and Wearne (1993), two senior members of the project management field taking an overview of current trends in big projects, conclude that "in engineering and construction, *despite* [my emphasis] the growing complexity of capital projects, the average speed at which they are designed, constructed and commissioned is much higher than ever before." But in fact the complexity of projects stems partly from this compression of project durations, since the compression *compounds* the increasing structural complexity we talked about above. This will be discussed in detail in Chapters 7–9 on systemic effects, but we can briefly say by way of example that as projects become shorter in duration, this enforces parallelism and concurrency, which by definition increase project complexity further as the intra-project reciprocal interdependencies increase both in number and significance (for further details, see Smith and Eppinger 1997).

None of this is to minimize the role of project clients and managers in trying to make projects less complex. Indeed, one of the most important responses to the increasing product complexity has been efforts by major procurers to take complex projects and decompose them into simpler sub-projects or programmes of sub-projects (see, for example, discussions in Williams 1997a). However, while this is sometimes a useful response, many projects are not easily reducible in this way and the underlying complexity of projects has to be recognised and managed.

If structural uncertainty in projects is increasing, what about the uncertainty measures? It is not obvious that there has been any significant increase in Goal Uncertainty—indeed, the tendency towards fixed-cost, prime contracts, with a tightly-written (perhaps performance-based) specification, suggests that, at least in the early 1990s, there may have been a general reduction in Goal Uncertainty. But many writers point to the increasing rate of change in technology (see Toffler 1971), suggesting that Uncertainty in Methods at least may well be increasing. This means that a high-tech project of any significant length has to consider the possibility of its technology becoming obsolete during the project, or new technology coming to market.

Covering all of the above, Laufer *et al.* (1996) have characterised the last four decades of project management by an evolution of models appropriate to changing dominant project characteristics: they characterise the 1960s by scheduling (control), for simple, certain projects; the 1970s by teamwork (integration); the 1980s by reducing uncertainty (flexibility), as projects became complex and uncertain; and the 1990s by simultaneity (dynamism) for complex, uncertain and quick projects—in other words, the very elements that we have defined as "complexity"—and these are the challenges that we will have to face in this book.

Tools and techniques—and the way ahead

Having now defined complexity, we are saying that classical project management techniques are unsuitable for dealing with such projects. Why? Well, let us consider how classical project management methods work. They were developed to deal with big projects—those with a large number of structural elements—by breaking them down hierarchically into sub-elements that can be managed (e.g. by scope, as in the WBS, or in time, as in PERT/CPM, etc.). But such methods:

- can only deal with certain well-defined types of interaction: so a PERT network can easily represent a finish-start relationship, but is not so useful for representing reciprocal interactions between activities;
- are not easily extended to include uncertainty: later, we will look at the simplest extensions to PERT and the use of stochastic networks, but these do not really comprehend the effects of Goal Uncertainty, and only mimic the effects of Methods Uncertainty in the simplest of ways;
- do not account for the systemic, holistic effects that are present in structurally complex projects, so cannot reproduce the effect that the "whole is more than the sum of the parts" (discussed in Williams 1995c);
- most importantly, certainly cannot deal with the sort of complex effects we have described when Goal and Methods Uncertainty impact upon a structurally complex project: the perturbations, feedbacks and dynamics that are set up, producing complex dynamic behaviour.

What is needed, then, is new ways of looking at modern, complex projects, new models and techniques for analysing them and (although this is strictly beyond the scope of this book) new methods for managing them—in fact, new paradigms to underlie our approach to them. In Chapters 5 and 6, we start by taking the bottom-up decomposition models and building on them. These chapters will add the dimension of uncertainty. But once we've considered some of the complexity issues highlighted in this chapter, and some of the "softer" issues that we need to model (in Chapter 7), we'll look at some of the top-level holistic models, in particular using System Dynamics (Chapters 8 and 9) which can capture some of the effects of structural complexity. But since these lack operational detail, they are neither useful nor credible to a practising project manager. So we'll then look at syntheses of methods, and hybrid methods that can produce models that comprehend the full range of our project complexity in a format that is accessible and useful to practising analysts and project management teams (Chapter 10).

5 Discrete effects and uncertainty

Introduction

If we're going to use models to look at the effects of various events on projects, the easiest place to start is by looking at individual effects, or effects that can be clearly delineated as discrete entities. Of course, much of what we want to model is not as neat as this, and as we move into the following chapters we'll start to look at effects that cannot be handled so neatly. But this level of modelling will allow us to look at events which have some degree of unknown-ness, and bring probabilistic ideas to bear on projects. Even with the type of models described in this chapter, we can add a useful tool to the project manager's toolbox, providing him with understanding that neither his unaided brain nor conventional project management tools can provide.

The key feature of modelling these types of events is that we can base our models on classical project management techniques, which decompose the project into discrete items. Since these are individual, discrete effects, we are in these simple models barely seeing the full Simon complexity effects discussed in Chapter 4, where the total is greater than the sum of the parts.

Adding in single effects to a deterministic project plan is straightforward, since essentially it is simply mirroring well-known project management methods. It is assumed that the reader is familiar with the ideas such as:

- adding a cost to, or amending a cost in, a cost spreadsheet; and
- amending the structure of or changing numbers on a project network.

Where these single events are not known with certainty, modelling can help to understand their effects. This chapter will start with some basic ideas of uncertainty and risk as it affects projects. We'll look at effects that can simply be added up. Of course, events that have an effect on the duration of activities cannot be analysed by simply summing them, so we will also look at models of some such events, and this leads into a discussion of the use of simulation to evaluate the effects of such events. (Some people would dispute the use of simulation in this context and advocate analytical techniques—generally extensions to standard network techniques—see below for details of these methods and their applicability to real projects.) This also helps to identify the important effects using ideas such as "cruciality". We'll have a quick look at how we might evaluate effects on the triple time/cost/performance requirement. In Chapter 6, we'll revisit the all-important questions of how to collect data for such models, and how we might fill in any gaps with default or generic data.

Uncertainty and risk in projects

To understand and model the effect of "uncertainty" or "risk" on a project, we must first understand what we mean by these terms, so we'll look first at the idea of probability. Then we'll look at what Project Risk Management is, and how it operates in practice—and in particular, the use of Project Risk Registers. This section ends with a comment on the two-dimensionality of project risk.

The nature of probability

What is probability? We use probability in a variety of ways in everyday life: "The next throw of this die is unlikely to produce a one"... "Eating too much fat reduces the chance of a healthy life"... "It is probably going to rain today". These are quite different usages of the term. Much research has been done on the question of what probability is, and this has led to the distinction of two types of probability statement. Shafer (1976) defines these two types as *aleatoric*, relating to intrinsically uncertain situations (from Latin *alea*: dice) and *epistemic*, relating to a measure of belief, or more generally to a lack of complete knowledge. (Oakes (1986) discusses this in much more detail.) For example, a machine that makes castings will cast a different amount of material each time, and the differences will lie in a recognisable distribution (*aleatoric*); but ask how much material a new machine will cast and, since you haven't tried out such a machine before, you will have to express a certain uncertainty (*epistemic*). This distinction is somewhat academic, and the two types of uncertainty tend to merge into each other, so that it can be difficult to distinguish them. However, project managers will realise that these two types are distinguished and treated differently in practice. And we will certainly distinguish between these two types throughout this book. In general, epistemic uncertainty forms the biggest problem in planning and prediction, where there is little historical evidence on which to base predictions.

Let us turn to the idea of *risk*. A world-famous book by Bernstein (1996) gives a history of the idea of "risk" from the Greeks, through the Renaissance and up to the present day. (The author is a well-known consultant to investment advisors, so knows something about taking risk! The book is recommended as being informative and extremely readable.) Much of that book was about *uncertainty* or *probability*. The idea of *risk* has two elements: *probability* and *impact*

Generally, the word "risk" has implications of negative or adverse impacts from an uncertain event: Ansell and Wharton (1992) discuss the origins of the word and some modern definitions, all referring to the uncertainty of the event, and the adverseness of the effect. But the key point is that both of these aspects must be present; the casual reader will be confused by a number of definitions of risk in the literature that (wrongly) define risk as simply a bad event. For example, Fishburn (1984) calls a certain bad event "risky", and Statman and Tyebjee (1984) define risk as "a high probability of failure". An event that is certain is not a risk—it's a certainty. If you're building a garden shed, you don't treat the possibility that it might need a roof as a risk, but as a certainty, so you include it in your planning. Similarly, an event that has no impact is not a risk. Whether or not it rains during your project to build the shed may be a risk. Whether or not it rains in Moscow while you are building your shed is unlikely to be a risk, since it won't affect you, unless you live in Moscow and are building your shed there!

The meanings of the words epistemic and aleatoric are by no means agreed in the literature. However, the division between them can be found to underlie a lot of the discussions of uncertainty in risk analysis. For example, the popular idea of likelihood/impact grids (where risks are plotted as points on a graph of likelihood versus impact (Williams 1993a, Chief Scientific Advisor undated) is extended by Charette (1989) into three-dimensional graphs with independent axes he labels severity (i.e. impact), frequency (i.e. likelihood) and predictability (i.e. the extent to which the risk is aleatoric rather than epistemic). (The interested reader might like to look at Wynne (1992), who takes this distinction further, distinguishing between situations where the "odds" are known, where the odds are not known but the main parameters may be known, where we don't know what we don't know, and where we have indeterminate causal chains or open networks.) Yeo (1995) defines three different states: certainty, controlled uncertainty and uncontrolled uncertainty, and discusses the idea of the "state of mental models". Pearson and Brochhoff (1994) have dimensions the same as those of Turner and Cochrane (1993) quoted in Chapter 4—uncertainty in means and uncertainty in goals.

Here, we will take the word "risk" to refer to an adverse event which is uncertain, either aleatorically or epistemically. But we'll often distinguish between these two types of uncertainty, as they require different attitudes and different management actions. In practice this covers most of the main requirements of project modelling.

Project risk management

The modelling of risks in projects, or *risk analysis*—and the more general *project risk management* (PRM), which incorporates risk analysis—is of course a popular topic in project management nowadays. The ideas have developed slightly separately in a number of domains. Construction is a major user of PRM, because of the size of the projects often undertaken (Perry and Hayes 1985). Similarly, information technology projects tend to be complex and high-risk (Charette 1989, Wolff 1989). R&D is an obvious field where risk is the main differentiator between projects (White 1982). The oil industry is also an important user (e.g. Hall 1986, Clark and Chapman 1987), but as well as being notoriously secretive, their requirements are somewhat unusual as there is more empirical data about two main areas of uncertainty—weather and geology.

It is instructive to look at the use of PRM in one particular domain, defence, because of its peculiarities here. In 1958, concern about starting major defence (mainly aviation) development projects prompted the setting up of the Committee on the Management and Control of Research and Development. Its report (the Zuckerman Report) recommended (echoing a Ministry of Supply proposal) that "project studies" should be carried out for all major projects before a development contract was placed. This idea came to full fruition with the crucial Downey Report (Ministry of Technology 1969) which fully defined the concept of a Project Definition (PD) study phase, gave it its strategic parameters (in particular, that it should take up 15% of the cost and 25% of the time of the project) and made detailed proposals on procedural changes. PD studies are now mandatory for large UK Ministry of Defence (MoD) projects. Although the PD was becoming effective in estimating absolute project parameters for MoD projects, problems continued because of the high-risk nature of defence development. For example, the National Audit Office's 1986 study on the control and management of 12 defence projects (National Audit Office 1986), showed real increases of £938mn, or 91%, since the initial statement of operational requirements. It became clear that the PD had to estimate risk as well as absolute parameters. The Downey Report was therefore extended by the Jordan *et al.* Report (1988) which, as well as endorsing the Downey procedures, called for MoD resources to be utilised in the technical scrutiny of proposals, particularly to assess the degree of technical risk at each project phase. These resources were placed under the chief scientific advisor, who has an important role on the MoD Equipment Acquisition Committee: see Humphries (1989), which was written when he was Assistant CSA (Projects and Research). PRM is now mandatory on all large projects (i.e. those going to the MoD central committees), and current procedures are given in the CSA Guidelines for Technical Scrutiny.

So, this more straightforward type of project modelling is not only accepted but indeed sometimes mandatory. However, although the simple cost-risk analysis has been around for some time (e.g. Coats and Chesser 1982, Hertz and Thomas 1983), even this has a long way to go before it is practised routinely; Ho and Pike (1992) and Pike and Ho (1991) describe a survey of its use in large UK firms, which suggests that only around one-quarter of such firms use any formal risk analysis.

Such analysis is important at the start of a project since, although spend on a project is spread throughout the project—often, in fact, the biggest rate of spend is in the second half of a project—cost causation is concentrated near the beginning of the project; in other words, the decisions made at the start of a project determine to a large extent how much the project will cost (see, for example, the graphs in Hirzel 1986).

We'll look at some examples, starting with the simplest. But, first, it would be useful to take a brief look at Project Risk Registers, which form the core of much of the PRM practised today. The reason for looking at Project Risk Registers (PRRs) is that we'll be considering how to model these risks, and their representation within the Project Risk Register is significant in this consideration.

Project Risk Registers

Later, we will look at how to model risks, and their representation within the Project Risk Register strongly influences their modelling. In fact, it gives a very useful starting point for the modelling, although we'll see that

PRRs are inadequate for a modern complex project later on. PPRs are really a project management tool, not a modelling tool, and we shall mention some of the management actions that flow from them—but it's the modelling implications we're really interested in.

Risk assessments are usually based around a Project Risk Register (PRR). This is a document kept under strict configuration control, usually within a proprietary database package. The PRR should first be a list of adverse *events* that might occur. It should not be a list of ill-defined difficult areas (such as "gearbox" or "weather"), but defined events (for example, "supplier goes bankrupt"). To be correct, it should be a list of binary ("0–1") events that either will or will not occur, each with a specific disbenefit to the project. In reality, risks are often not this straightforward; in particular, the amount of disbenefit can take a probability distribution (e.g. X might be overweight—but the extent might be anything from 0 to 10 tons). In this case, the PRR must record this distribution of adverseness, and modelling is required of the effect in the analyses listed below. Alternatively, in some cases the risk can be discretised into a very small number of mutually exclusive events which adequately cover the range (zero or 2 tons or 10 tons overweight) and to which probabilities can be attached.

The PRR must contain all the important epistemic risks, since it reflects the lack of knowledge at the start of a project and the gradual resolution of those uncertainties. The major aleatoric uncertainties should also be held in the PRR. Run-of-the-mill aleatoric uncertainties are taken as read, and only come into play when risk analyses are carried out. Thus, the epistemic risk that a new casting proves unsuccessful should be in the PRR; the fact that casting time varies by $\pm 10\%$ (aleatoric uncertainty) will be taken into account in the temporal risk analyses, but needn't be in the PRR unless it is likely to be an important determinant of project success which will change management actions.

Details of each risk come in four categories, as follows.

1. *Event*: Details need to include (a) a description of the risk, (b) its estimated likelihood of occurrence (often initially classified as "High", "Medium" and "Low", becoming more quantitative as the analyses proceed—quantitative definitions of these categories can be established (Ireland and Shirley 1986), although difficulties arise for events which are not binary ("0–1") events, and (c) its "owner": this is the body who will feel the effect of the risk, and who is also responsible for its removal or amelioration—these two phrases usually describe the same body (if there is a good contract), but if the body feeling the effect is different

from the body responsible for the risk these two need to be recorded separately.

2. *Impact*: the project objective on which the risk impacts (time, cost or a performance measure) and the estimated severity of its impact (again often initially classified as "High", "Medium" or "Low", and becoming more quantitative; these categories are more problematic to define quantitatively; the risk analyst can often sustain a subjective definition until quantitative data can be collected). Also needed for temporal risks are the network (CPM/PERT) activities or groups of activities affected and, for cost risks, the WBS items affected, or the probability of spread of costs.

3. *Actions*: both risk reduction actions (actions required to reduce the probability of the risk occurring) and contingency plans (actions in case the risk does occur) should be investigated for each risk; the formal collection of these is described below. Furthermore, where the actions themselves are risky, which can give rise to iatrogenic risks (Stringer 1992), these secondary risks also need to be recorded.

4. *Contractual*: the degree of risk transfer that can take place also needs to be categorised and recorded, as discussed below.

The PRR, then, has two main roles. The first is that of a repository of a corpus of knowledge. A small tight-knit PD team in which all members have a good project overview has less need for this (Williams 1993a). However, in major projects, few project members have such an overview. Indeed, many such projects are undertaken not by individual companies but by consortia with, for example, in defence projects, one company manufacturing the vehicle body, one the motive power and a third the weapons-set. Often engineers involved in one aspect of the manufacture will have a surprisingly hazy view of the issues involved in other aspects, and many of the major problems of recent defence projects stem from the interfaces *between* aspects rather than *within* them. Thus a formal repository of project risk knowledge is useful; indeed, the risk manager rapidly becomes one of the few people in the project with a good overview of it. However, in consortia projects, the PRR must be seen as having been developed in an unbiased way, either by an independent risk manager, or because some sort of risk management committee with representation from all the companies involved has compiled the risk data (Williams 1993a).

The second role of the PRR is to initiate the analyses and plans that flow from the Risk Register, the main subject of our discussion here. Figure 5.1 (taken from Williams 1994) shows this flow. It starts with the Register; this provides data for cost, time and technical analyses when combined with the

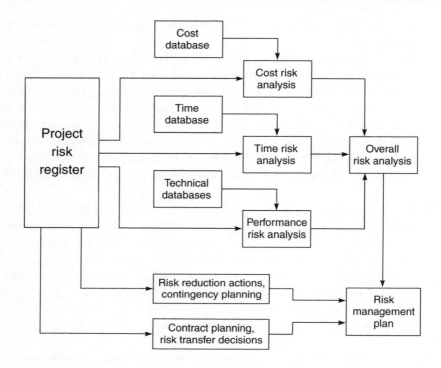

Figure 5.1—The role of the Project Risk Register

deterministic and other aleatoric data. It also provides the foundation for the Risk Management Plan and aids decisions on which risks the tenderer should accept. These aspects are briefly discussed in turn below.

The first analysis shown is the risk to the project cost; combining probabilistic costs to give an overall risk assessment is well understood, and we'll discuss some of the methods involved in this chapter. The important point here is that two separate sets of uncertainty need to be combined: the ordinary engineering aleatoric uncertainties, and the epistemic and major aleatoric risks in the PRR. The former will generally be smooth distributions, the latter mainly discrete 0–1-type variables, but these can be combined using simulation; analytical approximations must be treated with care, since although they may be very accurate in estimating mean and standard deviations, they may be inaccurate in estimating the tail of the distribution, which is our main interest here. Additional care must be taken to avoid double-counting: the uncertainty contained in the aleatoric data-set must assume that *none of the epistemic risks occur*; otherwise that risk's uncertainty is being counted twice. Thus, when collecting the "ordinary" uncertainties to be included in the aleatoric set, estimators must be aware that these assumptions are being made, and remove any contingencies they would make separately for the risks.

Second, the summation of temporal uncertainties is not a simple additive process, as it is in cost analysis, but the techniques available are well-known. This is treated in detail in the section below on Time risk: effects in a network. Much of the process for gathering data mirrors that for cost data, with similar warnings about double-counting etc. The part of the process that is generally less well-defined in practice is the quantification of aleatoric uncertainty within activities. Indeed, the definitions of the parameters of interest are often controversial (Williams 1992b). An agreement has to be reached, in particular, about which central parameter is being estimated; this will frequently be the mean or most-likely value, but has often been found by this author in practice to be a "safety figure" (e.g. "these figures represent the durations we are 80% confident of achieving"), and exactly what this global level of "safety" is must be established. Superimposed on these central figures will generally be absolute maxima and minima, or 10% and 90% confidence figures. Also required are the correlations and third-party effects linking activities (see section titled Time risk, below).

After all the uncertainties have been established, the risks can be listed against the activities which they affect, and then attention given to the activities subject to many risks. This also provides a visual aid to management, showing the list of risks associated with a particular activity, and this in itself can change attitudes towards the activity or the risks themselves. Some projects started off by the author in their early stages have now automated this process. (For example, an activity with, say, three "high" time risks is given a certain spread (say, standard deviation = 0.5 × mean), while one with only two "medium" time risks is given a fixed lesser spread (say, 0.1 × mean); this can be effective under certain limited circumstances (an automatically-run risk register, a strong requirement to demonstrate impartiality, and a lack of expertise/time to consider activities individually), but in the PD stage, some human intervention is needed to ensure good results.

The third analysis is of the risk to achieving the required technical specification; this cannot be commented upon in general, because different projects have different types of measure of project success, although again the risk is the combination of the engineering aleatoric uncertainties and the epistemic uncertainties in the PRR. Where a measure can be quantified and is additive (such as weight), combining uncertainties to give an overall assessment of risk can use similar methods to those above for cost. Where a project has many such target measures, and each is subject to Liquidated

Damages (LDs) or some such contractual device, a simulation of the correlated distributions of the measures will show the probable distribution of LDs likely to be imposed, or alternatively the probability of achieving all aspects of the specification. Where measures cannot be quantified, Probability Impact Grids (mentioned earlier) can be a visual way of categorising the risks in the PRR, although the aleatoric uncertainties are not included in the analysis, and thus their combined effect is often forgotten about.

The need to combine the effects of time, cost and technical risk must be recognised. The use of the PRR as a central analysis tool means that these three aspects are not assumed to be independent, while still enabling separate analyses. However, integrated analyses are required when management has the freedom to set some of the project parameters at the end of PD (Williams 1994).

In the above description of the contents of the PRR, (3) was a description of management actions, both risk reduction actions to reduce the probability of the risk occurring, and contingency plans reducing the consequences of the risk in case it does occur, either within the PD phase or to be carried out in the development phase. The collection of these actions in this formalised way provides two benefits. The first is well-known: it stimulates thought on how to reduce the likelihoods and impacts of risks, and this in itself makes the risk analyst a catalyst for better project management, as well as showing senior management which of the key risk items has no risk reduction measure (thus this element of the project is not being risk-reduced) or no contingency plan (thus this element is leaving them exposed). The second benefit is perhaps less often observed, and is a benefit to the procurer. The set of risk reduction measures/contingency plans to be carried out in development can be directly taken from the PD report and used as a checklist to ensure that tenderers are going to carry out all these activities, thus ensuring that the risk is managed, and allowing the PD experience to carry over into development.

Perhaps the most critical link with the PRR, only made in recent years, is the link with the contract itself. This is a clearly recognised need—for the UK MoD, for example, the key House of Commons Defence Committee report (House of Commons 1988) stated that "MOD's relationship with industry has in the past been characterised by . . . loose contractual specifications . . . payments made to suppliers under cost-plus arrangements", and welcomed the move towards Prime Contractorship—although it pointed out that fixed-/firm-price contracts do not imply no risk at all, because of the need for tightly-drawn specifications. So how does the PRR link to the contract?

The first requirement is to identify all the relevant risks, as described.

Then the tenderer can select those risks which can be reasonably transferred to him, and those best left with the procurer. This brings an immediate benefit, in that the bearer of each risk is stated specifically and visibly. Robinson (1987) claims that certain contract types overrun much less often because the contract is clear who bears the risk. The risks can then be categorised by the feasible level of transfer from the procurer to the tenderer (whether or not desirable). Typical categories may include:

1. *Legally unavoidable*: risks that the tenderer must by law take on, such as accidents covered by the Health and Safety at Work Act, or product liability law, cannot by definition be the subject of a risk-transfer decision;
2. *Quantifiable risks*: straightforward aleatoric risks (and perhaps some epistemic risks) which management feel comfortable about estimating, can be quantified and a contingency calculated to cover the transfer of the risks, if that is agreed;
3. *Epistemic risks*: the extent of some risks will not be known until the development is actually tried; in general, these will be covered only by a qualified transfer with a contingency;
4. *Actuarial*: it is not generally feasible to cover very-low-probability but very-high-impact risks by a contingency (e.g. the risks of a nuclear accident when setting-to-work a nuclear power-station): such a calculation will add greatly to the price of the project, with a payment that is extremely likely to be nugatory; under the same principle that large bodies such as the MoD and the Crown do not insure property, so the transfer of actuarial risks is not generally worthwhile.

Having collected and categorised the risks, the risk analyst can act as a facilitator to senior management in making a decision on each of the risks: whether to offer to transfer the risk to them (at a price) or whether it would be more economic for the procurer to retain the risk. In very large projects, senior management may of course only deal with the "most significant" of the risks—but it should be noted here that the "most significant" are those with the largest *impact*, with the likelihood of the risk occurring being less relevant to the decision of whether they should be transferred. Finally, the categorised list of risks is a significant asset to the procurer. It provides a checklist of the risks against which the tenderers must indicate whether or not they are offering to transfer each risk; thus tenders equal in all other respects can be adjudicated on by this aspect.

This formalised structure built around the PRR then gives us the following.

1. It enables time-, cost- and technical risk analyses and risk-reduction and risk-transfer planning, with a configuration-controlled document to maintain the analyses throughout the study.
2. It provides a central repository of knowledge about which to build risk management.
3. It forms the basis of the outputs required of the risk work, namely the Risk Analysis paper, the Risk Management plan, and the risk transfer input to the contract.
4. It also provides an audit trail so that decisions made can be traced to the assumptions, judgements and calculations that formed their basis.
5. It forms an important interface with the following phases of the project, in the MoD's case Full Development and Initial Production, which will take up the Risk Management plan.

A comment on the two-dimensionality of project risk

It has become quite popular to list risks using a product of probability and impact: a typical scheme might be to rank risks by $R = P \times I$, where R is the degree of risk, within $[0,1]$, P is the probability of the risk occurring, within $[0,1]$, and I is the degree of impact of the risk, which is defined as being within $[0,1]$. That ranking of the risk factors can be used to provide a basis for considering the priority of the response to the various risks. (This is taken from Zhi (1995), who does precisely this—answered by Williams 1996a.) This idea of multiplying likelihood and impact pervades the literature. The top-level guidance in the UK MoD (1992) *defines* risk as "the product of the probability of an event occurring and the impact of that event. . .". Turner (1993) says, "the impact of a risk factor depends on its likelihood of occurring and the consequence if it does occur: Impact of risk = (Likelihood of risk) $\times$ (Consequence of risk)."

But proper consideration of project risk clearly requires consideration of both impact and likelihood; furthermore, multiplying impact and uncertainty to "rank" risks is misleading, since the correct treatment of risks requires both dimensions. Obviously, this is acceptable when dealing with a single risk, but Project Risk Analysts usually produce lists of risks to be considered by managers; the production of a list *only* ranked by the multiplied figure, so that managers only pay attention to the "most risky" risks (according to such a list), is dangerous. Haimes (1993) says "the expected value of risk, which until recently dominated most risk analysis in the field, is not only inadequate, but can lead to fallacious results and interpretations."

We can look at the use of the two dimensions of risk in practice by referring to Figure 5.1. The point of the risk analyses is to calculate the expected cost, time and technical outcomes and, where necessary, to calculate contingency levels that need to be set to provide acceptable risk levels. It is obvious that in order to carry out such analyses, both likelihood and impact levels need to be given, as the effect of a likely low-impact risk will be quite different from that of an unlikely high-impact risk. To give a trivial example: a project with a base cost on top of which are 20 risks, each with a probability of 0.01 and an impact of £10 000, has a 16% chance of costing an additional £10 000 and a 2% chance of costing an extra £20 000 or more; a second project with a base cost on top of which are 20 risks, each with a probability of 0.1 and an impact of £1000, has a one-in-a-million chance of costing an additional £10 000 or more—all of these risks would be seen as equivalent in a ranking by probability multiplied by impact, but their effect in combination is obviously quite different.

Consider the setting of contingencies. Suppose again that a particular risk has a probability P of occurring, and of incurring a disbenefit of I if it does occur. Then if a rough calculation is done using Normal-distribution approximations, it can be shown that

mean disbenefit	$= PI$	$= R$
variance of disbenefit	$= P(1 - P)I^2$	$= R(I - R)$

where R represents the product $P \times I$. This means that for a constant "risk level" (i.e. product term R), the larger the I, the larger the variance of the effect, and thus the larger the contingency that is needed. In other words, as we would intuitively expect, for risks with the same product term, likely, low-impact risks require a smaller contingency than unlikely, high-impact risks. So ranking risks by their product term will often mean considering risks that imply only a small contingency being considered earlier as "more important" than risks that imply a large contingency.

Consider the use of the PRR as a basis for the contract, and in particular for decisions on which risks to consider taking on by the contractor and which to leave with the client. The decision about *how* to treat the risks contractually is made on the basis of *impact only*, and should not consider probability at all. A Project Risk Analyst who has to pass the "most important" risks to management to consider whether the contractor should take them on, *only* considers the nature of the risk and its impact. Thus, an actuarial risk—one whose impact is so large the company could not consider taking it on (the obvious example being the risk of explosion when constructing a nuclear power plant or nuclear submarine)—is deemed to be such because of its impact, and the risk is explicitly written out of the contract; the probability is thus irrelevant. In this case it is obvious that a 10^{-8} probability of a loss of $£10^9$ is not the same as a 0.1 probability of a loss of $£100$. This might appear extreme, but project risk analysis does tend to consider unlikely events (although usually not that unlikely) and the principle remains the same with less extreme data—a computerised "ranking" of risks by $P \times I$ will not necessarily highlight those risks which need to be considered when writing the contract.

The third item flowing from the PRR is the action plan of how to reduce the risks. Here again, there are two different types of action that can be taken: probability reduction actions, to make the event less likely, or impact reduction actions, to make the impact less if the risk does occur (this might include contingency plans, which are a special type of impact reduction plans). Again, these operate independently in the two dimensions of project risk, and which is more important depends on the values of the two dimensions, and where there is more scope for reduction.

So calculating "expected" risk as probability multiplied by impact has limitations, and ranking risks according to this figure is misleading. Computerised "risk lists" thus ranked should not be relied upon. Both probability and impact must be considered at all times.

Cost risk: additive calculations

Adding up costs

When we start looking at examples of analysing discrete uncertainty events, the simplest example is where we try adding up uncertainties in costs. In a sense, analysing the sum of cost risks is easy, as costs can simply be added together. In other words, if one work package costs an extra $£1$ and another costs an extra $£1$, you have cost an extra $£2$ in all. This is quite different from time risks (discussed below), where if one work package takes an extra day and another takes an extra day, the total extra time depends on the relationship between the two work packages (in particular, whether they are parallel or serial). Calculations can be even more complex with some technical performance parameters (although some are also additive—for example, weight).

This means that we can carry out simplistic calculations, such as the addition of simple cost distributions. Suppose that a project is the sum of three components:

A costs	£4mn	with probability 50%	and	£5mn	with probability 50%
B costs	£3mn	with probability 20%	and	£4mn	with probability 80%
C costs	£5mn	with probability 20%	and	£6mn	with probability 40%
			and	£7mn	with probability 40%

then (A + B)

costs	£7mn	with probability	0.2×0.5	= 0.1
	£8mn	with probability	$0.5 \times 0.8 + 0.2 \times 0.5$	= 0.5
	£9mn	with probability	0.5×0.8	= 0.4

so (A + B) + C

costs	£12mn	with probability	0.1×0.2	= 0.02
	£13mn	with probability	$0.1 \times 0.4 + 0.5 \times 0.2$	= 0.14
	£14mn	with probability	$0.1 \times 0.4 + 0.5 \times 0.4 + 0.4 \times 0.2$	= 0.32
	£15mn	with probability	$0.5 \times 0.4 + 0.4 \times 0.4$	= 0.36
	£16mn	with probability	0.4×0.4	= 0.16

The resulting distribution is shown in the graph in Figure 5.2.

Cooper and Chapman (1987) give an illustration where costs have some dependency. They describe a hypothetical example where the cost of a project is equal to the sum of the labour cost and the equipment cost; there is uncertainty about equipment prices, depending partly on whether an equipment-intensive or labour-intensive approach is taken, and the distribution for labour is thus dependent on the equipment cost. The calculation of total cost must then take this relationship into account by a simple conditional probability calculation.

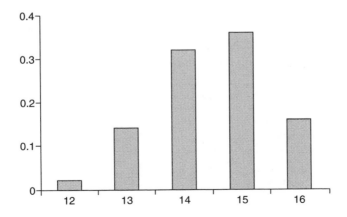

Figure 5.2—Graph of costs

These calculations are of course very trivial. A more common usage is the so-called "method of moments". We will look at this method here because it illustrates some ideas that are used in practice, but we'll see it has some significant problems, and may be discredited. However, we'll see some equations that are commonly used, and noting the inherent problems will be of use when looking at other methods later.

Method of moments

The idea of the method is to use the expected or mean value and the variance of the main activities of a project to derive the overall outcome. Suppose we have a project to develop a new sonar, and we break down the product we are developing into six cost components, as in Figure 5.3. Then suppose the analyst has taken expert opinion on how much each element will cost to develop: both the *most likely* cost and *minimum* and *maximum* probable costs. Now, you might well ask, why did he choose these parameters? Clearly the idea of a "maximum" cost is problematic—if you asked an expert what the "maximum" cost of the Channel Tunnel was before it was dug, I guess he'd come up with a value less than what it actually cost—and the calculations used, as we'll see, are sensitive to these (rather problematic) values. Even the choice of the "most likely" is not necessarily obvious—is this different from "expected" in an expert's mind? And how do you collect these data in a robust way? The "method of moments" assumes that these parameters are available, but we can see problems, and we'll come back to these problems in Chapter 6. But, for now, we'll assume the parameters are available.

Now we calculate the approximate expected value (mean) and standard deviation. These are taken from old equations that were popular when PERT started, although there has been much recent discussion about their validity. They are based on the ideas that:

Product element	Minimum	Most likely	Maximum
Hydrophones	30	32	34
Analysis programs	50	60	100
Computers	50	60	65
Integration	10	15	30
Display programs	20	25	45
Display terminals	20	22	24

Figure 5.3—Development of new sonar system: costs

- the distributions are beta-distributions (why, you might well ask. It's just a hangover from the original PERT days; we'll revisit this question in Chapter 6, but there is no empirical validity to this assumption), and
- the range used is six standard deviations or, alternatively, an assumption that the standard deviation is ⅙ of the range; again, this is another suspect assumption, based on the idea that if you ask someone for a "maximum" and "minimum", the values given are the 99% range of a normal distribution.

If we accept these assumptions for now, we can derive approximate equations as follows (we'll discuss the derivation of these equations in a few paragraphs):

Expected value   = $(a + 4m + b)/6$
Standard deviation   = $(b - a)/6$

This means that we can extend Figure 5.3, as shown in Figure 5.4.

The total expected (or mean) cost is equal to the sum of all the expected cost component values. The standard deviation (SD) of the total cost is calculated by taking the square root of the sum of all the component variances. We then have a mean and standard deviation of costs, and a Normal assumption allows us to derive confidence intervals.

Note that this assumes independence between the elements—which is itself a dangerous assumption, particularly as we've already discussed the idea that risks will often impact on a number of project areas simultaneously. Where dependence between the items is identified, the method of moments has a

Product element	Minimum	Most likely	Maximum	Mean	SD	Variance
Hydrophones	30	32	34	32.0	0.7	0.4
Analysis programs	50	60	100	65.0	8.3	69.4
Computers	50	60	65	59.2	2.5	6.3
Integration	10	15	30	16.7	3.3	11.1
Display programs	20	25	45	27.5	4.2	17.4
Display terminals	20	22	24	22.0	0.7	0.4
Sum		214		222.3		105.1

Mean	222.3
SD	10.25

SD = standard deviation

Figure 5.4—Development of new sonar system: cost calculation

simple and conservative calculation method: the standard deviations are simply added and then squared to find the variance. You can work out that this is equivalent to an assumption of straight linear dependence between the items; obviously it takes no account of the type or degree of dependence. (In the example above, if "display programs" and "display terminals" were considered to be dependent, then their standard deviations would be added to give $4.17 + 0.67 = 4.83$, squared to give a variance of 23.36, and this is used to give a total variance of 110.6, somewhat higher than the figure in Figure 5.4.)

In passing, we should perhaps also note where these two PERT equations come from, since they've come into project management folklore, with little remembrance of their derivation or justification. Indeed, in 1986 Sasieni (1986) asked where the equation for the Expected Value came from. Two answers immediately appeared to this question. The first was by Littlefield and Randolph (1987), who repeated the historic derivation, using four assumptions: that the activity duration distribution is beta, that the estimates of a, m and b are good, that the equation for the standard deviation holds, and that a linear approximation, which leads to the equation for the Expected Value, is good. The second was by Gallagher (1987), who approximated the same equations assuming the duration has a beta distribution with parameters summing to 4. Further developments of these derivations have come from Farnum and Stanton (1987) and Golenko-Ginzburg (1989), both following similar lines but giving further steps to refine the approximations. More accurate estimates of moments of beta distributions are given in Keefer and Verdini (1993).

So while we've found a number of problems with this method, these problems have highlighted some issues that will crop up over the remainder of this chapter. The problem of interdependence between the risks can now be considered, because the section on Uncertainty and risk in projects set up a system for collecting our risks and defined different types of risk via the Project Risk Register. Now we'll look at two examples of how this could be used to model the risks as they appear in the PRR in practice.

Spreadsheet calculations using the PRR

The first example is shown in Figure 5.5, and is much like how a PRR-driven cost risk analysis would look. We have a project divided up with a hierarchical WBS, and PRR containing four major epistemic risks that may or may not happen, that will affect the cost of the project.

WBS item	Aleatoric mean	St.Dev.	Epistem Prob. Effect	Risk 1 0.25 mean	st.dev.	Risk 2 0.1 mean	st.dev.	Risk 3 0.3 mean	st.dev.	Risk 4 0.05 mean	st.dev.	expected value
1.01	3.2	1				1	0.1			2	0.3	3.4
1.02	5.1	1.1		2	0.2			1	0.1			5.9
2.01	4	0.9										4.8
2.02	2.5	0.3				2	0.3			2	0.8	2.8
2.03	7.7	2.3		3	0.5							8.45
3.01	3.1	1.1								3	1	3.25
3.02	5.2	0.3						0.5	0.1			5.35
3.03	1.7	0.1										1.7
											mean	35.65

Simulation:	
mean	35.8
st.dev.	4.25
70%	38
80%	39
90%	41
95%	44

Figure 5.5—Cost risk based on the PRR

On the left is the WBS. Each item has a cost, and a spread of costs has been assessed for each one (that is, we have assessed aleatoric uncertainty within each WBS item). The four major risks from the PRR are shown along the top of the figure. These each have a particular probability of occurrence, and each will affect the cost of some of the WBS items to a degree (which itself has some uncertainty), as shown.

This data has been typed into a Microsoft Excel spreadsheet and a macro used to perform a Monte Carlo simulation. The resulting total cost is shown in the box below the spreadsheet. Three issues are of interest here:

- the uncertainties in the WBS items are now *not* independent; major risks often cut across activities and work packages, and this is modelled, albeit very simplistically, here;
- the mean of the simulation is pretty close to the theoretical mean (also shown)—a good check!
- as well as the mean and standard deviation of cost, 70%-, 80%-, 90%- and 95%-iles are also shown—so the decision-maker could set his budget with a certain confidence of success.

Now, Excel macro simulation is rather clumsy, and there are packages to perform much of the donkey work for you. The following example illustrates the use of one of these packages, perhaps the most popular, called @RISK. This example is small, but it is designed to give a feeling for the overall process, and we'll be continuing with this example in the next section on time risk. Don't forget we'll be looking at estimating such data in Chapter 6—let's take the data as read for now and see how we might analyse it.

The Greenhouse example

A friend and I are going to build a greenhouse. The project has been planned, and will consist of five activities:

(a)   Planning   (will take 3 hours)
(b)   Preparing the ground   (will take 4 hours)
(c)   Erecting the walls   (will take 6 hours)
(d)   Inserting the door   (will take 3 hours)
(e)   Putting on the roof   (will take 5 hours).

The first two activities can start immediately. The third cannot start until the first two have been completed. The last two cannot start until activity (c) has been completed.

The costs will come from the stones/rubble for the base, glass (which costs 50p/sq. ft.) wood and various miscellaneous items (nails, etc.). These costs are as follows:

Activity	Stones £	Glass sq. ft.	Wood £	Misc. £
(a)				2
(b)	40			
(c)		100	10	2
(d)		12	5	3
(e)		30	15	3

The uncertainties are as follows:

1.   The exact state of the ground isn't known: £40 is the mean estimate; it is considered to be 95% likely that it's within ±£8.

2.   In addition to (1), it is considered that there is a 20% chance that the soil will be sandy, adding an extra 2 hours and £20 cost to activity (b).

3.   As inexperienced constructors, we estimate that there is a 1 in 10 chance that the walls will not be square on the first erection, which will add 3 hours to activity (c).

4.   the glass cost is not certain. The average value is likely to be 50p, with a standard deviation estimated at 30p, a minimum of zero but no obvious upper limit.

5.   In addition to (4), the quality of the glass might be poor, causing extra care to be needed and extra glass needing to be bought; this is considered to be only 5% likely, but if it occurs, it will add one hour to *each* of activities (c)-(e), and add 3 sq. ft. of glass to each of activities (c)-(e).

ID: [1]

Title: [Walls not square]

Prob: [0.1]

	IMPACT: Time	IMPACT: Cost
Activity no (1): [3]	[3]	[ ]
Activity no (2): [0]	[0]	[ ]
Activity no (3): [0]	[0]	[ ]

Contingency plans: [ ]

Risk-reduction plans: [ ]

ID: [2]

Title: [Sandy soil]

Prob: [0.2]

	IMPACT: Time	IMPACT: Cost
Activity no (1): [2]	[2]	[20]
Activity no (2): [0]	[0]	[ ]
Activity no (3): [0]	[0]	[ ]

Contingency plans: [ ]

Risk-reduction plans: [ ]

ID: [3]

Title: [Poor glass]

Prob: [0.05]

	IMPACT: Time	IMPACT: Cost
Activity no (1): [3]	[1]	[3@glass cost]
Activity no (2): [4]	[1]	[3@glass cost]
Activity no (3): [5]	[1]	[3@glass cost]

Contingency plans: [ ]

Risk-reduction plans: [ ]

Figure 5.6—PRR for Greenhouse example

Greenhouse project

		Costs including all risks			Time inc. all risks	
Activity	Stones	Glass	Wood	Misc		Hours
Plan	0	0	0	2		3.00
Prep	40	0	0	0		4.00
Walls	0	50	10	2		6.00
Door	0	6	5	3		3.00
Roof	0	30	15	3		5.00
				TOTAL	166	TOTAL 15

ALEATORIC UNCERTAINTIES

Glass cost	0.5	£/sq.ft.
Ground diff	1	scaled

EPISTEMIC UNCERTAINTIES

	Prob	Extra hrs	Extra cost
Walls not square	10%	3	0
Sandy soil	20%	2	20
Poor glass (EACH act'y)	5%	1	1.5

Figure 5.7—Greenhouse data as presented on the @RISK screen. @RISK for Excel package, copyright © Palisade Corporation, Newfield, NY, US. Reproduced by permission of Palisade.

Two of the risks are simple aleatoric uncertainties that we can build into the cost and time distributions; the remaining three would go into a risk register. Figure 5.6 shows a simple risk register containing these three risks.

How do we analysis this data? Figure 5.7 shows a spreadsheet containing the data. But in fact, although this is an output from an Excel spreadsheet, in fact it is running with the package @RISK superimposed on Excel. @RISK is a package produced by the Palisade Corporation (Palisade Corp. 1997) and runs on Excel (there is also a Microsoft Project version available, described later in this book). The idea is that you work with Excel, with all the functionality that this gives you, but instead of typing a number into any cell, you have the capacity to replace it with a probability distribution. The figures shown in Figure 5.7 are not what I typed, but @RISK is showing the mean values. In fact, I entered the data including probability distributions: Figure 5.8 shows the data concerning the costs as actually typed in. (Figure 5.7 actually has a time analysis of this very simple example, although of course for a proper-size network this wouldn't be practical—we'll look at methods for this in the next section.)

Some of this data may well be self-explanatory, and the reader is referred to the @RISK documentation for full information (Palisade Corp. 1997). But three of the in-built functions can be seen in Figure 5.8:

- The *RiskNormal* function gives a Normal distribution. To calculate the preparation cost, the example stated that "The exact state of the ground

	A	B	C	D	E	G	H	I	J	K	L
1	Greenhouse	project									
2											
3		Costs including all risks									
4	Activity	Stones	Glass	Wood	Misc						
5	Plan	0	0	0	2						
6	Prep	=40*B15+RiskDiscrete(K16:L16,G16:H16) 60	0	0	0						
7	Walls	0	=100*B14+RiskDiscrete(K17:L17,G17:H17)	10	2						
8	Door	0	=12*B14+RiskDiscrete(K17:L17,G17:H17)	5	3						
9	Roof	0	=60*B14+RiskDiscrete(K17:L17,G17:H17)	15	3						
10					TOTAL	=SUM(B5:E9)					
11											
12											
13	ALEATORIC				EPISTEMIC UNCERTAINTIES						
14	Glass cost	=RiskGamma(2.5,0.2)	£/sq ft.			Prob		Extra hrs		Extra cost	
15	Ground diff	=RiskNormal(1,0.1)	scaled		Walls not square	0.1	=1-G15	3	0	0	0
16					Sandy soil	0.2	=1-G16	2	0	20	0
17					Bad glass (EACH acty)	0.05	=1-G17	1	0	=3*B14	0

Figure 5.8—Greenhouse @RISK equations. @RISK for Excel package, copyright © Palisade Corporation, Newfield, NY, US. Reproduced by permission of Palisade.

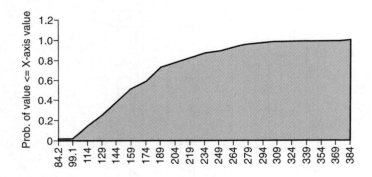

Figure 5.9—Cumulative cost distribution for greenhouse example

isn't known; £40 is the mean estimate of the cost of preparing the ground; it is 95% likely to be ±£8."; this has been judged to be a Normal distribution, and it is straightfoward to calculate then that it is 40 times a Normal distribution with mean 1 and standard deviation 0.1; a metric of "difficulty" (with mean 1) has been put into cell B15 and the preparation cost (cell B6) is dependent upon this.

- The *RiskDiscrete* function simply gives a discrete distribution, used for the epistemic Boolean risks. Still with the ground preparation costs in cell B6, it can be seen that this cell uses the data in cells G16:H16, which give the probabilities of sandy soil, and cells K16:L16, which give the extra costs of sandy soil.

- The *RiskGamma* function gives a Gamma distribution, allowing variables which are non-negative but can grow without a known maximum; in this case, the glass cost has been modelled with a Gamma distribution, whose parameters (as defined by the @RISK package) can be derived from the known mean and standard deviation in the example.

Of course, the value of @RISK is not only in its capacity to take in uncertain values. It can then carry out a Monte Carlo simulation (with various different parameters available for carrying out the simulation under different methodological assumptions), and then display the results in graphical form. When a simple simulation is carried out on the greenhouse data, the cumulative distribution for project cost is as shown in Figure 5.9, and percentiles, etc. are also given in text form (if you're interested, the mean simulated cost is £170, a standard deviation of £55, a skewness of 1.09, a kurtosis of . . . well, you get the idea).

Endnote

This section has introduced us to modelling. We've seen some of the data we might use for the simplest modelling—discrete events which combine only in the most straightforward of ways. Essentially, costs are simple, because they can be added together. However, there are various ways in which the above analysis may need to be extended. These include:

- We have only considered a single level of costs. Exactly the same analysis—only slightly more complicated—can be carried out in a more realistic situation in which there is a hierarchical structure of costs (see, for example, Cooper and Chapman 1987).
- We have also only considered overall cost. In practice, especially with modern structured-finance projects, it is the cost *profile* that is important, and risk to the cash flow is as important as risk to the total project cost. This will be considered further in the section, The three criteria and beyond.
- More sophisticated calculations can be made using exactly the same principles, and the interested reader is referred to Cooper and Chapman (1985), who describe a slightly more complex summation; Burke and Ward (1988), who describe more sophisticated methods for carrying out full probabilistic financial appraisals of projects; and Ho and Pike (1992), who provide a useful summary of methods, carrying out both a simple risk adjustment and full probabilistic risk analysis.

But we've said that discrete effects in cost risk are simple because of their additive nature. Schedule is the other main driver of projects, and we can't simply add schedule delays together. So let's have a look at what happens when we take similar uncertainties to our cost risks, and look at schedule risks.

Time risk: effects in a network

Let's look first at the type of effects we wish to model, then we'll consider the solution and implications of those models in the next two sections. Since we're looking at discrete events, we've already said we'll be basing our modelling on the project network, and looking at the effects of uncertainty upon this network—either on a single activity or (more especially) where risks cut across a number of activities. (It has been assumed that readers know the basic elements of project management, in particular the fundamentals of CPM/PERT, including both activity-on-the-arrow and activity-on-the-node nomenclature, the concepts of float and the critical path, and the basic idea of resource levelling/smoothing.)

Simple deterministic network analysis looks at two questions:

- How long is the project going to take?
- Which are the most important (i.e. critical) activities?

In the forthcoming sections, we'll look at these same two questions, but for networks where there are uncertainties. We'll consider the different effects in this section, then look at analysing the project duration, then look at questions of criticality and then in Chapter 6 we'll look at data collection.

What type of risk or event are we considering? We want to be able to use tools which can help us with the types of problem we are going to face in real-life projects. A single event affecting a single activity in one way would clearly be simple to analyse. But we might be considering a number of independent uncertainties, each affecting individual activities on the network in simple ways—and even that becomes quite difficult to solve analytically. Moreover, each uncertainty might affect a number of activities simultaneously; and these effects might not be simple but more complex to model; and the uncertainties might not be independent. So we could end up with some complicated models. Let's look at some typical complications, but still retain the simplification that these are discrete, separable effects that we can model on the project network. This still raises some problems, which we'll deal with in later chapters, but allows us to build some useful models.

Let's look now at some typical effects that we need to be able to model. (Where these refer to the real-life projects from Chapter 2, note that we are discussing *hypothetical* instances of the type of effect typical within those projects.) No solutions will be given here, but some of these will be revisited in later chapters and solved there.

1. First, of course, come projects where activities have uncertain durations. Even projects which are apparently straightforward construction projects, whose element durations should be known, can have a number of significant time uncertainties. Take, for instance, the Sydney 2000 project. This, of course, had an absolute deadline (the time of the Games). It involved largely construction but included (taken from Cleland *et al.* 1998):
   - Software development activities: this includes activities to develop software to monitor the Games' progress, establishing the Games

database, and development of systems to disseminate the infor- mation to the general public. Each of these three activities will have inherent uncertainties significantly greater than in construction activities. The latter, in particular, is also affected by the unknown potential development of new technology, which could mean significant levels of redesign or rework late in the activity.

- Activities that depend upon "inspiration", such as development of the cultural events and the opening and closing ceremony perform- ances. Predicting the time required for such activities is clearly difficult.

A PERT/CPM network of this project would have to include signifi- cant uncertainties upon at least these activities.

2. Second come uncertainties that operate across a range of activities and/or resources, such as third-party effects, or common-cause effects: the major risks within a project usually involve more than one activity.

     An example of this could be the development of a sonar system. Obviously, in practice this is a complex set of projects involving multiple companies, but a simplification of the project network could be as shown in Figure 5.10:

     In this network, how well the project definition phase was carried out would affect all of the other activities—so there would be complex correlation effects between the duration distributions of the four suc- ceeding activities.

3. Domain-specific uncertainties can have very particular uncertainty profiles, such as the random failure of test rigs, or weather windows in deep-sea oil work etc. An instance of the former is given in the more detailed example below. Examples of the latter would include:

- Construction project X. The project plan here consisted of a num- ber of design activities leading to a number of construction activities.

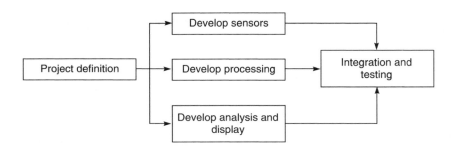

Figure 5.10—Simple sonar development network

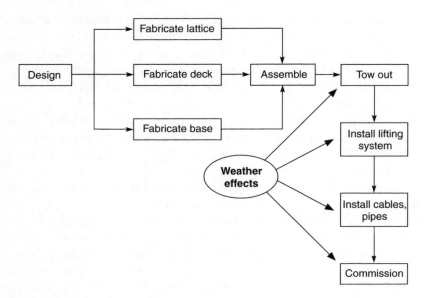

Figure 5.11—Simple oil platform crane installation

For the most significant element of the work, early in the construction programme was the milestone "make building weatherproof". If you were to model uncertainties in the design programme activities, this would imply a probability of reaching this milestone before the winter. In fact, this milestone date was not met, and construction work between that date and the building being weatherproof, since it was being carried out outside in temperatures of around $-40°C$, was only, say, 25% as productive as the work would have been had it been undertaken before the winter. So modelling this project would need to take into account not only the uncertainties in the design activities, but also the implications for downstream activities if the milestone date is not met. This project will be modelled in Chapter 8.

• Similar considerations apply to North Sea oil platform projects, which clearly have weather-dependent effects. Consider a project to install a crane on a North Sea platform, with the network shown in Figure 5.11. In this project, the first five activities shown are shore-based, and can be predicted with a certain amount of aleatoric uncertainty. The last four activities, however, are weather-dependent (in particular, wave-height dependent) and each activity has to be completed before the next one can start, which increases dependence on weather. The activities have a duration around four to five months, so need to be started at the beginning of summer to avoid getting into winter bad weather. A more detailed analysis of this network is given in the section below on Analysing time risk: simulation.

- The Montreal Olympics 1976 project also had significant weather implications (too cold), as did the Kuwait Oil Field Reconstruction project (too hot!).

4. Then, modelling these effects might imply different or unusual distributions to describe the duration of activities. One obvious instance that frequently occurs in practice is the need to combine 0–1 and continuous uncertainties, where several risks combine in an activity, particularly where some of those risks are epistemic and others are aleatoric. This was seen for cost risk in Figure 5.5 where the cost distribution of each WBS element is not easy to express analytically. Another example is the need to model Parkinson's law in activities. This type of modelling is going to be described more fully in Chapter 6.

5. We might need to model resource availabilities or requirements that are themselves uncertain (and possibly with uncertainties that vary over time): these can sometimes be the critical uncertainties, for example, the precise timing of the availability window for a vital resource can be the deciding factor in whether a project meets its deadline. Again, an instance of this is given in the more detailed example below.

6. We might need to model uncertainties in the project network structure itself: all classical network methods assume that the network itself is fixed; however, in practice there can be branching, either probabilistic (where one path or another in the network is taken depending on a probabilistic event, such as the weather) or conditional (where management will choose one path or another, depending upon a project parameter; for example, on a project to develop a vehicle, at a certain point if the current vehicle weight is too high they might move into the development of a light engine, but if it is acceptable they might move into adapting an existing, heavier, engine). An instance of this is given below.

Let's look at one example in more detail.

Example: development of military aircraft

This section describes an example which is simple enough to be coded in Excel. Obviously, that isn't very realistic, but it means the reader can check this example and try it out for himself. It is a fictional example, but it is based on real work done by the author and John Bowers for the Ministry of Defence (more detail on this work is given in Bowers 1994), and covers many of the points (1)–(6) in the list above. A simplified project programme is shown in Figure 5.12. It shows a unified programme consisting of three strands: development of an engine, airframe and avionics.

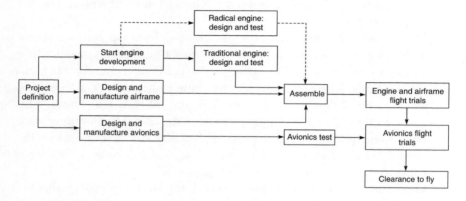

Figure 5.12—Simplified military aircraft problem

Let's suppose some of these activities have a fixed duration:

1	Project definition	6 months
2	Start engine development	2 months
7	Assemble	3 months
11	Clearance to fly	2 months

But let's suppose that there are four complications.

1. There are two possible engine developments, and which one occurs depends upon the "Start engine development" activity. Suppose for simplicity that there is a 70% chance that the decision will be made to go ahead with the radical engine rather than the traditional engine.

2. The design activities after the project definition stage have some uncertainty:

3	Traditional engine: design and test	Mean 6, st. dev. 1, months
4	Radical engine: design and test	Mean 9, st. dev. 1, months
5	Design and manufacture airframe	Mean 12, st. dev. 1, months
6	Design and manufacture avionics	Mean 10, st. dev. 2, months
9	Avionics test	Mean 6, st. dev. 1, months

(st. dev. stands for standard deviation)

Similarly, the testing activity is of variable duration, depending upon the requirement for flight-test hours. There are two test aircraft, which each fly 100 hours per month. The flying hours for each activity are:

8	Engine and airframe flight trials	mean 1000, st. dev. 20 hours; *plus* a further 200 hours if the "radical" engine option has been chosen.
10	Avionics flight trials	Mean 400, st. dev. 10, hours

3. All of the four design activities (3–6) will depend on the success or otherwise of the project definition phase. While this activity is of fixed duration, if it is done badly, all of the following four activities will be affected. So let us model this in the simplest way possible: by a parameter x between 0 and 1, chosen with a Uniform Distribution, and let us add x to activities 3–5 and $2x$ to activity 6 (since it will affect the development of the avionics twice as much as the other development programmes).

4. Test aircraft can crash, which will affect the flight trials activities. Let's suppose for simplicity that one crash will happen after a period of testing with a negative exponential distribution, with an average of 2000 test hours, then the second happens after a further period of testing with a negative exponential distribution, with an average of 2000 test hours. Suppose further that, if both planes crash, six months is added to the program to rapidly build a further test plane to complete the testing.

Now as we said, this is grossly simplified. In reality, each of the four effects would be more complicated—Normal distributions would not be used, and in particular, test aircraft crashing would have a complicated effect on the test activities taking place at that time. Furthermore, there might be effects such as resource requirements, perhaps particular windows of resource availabilities (such as test rigs). However, when the solution to this problem is described below, this problem is simple enough to be coded in Excel (although obviously, coding a network in Excel isn't very efficient generally!). Slightly more easily, it could be modelled in the @RISK package, which would make different distributions available, take away the tedious requirement to generate random numbers, and greatly simplify the graphing and analysis process. But since many readers will not have @RISK, we have stated a problem simple enough for Excel to be used.

Analysing time risk: simulation

Now we've got a model based on the project network, what can we do with it? We said that deterministic network analysis looked at:

- calculating the duration of the total project, and
- evaluating the most important (critical) activities.

This section will look at the first of these for uncertain networks. It will first consider the original PERT method, and illustrate why it doesn't work. It will then briefly consider analytical methods, before rejecting them and discussing Monte Carlo simulation. The next section will look at the second element, criticality, for uncertain networks.

PERT methods

The original PERT methods allowed for uncertainty within activities. So why not just use that? Well, let's consider how PERT worked. As we mentioned above, four assumptions were made for each activity's duration:

- there is a min (a), max (b) and most likely (m);
- standard deviation is ⅙ of the range (b − a);
- the distribution is Beta;
- the activity durations are independent.

These assumptions themselves are suspect:

- What is a maximum or a minimum? An absolute maximum is often infinite—or should there be a more practical maximum? And even the "middle point" isn't very well defined. We'll discuss this in more detail in Chapter 6.
- Since the definition of a and b are not clear (and the calculations are quite sensitive to them), clearly the use of (b − a)/6 is not very robust.
- As we've already discussed, why a Beta distribution? In fact, as we shall see in Chapter 6, other distributions are simpler and easier to explain to a non-modeller.
- Activity durations are rarely independent, as we saw in the previous section. Furthermore, management take various actions to bring a project back on course if they do go wrong. In fact, we'll see in Chapter 10, this is important in modelling uncertain time-networks, and will lead us to rethink some of our models.

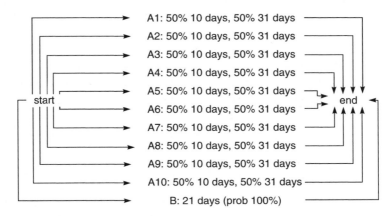

start

A1: 50% 10 days, 50% 31 days
A2: 50% 10 days, 50% 31 days
A3: 50% 10 days, 50% 31 days
A4: 50% 10 days, 50% 31 days
A5: 50% 10 days, 50% 31 days
A6: 50% 10 days, 50% 31 days
A7: 50% 10 days, 50% 31 days
A8: 50% 10 days, 50% 31 days
A9: 50% 10 days, 50% 31 days
A10: 50% 10 days, 50% 31 days
B: 21 days (prob 100%)

end

Figure 5.13—Problems with PERT

But leaving all these problems aside, PERT then makes the technical assumption that: *The expectation of the maximum of variables is approximately the maximum of their expectations.* What does this mean? It means, in other words, to find the distribution of the critical path, PERT:

- finds the mean of each activity's duration distribution;
- finds the deterministic "critical path" based upon these mean durations;
- considering *only these activities on the "critical path"* it finds the distribution of the "critical path"; and
- assumes that this is the same as the distribution of the project.

This is now widely recognised to be wrong, since sub-critical paths are not considered. And as projects are becoming more and more parallel, PERT is becoming increasingly wrong. But let's see an example of the error. Figure 5.13 shows an extreme example. The network consists of 11 activities, all independent; 10 have a 50/50 distribution of 10 days and 31 days; the eleventh will take 21 days.

The PERT algorithm:

- finds the mean of each activity's duration distribution *(20.5 for the 10 A activities; 21 for activity B)*;
- finds the deterministic "critical path" using these mean durations *(activity B: the others each have a float of 0.5)*;
- considering *only these activities*, it finds the distribution of the "critical path" *(the "critical path" has a constant duration, since activity B is constant)*;
- assumes that this is the same as the distribution of the project.

So the PERT algorithm says the project will take 21 days, with no uncertainty.

But in fact we can use simple probability to analyse this network. There are 10 activities which are each 50% likely to take 31 days. So the probability that the whole project takes 31 days is equal to one minus the probability that none of the 10 activities takes 10 days, or:

$$1 - (0.5 \times 0.5 \times 0.5 \times 0.5 \times 0.5 \times 0.5 \times 0.5 \times 0.5 \times 0.5 \times 0.5)$$

which is roughly 0.999. In other words, there's a 99.9% chance the project will take 31 days (otherwise, it takes 21 days).

These two answers are clearly totally different! Now, the error might be obvious in this small example. However, we're looking for automatic systems that will work, so we can analyse networks with computers; when large networks are being automatically analysed an error such as the above, and the correct solution, might be totally obscured.

We should consider briefly *why* PERT was wrong. Clearly, the error is that when you disregard paths that are not critical in the mean sense, you forget that these paths might become critical in some realisations of the uncertainties. In other words, we have to be worried when there are a number of sub-critical paths that could become critical. But when we discussed project complexity in Chapter 4, we said that precisely this was becoming more common in today's modern projects: concurrency, and multiple paths through a network that are sub-critical. So it is important that we do not make the error of only considering the single (deterministically determined) critical path.

Solutions

Where a network is not subject to resource constraints, and has simple uncertainties which each apply independently to individual activities, a number of analytical methods have been tried to calculate the duration of the whole project. Some can deal with resource constraints. In order not to interrupt the flow of the book, we won't discuss them here but they're discussed in detail in other literature. They cover, for instance:

- Exact analysis is what is known as "NP hard", that is (expressing it loosely), no simple method can be found to solve the networks in a short time. Branch & Bound/Integer Programming techniques have been used, but without much practical success.

- Analytical bounds and inequalities can be found, but they're computationally very complex, and don't necessarily reach close approximation.
- Approximations use methods such as:
  - extreme value theory
  - multivariate between paths
  - fuzzy sets
  - new distributions to make calculating the maximum easier
  - continuous network collapsing to simplify the network
  - approximations for criticality indices, none very successful (see the section below on the three criteria).

Progress has been made on all these in an academic sense (see, for example, Appendix A in Williams 1995a), but none are really used in practice. For more complex problems, Elmaghraby (1995) gives a good summary of many such methods, in a large, effective review covering PC software, floats, network complexity, crashing under general precedence relationships, resource constraints and bidding (calculating Net Present Value etc.). Soroush (1993) also gives a useful summary of the methods, including also in the decision-maker's attitude to risk. Dawson and Dawson (1994, 1995) give a summary of GERT/VERT, concluding that the resulting network must be simulated; they give a full description of all input/output possibilities at a node, giving a fuller foundation for such networks.

But even if we could solve these simple networks, we've seen over the course of this chapter that our uncertainties are rarely that simple: they might cover many activities, they might set up complex correlation effects, they might affect resource requirements or resource availability, or they may affect the structure of the network itself (the precedence relationships or even the existence of particular activities or paths). The types of uncertainty covered in the above section are certainly not amenable to analytical solution.

For resource-constrained networks where the durations have uncertainties, many project management packages include "add-ons" to run simulations (OpenPlan has OPERA, Primavera has Monte Carlo, Artemis has various ones, PAN and RISK7000 being two older ones). But the capabilities are almost as limited as those of analytical solution. Again, to model the complexities found in a real-world project network, such as those discussed above, we need more.

So simulation seems an obvious solution. This has been used widely even for simple networks. Simple "crude" simulation is usually used, although (especially in the days of slower computers), various techniques were used to gain more information from a simulation run, such as conditional sampling (choosing particular arcs or "cutsets"—a complicated technique) or variance reduction techniques (choosing replications that are negatively correlated, or stratifying the random numbers) but I don't think these need concern us here.

There are a number of mechanisms now available which enable the analyst to take a project network and simulate it with various uncertainties impacting upon it. Even a decade ago, many authors were doubtful that computers were powerful enough to undertake such analyses (e.g. Ragsdale 1989). However, early papers espousing this technique include Williams (1990), who described the RiskNet package; this was one of the first successful commercial packages allowing networks to be manipulated in a Monte Carlo simulation framework (see also the VERT approach; Kidd 1990). And as well as answering the question of "How long will the project take?", we'll see in the next section that simulation will allow us to answer the second question posed at the start of this section: "What are the most important (or 'critical') activities?"

It is assumed that readers are familiar with simulation methods. In these simple methods, parameters are represented by random variables, then streams of random numbers are used to populate the network. This is repeated either for a predetermined number of replications or, after the cumulative behaviour of the network has been observed to converge (see Figure 5.14).

The two most popular packages at the time of writing this book are probabilistic packages imposed on well-known project planning tools. The first is @RISK for Projects (Palisade Corp. 1997), which is a sister package to @RISK, the main difference being that it is imposed upon a Microsoft Project file rather than an Excel file; as in @RISK, the input is a normal

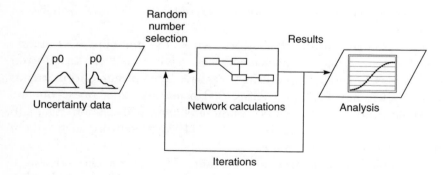

Figure 5.14—Monte Carlo analysis of networks

Microsoft Project file, but various parameters are allowed to be replaced by the @RISK probabilistic statements. The second package is called Monte Carlo (rather cheekily annexing the generic name for itself). This is a package for Primavera (Primavera 1995), based upon Primavera Project Planner (P3), widely used project-planning technique. This has a number of predefined capabilities, such as conditional branching and probabilistic resource requirements. Having said all that, the dedicated project risk analyst may well wish to develop his own tools, or at least supplement these existing tools with pieces of self-written code, to allow modelling of the full effects discussed in this chapter.

Examples

Let's look back to the development of military aircraft example we discussed above. This is easy to code into any network simulation, since we've defined it so simply. In fact, it can very easily be coded into an Excel spreadsheet. Normally distributed random variables are provided by Excel, as are Boolean (0/1) random variables; the network logic can, in a few minutes, be "hard-wired" in, and negative exponential variables ("random occurrences") found from taking the log of uniform [0,1] randomly distributed variables. This will give a probability distribution of the time to the end of the programme as shown in Figure 5.15.

This is from a very simple 400-iteration simulation (so as a rule of thumb, proportions quoted should be regarded as having a $\pm 2/\sqrt{400} = \pm 0.1$ confidence interval around them). The mean and standard deviations of this distribution are around 37 months and 7.5 months respectively, and the 90%-iles and 95%-iles are around 50 months and 54.5 months

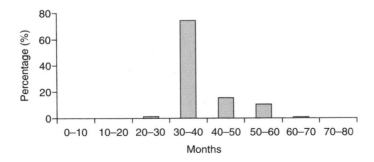

Figure 5.15—Results of development of military aircraft example

respectively. Of course, we can get a lot more from this simulation, but we'll look at this in the next section.

Take a second example. We said above that we'd revisit the North Sea oil platform project example, whose installation programme is shown in Figure 5.11. Modelling this project would require understanding of the behaviour of weather, in particular as measured by wave height. This requires knowledge not only of the distribution of wave heights over time, but also of statistical features such as their persistence, or their auto-correlation (that is, the intra-relationships within the wave series).

Suppose for simplicity we assume that the maximum wave height during a day (call this X_t at time t) follows an autoregressive pattern, so that

$$X_t = 0.8 \times X_{t-1} + 0.2.\mu + \varepsilon_t$$

Where ε_t (t = 0,1,2,3......) is a series of independent Normally-distributed random variables with mean 0 and standard deviation 0.5, and μ is the mean wave-height for the month, which let us suppose is:

Jan	Feb	Mar	Apr	May	Jun	Jul	Aug	Sep	Oct	Nov	Dec
6.5	6.5	5.5	4.5	3.5	3.5	3.5	4.5	5.0	5.5	6.5	7.0

(in feet) (these are NOT real data!).

Now let us suppose that the duration of the activities is as follows—and, for simplicity, let's just lump together the first five activities. Again this exposition has been grossly simplified, in particular in using a simple serial network—but of course, for a bigger network with resource constraints and cross-activity effects, and more realistic wave height constraints, clearly a network model within a general purpose programming language would be needed.

Start of the project: design, fabricate lattice, deck, base, assemble	Duration uniform between 3 and 4 months
Tow out	Task requires 6 days where max. wave height is less than 4 ft (will remain tethered during other days)
Install lifting system	Task requires 6 days where max. wave height is less than 3 ft (will remain tethered during other days)
Install cables/pipes	Task requires 12 days where max. wave height is less than 3.5 ft (will remain tethered during other days)
Commission	Duration uniform between 1 and 2 months

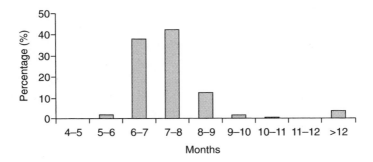

Figure 5.16—Results of North Sea oil platform project example

Assume that the project starts at the beginning of a year. Then we can simulate the network, and we'd find that the duration is as shown in Figure 5.16.

This is from a 1000-iteration simulation. There is thus around an 83% chance of the project being complete before August, and a 12% chance of it finishing in August; but then the weather gets bad, so that for the remaining 5%, the project will probably not be complete within the year. Again, we can get a lot more from this simulation, and we'll revisit this example in the next section.

Management decisions

One key element not generally included in analytical or simulation models is management control—decisions made during the course of a project in response to the progress of the project. This is a key element that we will need to consider and include in our models, and we will look at this in Chapters 7–10. It is still a feature of many network simulation outputs that the distributions are often very wide. A report that gives a 95% confidence interval (CI) to the project duration falling between (say) two and eight years will simply be ignored. A key reason for this problem is that the simulations described above simply carry through each simulation run in a "dumb" fashion. In reality, of course, management would take action to control a project going out of control but, until recently, simulations were unable to take cognisance of such actions. This has significantly weakened the credibility of the time risk analyses used in common practice (Williams 1999a). A few authors have attempted to include such management actions within analytical models or complex mathematical models, using simulation to reach a solution. Key amongst these is Golenko–Ginzburg, (1988b) who describes a line of work through GERT leading to CAAN (Controlled Alternative Activity Networks), which attempts to make decisions to optimise the networks, although these decisions do not depend on the state of the project at that time. The author understands that such methods are not widely used in practice, since they have a high level of complexity while still not incorporating sufficient generality with sufficient transparency for practitioner acceptance (although see a defence of this area and subsequent discussion in Williams 1997a). (For more on this work, see for example, Golenko–Ginzburg and Gonik 1996). But whatever type of modelling is used, it must recognise the multiple ramifications of management actions (Williams 1999a), which will be discussed in Chapters 7–10.

Criticality and cruciality

Using simulation, we can evaluate the duration of the project and the time to key event milestones. But just as deterministic network analysis provides the answer to the question, "Which activities are critical?", so we can use our probabilistic networks to look at the question, "Which items do management need to pay attention to in order to reduce the risk?" "Which items" here might mean activities—but could also mean "which risks?" or "which decision points?" or "which resources?"—and so on. That point immediately shows us that this is a more difficult question than in the deterministic case. But it is the basis on which tactical decisions are made— that is, decisions on how to run the project (rather than larger decisions such as whether to proceed, or how much to bid).

One definition of "criticality", has been long established and was widely used for decades. More recently, however, a number of authors, following pioneering work by Bowers and Williams (Williams 1992a, 1993b), demonstrated problems with this definition, and defined a new metric, known as "cruciality". This doesn't replace criticality but for decision-making requires both metrics to be taken into account. On the other hand, it is a much more general definition, and can be used to answer some of the questions posed in the previous paragraph. We'll look first at problems with the traditional definition, then look at cruciality, then how to use the two metrics together; finally, we'll go through a number of examples.

Standard criticality

Let's look first at the traditional definition, which for the purposes of this section we'll continue to call by its accepted name, "criticality". In a deterministic PERT network, with no resource constraints, the concept of "criticality" is well defined, easy to establish and easy to understand. When uncertainties are introduced to the activity durations, a definition of criticality has become generally accepted without question (uncritically!). Dodin and Elmaghraby (1985) define the criticality index of a path through the network as the probability that the path is a critical path. They then define an activity's "criticality index" as the sum of the all the critical indexes of paths containing that activity. This is equivalent to defining the criticality index of an activity as *the probability that the activity lies on a critical path.*

Of course, once you've simulated the network this can be estimated quite easily from the simulation output. Dodin and Elmaghraby is a well-known reference on the subject, so it will be used here to illustrate traditional thinking on criticality.

The first problem with this definition is that it can be misleading. Management expects activities with a high criticality index to be those causing high risk to the project, thus requiring more attention than other activities. Dodin and Elmaghraby state that "Evidently the larger the value of CA [the standard criticality index] the more crucial is the activity, and conversely." In fact, this is not so; this can be easily seen by considering a simple example, as follows. (The examples in this section might appear slightly impractical, but they are extreme cases used to illustrate the behaviour of indices under common circumstances. We need to know how these metrics operate and what they mean, and studying them for networks that we can easily understand will enable us to understand the output from computer programs analysing big networks in which we cannot easily see the effects.)

Example (a) is illustrated in Figure 5.17. This shows two independent activities, one of which has a duration of 0.1 or 0.2 days (50% probabilities) and one of which will probably be zero duration, but with a 1% chance of taking 100 days.

The criticality indices of A and B are easy to calculate: B is critical only 1% of the time, and A is critical the other 99%. Thus the activity "criticality" of A is 99%. Thus, the metric identifies A as the overwhelmingly "critical" activity. But a risk manager might well feel that the risk lies in activity B—small adjustments to A aren't going to make much difference, whereas the risk of the project taking 100 days lies in B.

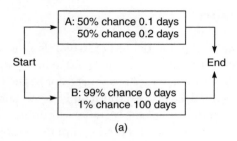

Figure 5.17—Criticality example (a)

This is a subjective "feeling", but something more objective can be said. The risk involved in an activity depends on the combination of the impact of various outcomes and their probabilities. The first problem with criticality is that it only considers probabilities. This means that, for example, activity A can be made more important to the total project risk without changing its criticality index. This can be seen by comparing example (a) with the two examples shown in Figure 5.18.

In example (b), the risk in A has become much more important to the project, and in example (c) it is the risk in A that is overwhelmingly important—a risk manager would probably apply all his effort to reducing the risk in A, and virtually ignore B. While these are still subjective statements, the fact remains that the relative importance of A and B has

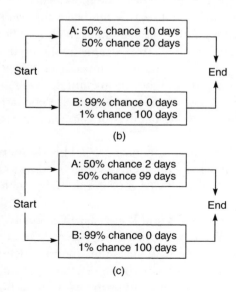

Figure 5.18:—Criticality examples (b) (top) and (c) (bottom)

changed drastically—but the criticality metric gives them indices of 99% and 1% for all three examples.

So we've identified two problems with the criticality metric:

- it's misleading;
- it doesn't distinguish between very different situations.

These are rather silly examples, but less extreme examples of this effect happen frequently in projects, for example where the bulk of a project has a fairly low uncertainty, but in parallel with this is a path of low mean-duration but very high uncertainty; possibly getting a safety case approved, or getting planning permission. A similar high-uncertainty path of activities could be the development of an item under a new technology, which will need to be redeveloped under a different technology if the first proves unable to meet the specification.

But there's also a third problem with the standard Criticality Index: it cannot be calculated in any but the simplest models. Even if there are only resource constraints in the network, the concept of a critical path ceases to be well defined, and thus criticality indexes also become undefined. (Any sensitivity analysis done would depend on the resource allocation algorithm used; Bowers is currently doing some ground-breaking work in this area.) Even more so, when the more complex modelling features we've discussed in this chapter are involved, traditional criticality is not useful.

Cruciality

These problems with the standard definition of criticality were the motivation for Bowers and Williams to propose alternative metrics. The metric that has become accepted, dubbed "cruciality" by Bowers, gives the cruciality index of an activity as (Williams 1992a, 1993b): *the correlation between the (activity duration) and the (total project duration).*

(It has been assumed here that the reader is familiar with correlation. Correlation (more specifically the Pearson correlation coefficient) is defined and discussed in any good statistics book (e.g. Chatfield 1970). It represents the degree of (linear) association between two variables—in this case, the duration of an activity and the total duration of the project—and thus indicates whether the two are likely to be related.)

Some similar work has been undertaken by Stjern (1994) (who reached a similar conclusion), Bowers (1996) (who looked at resource constrained networks), Soroush (1994) (who looked for paths that minimise the probability of completion by the deadline—although this leads to overesti- mation) and more recently Bowman (personal communication), but cruciality and criticality are the two metrics in common use.

Thus, if the project is always long whenever activity n is long, and always short whenever activity n is short, then activity n has a high "cruciality": its length is a good indicator of the length of the project, and thus presumably is to a large extent a determinant of the uncertainty in the project length (although see the discussion of causality later in this section). This index has been used for many studies of large projects, to identify activities requiring particular attention, and to identify problem areas that standard criticality analysis would not have picked up.

Does this metric solve our problems with criticality? Well, let's first consider our three examples. Cruciality can be easily calculated as:

	A	B
Example (a)	0.5%	99.999%
Example (b)	50%	86%
Example (c)	99%	10%

Thus, this metric appears to give figures that are more intuitively reason- able: so in the first example, B is by far the most crucial, while A grows more important and B less important through example (b) to example (c), where A is much more important; this seems to agree with our understanding of the examples. And of course it does distinguish between the three ex- amples. So we appear to have addressed the first two of our three problems. Turning to the third problem (that criticality can only be used under certain circumstances), cruciality can of course be used in any network problem that can be simulated—so long as a simulation can be run, statistics can be collected on activity durations and total project duration, and a correlation collected.

But, much more than this, the idea of cruciality can be used for any uncertain aspect of a project. As an example, suppose a network has a stochastic branch. Define a variable $x = 1$ if one path is followed and $x = 0$ if the other path is followed. Then

$$C = |\text{ correlation } (x, \text{ total project duration })|$$

is an indication of the effect of the path-choice on the path-choices. Thus we can compare this effect with the effect of activity durations, resource uncertainties and so on. In fact, since the standard deviation of C can be shown to be

1/(number of simulation iterations)

if the project duration is independent of path-choice, it allows conclusions to be drawn as to the significance of the statistic.

Care must be taken in interpreting cruciality indexes obtained from complex simulation models, since the causal link between the activity and the uncertainty in the project duration cannot be drawn directly from the high cruciality index. Inferring a causal link is usually reasonable (since the project duration is derived from activity durations) but sometimes other modelling aspects cause this effect. A typical example where a high cruciality does not imply a causal effect is when a number of activities are all assumed to depend on a single outside factor (a "common cause" or "third-party" effect, such as development activities all relying on the effectiveness of the initial Project Definition study in the sonar example above). In this case, if the common-cause effect has a high impact on the project duration via one of these dependent activities, all of the dependent activities will have a high cruciality index; for some of these, the high index may only represent the correlation via the common-cause effect rather than a causal effect. (This effect has been recognised in the successive principle of Lichtenberg and Moller (1979) where activity uncertainties are evaluated while identified common causes are fixed or "frozen", then the effects of artificial "common-cause" activities are added linearly.)

Using both metrics

So does cruciality solve all our problems? Well, no, as it can give results that initially appear counter-intuitive. It only measures the effect of an activity on the *uncertainty* in the project duration. Thus, if an activity has a large effect on the project but that effect is deterministic, it will have a low cruciality. The obvious example is when an activity is assumed to have no uncertainty, as in example (d) in Figure 5.19: if a project has two activities in series, the first taking 100 days and the second taking 0.1–0.2 days, the first will have a cruciality of 0% (since it is constant) and the second a cruciality of 100%. (As we said before, this example is of course impractical, since the

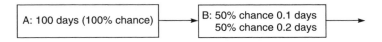

Figure 5.19—Cruciality example (d)

error in estimating a 100-day activity will generally swamp the smaller uncertainty in the second activity; however, as we also said before, this is an extreme case, to illustrate the common occurence of long, critical, relatively low uncertainty activities.).

Here, clearly A is the most important, since it contributes much more to the absolute duration. However, the uncertainty in project duration is entirely dependent upon B—but, as a risk manager, it's activity A that would be likely to keep me awake at night.

So, what's going on? Well, the two metrics are measuring two different effects in the network, and both can be important to the decision-maker. First, there is the effect of identified uncertainty causing *uncontrollable risk* to the project, measured by the cruciality index. Activities with a high cruciality need to be carefully assessed by management to see if their spread of uncertainty can be reduced—in other words, *risk reduction* is required for these activities.

The point of example (d) is that, if an activity really is of fixed duration (thus has zero cruciality), it would in theory be of no interest to the risk analyst. In practice, of course, durations can usually be reduced if effort is applied to so doing. This highlights the second effect being measured: for activities with a high criticality, there would be a benefit in *reducing their absolute durations by management control*—in other words, "expediting" is particularly desirable for these activities. Dodin and Elmaghraby (1985) again state that "Specifically, the CAs [standard criticality indexes] indicate which activities are the bottleneck activities, and should be expedited if the entire project is to be expedited", which agrees with our findings.

The answer, then, if there are no resource constraints or other such difficult modelling which inhibits use of the criticality index, is to measure *both* indices for each activity:

- the cruciality of the activity, which shows the total effect that its uncertainty is having on the project; and
- the criticality of the activity, call it C_A, which shows the probability that it is critical, and thus shows that if its duration were reduced by a small δ, then the expected project duration would be reduced by δC_A

The first of these reflects the impact of uncontrollable risks; that is, the effect of the uncertainty levels and impacts that have been modelled in the simulation, and the latter reflects the benefit that could be drawn from management reduction in absolute activity durations.

Activities are often found to have high criticality but low cruciality, or low criticality and high cruciality. These activities need to be viewed in quite different fashions. The former activities are known to be likely to be critical, so that it is worth management working at reducing their durations, or removing them from the critical path; however, they are not risky activities as a risk analyst would view them, and work to reduce their uncertainty would have little effect on the project out-turn. The latter activities are quite different—they are unlikely to fall on the critical path, so reducing the expected duration would have little effect; however, the high cruciality shows that in the event that they do become critical, their impact is very high (due to a long "tail" in their probability distribution), so that effort must be applied to ensuring that the uncertainty is reduced, so that the duration does not come into that distribution "tail". Obviously, activities whose criticality and cruciality indexes are both high warrant both types of attention.

Examples

Probably the first important time the idea of "cruciality" was explained to a client entirely unfamiliar to the idea, was a major study managed by the author of the time risk of a major defence programme. As a gross simplification, the programme can be summarised as shown in Figure 5.20.

The important parts of the programme (for this purpose) consisted of three major strands: building the first of a new class of naval vessel, developing and building a new computer to fit into it, and building the base to service the class of vessel, each of which consisted of a stream of activities. Each of these streams had quite different risk characteristics—as indeed could probably be guessed from the type of activity:

- the first, "Build base", allowed many work-arounds, so the risk could be avoided; this is typical of such a facility, where (say), if a power unit can't be built on time, a temporary power source can be provided, and so on;

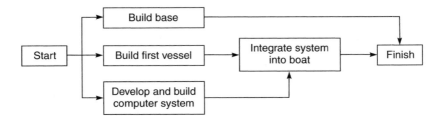

Figure 5.20—Simplified defence programme

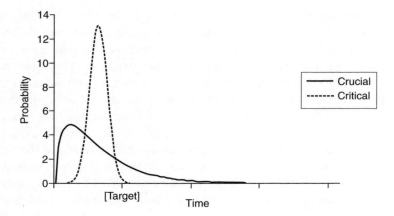

Figure 5.21—Typical completion times for crucial/critical streams

- the second, "Build first vessel" was critical: here lay the expected critical path, which needed to be managed carefully to complete on time but, being a manufacture, was not high time-risk, and was not crucial;
- the third, "Develop and build computer system" had an expected completion time less than "Build first vessel" but, as in any IT development, had a high time-risk, so this stream was highly crucial, but not critical. Typically, the distribution of completion times of the second and third stream would look something like Figure 5.21.

This figure shows a critical stream of activities, which should finish on time, and also a crucial stream of activities, which will probably finish before the critical ones, but have a long "tail" of distribution, so give the risk of lateness. Such crucial activities are of course commonplace: activities such as "obtain planning permission", "provide satisfactory safety case" or "obtain client permission to proceed" might be well off the critical path, but might have the potential (although low-probability) of very long delays which would cause a project to be very late.

For a numerical example, let's look back to the development of military aircraft example discussed above. Having simulated the project, it is easy to find out which activities are critical and which are crucial:

Activity		Criticality	Cruciality
1	Project definition	1	0
2	Start engine development	0.193	0
3 or 4	"Traditional engine: design and test" or "Radical engine: design and test"	0.193	0

5	Design and manufacture airframe	0.583	0.03
6	Design and manufacture avionics	0.225	0.00
7	Assemble	0.997	0
8	Engine and airframe flight trials	0.997	0.95
9	Avionics test	0.003	0
10	Avionics flight trials	1	0.97
11	Clearance to fly	1	0
	Success of PD programme	—	0.02
	Number of test aircraft lost	—	0.86
	Choice of engine	—	0

(This, you will recall, is from a 400-iteration simulation). So what do we draw from this? Well, first there is a clear set of activities which are highly critical: the Project Definition phase (which would probably be time-limited anyway), and the assemble, engine/airframe flight trials, avionics flight trials and clearance to fly activities. It is vital that these are not allowed to slip. However, a subset of these, namely the engine/airframe flight trials and avionics flight trials, are highly crucial thus contribute much of the uncertainty to the programme—these are the activities whose uncertainty needs to be limited. The reason for this is partly the inherent uncertainty within these activities, but mainly the loss of test aircraft—and the other key parameters (which engine is chosen, and how successful the project definition phase is) have an insignificant effect in comparison with this. Now, it is obvious that a lot of this could have been guessed from the original statement of the problem, since the problem is stated so simplistic- ally; however, it does illustrate how metrics can be established to give useful guidance to managers.

Final points

These definitions of criticality and cruciality still beg some questions, and two should be noted here.

● We have assumed that a project has a single end-point, and looked at the risk of achieving that. Of course, many projects will have a series of milestones which must be achieved on time due to external constraints. For example, consider the Los Angeles Oympics example, and look at the bid phase only: Figure 5.22 shows the activities to be undertaken, and some externally imposed deadlines. Cruciality analyses, then, must consider the cruciality to each end-date, as failure to meet *any* of these deadlines would have meant failure of the project.

- In the presence of resource constraints, or more complex modelling features, cruciality becomes even more useful, however, the standard criticality definition cannot be used, and this is an area still under study. Recent work by Bowers (2000) has finally redefined criticality in resource-constrained networks, but the implications of this have yet to be worked out in practice.

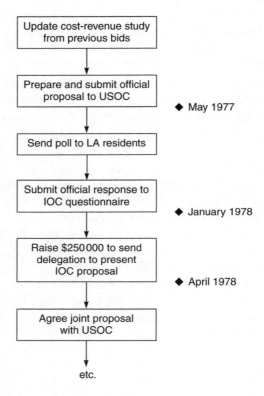

Figure 5.22—Illustration of multiple key dates based on Los Angeles Olympics. USOC = United States Olympic Committee; IOC = International Olympic Committee.

The concept of cruciality can be extended beyond analysis of risk to aiding decision-making. One typical use is in apportioning contingency between activities in a probabilistic network, as described in Williams (1999d). This method distinguishes between two requirements for contingency: for high-variance crucial activities, and for high-float, non-critical activities. This allows us to have a logical two-step apportionment, the first based upon the idea of cruciality and the second based upon standard ideas about float.

The three criteria and beyond

We've looked at time risk, and before that at cost risk. But we said back in Chapter 2 that projects have at least three objectives: completion of (a) some technical objective to a certain level within (b) time and (c) cost constraints. Indeed, Morris (1988) claims (with a literature list to back up his point) that "research has shown time and again, projects fail because the technical content of the program is not controlled strictly enough or early enough." We've also said that there are trade-offs between these three (remember "Good! Fast! Cheap! Pick any two"?). Klein (1993) goes one step further and says that the total "intrinsic risk" cannot be reduced but has to be shared between time, cost and quality risk—he illustrates his analysis with a cognitive map of trade-offs. So shouldn't we be looking at the three (or, as is usually the case, more than three) objectives simultaneously?

There is little in the literature about the analysis of performance risk (i.e. risk to the achievement of the total technical objective). While the addition of time elements is more difficult than the addition of cost elements, the summation is at least feasible, being the summation of a similar type of item. For performance risks, the different measures making up the overall required technical performance are not commensurate with each other.

Let's take an example. A shipyard has a contract to build a warship. It has technical targets for speed, weight, reliability/availability and infrared signature, radar cross-section and so on. Under the type of contract now common in most countries, failure to achieve the target on any of these measures will involve damages. For example, in a contract studied by the author some years ago, to build a number of warships at the rate of one per year, one element of the contract value was for availability. This element was not paid until after four years, when 10 ship-years had been achieved—one ship having sailed for four years, one for three years and so on—and the total availability over those 10 years was tested against the target. Furthermore, there might be trade-offs between these measures and between them and time and cost—making a ship more reliable implies redundancy; more available implies carrying spare; these both mitigate against a lighter, faster and cheaper ship. Big, powerful engines to make the ship go faster will increase infrared signature, and so on. However, the measures cannot be combined in any sensible way.

It must also be remembered that distributions or probabilities of these parameters will not be independent, but rather will be highly correlated, sometimes negatively (i.e. the achievement of one target—say, weight—is likely only to come with a lower probability of the achievement of the other target—say, speed). The calculation of the risk profiles of the individual measures themselves will be different depending on the type of measure involved. Simple additive measures, such as weight, might be carried out exactly as the simple cost summations in the section earlier this chapter on uncertainty and risk. More complex summations, such as for infrared signature, must be carried out in ways specific to that measure.

Once the technical performance measures themselves have been made commensurate, there is a further problem of making the (overall) technical performance commensurate with the temporal and financial performance. Only then can a proper measure be provided of the "success" (and hence risk to, or progress towards, success) of a project, as we're looking for.

To carry out such an overall analysis, a common measure must be used. The most obvious seem to be probability or cost. Let's look at probability first: that is, calculate the total probability of achieving the technical target (i.e. all of the individual measurements). If we can work out the probability of achieving each target under different conditions, then we can calculate the probability of achieving our overall project objectives. Again, there is some work involved in trying to do this analytically—for example, Bushuyev and Sochnev (1994) use a complex matrix methods to give the p.d.f. (probability distribution function) of cost and the probability of achieving goals. Hazelrigg and Husband (1985), in evaluating R&D projects, propose a model that combines the probability density functions of "technological advancement", time and cost, although it is not clear whether this would transpose successfully to the analysis of individual projects. As in all our models, real life is usually too complex for analytical methods, and simulation has proved more successful.

Let's turn now to the second option—cost. Probability allows us to work out the probability of achieving all the objectives, but doesn't distinguish between only just missing the objectives and missing them by a long way—unless you plot the probability distributions separately, which loses the overall view. A similar "pass/fail" approach is taken by Riggs *et al.* (1994) who use Saaty's (1998) AHP (Analytical Hierarchy Principle) on the three criteria of time/budget/technical. The neatest solution, where it can be done, is to turn all the impacts into costs. In fact, in modern contracts this is often very easy, as Liquidated Damages or (the reverse) Incentives are given in the contract. This has been an aim in risk analysis for some time (e.g. Kohrs and Welngarten 1986 and Franke 1987), but it is difficult to achieve unless the project has been modelled and then simulated. An alternative to cost is utility—Canal (1996) simply uses utility curves for the different objectives, thus perhaps avoiding some of the quantification problem but taking the result one step further away from the managers' understanding.

Where such an analysis is feasible (and often data collection issues are problematic) the models are either trivial or too large to be used here as illustrations. A common use is in comparing two distinct high-level design options: should we build a nuclear submarine with reactor X (less powerful and older technology) or reactor Y (which requires a change to the hull diameter to fit it in)? Another specific example is in the spares provisioning problem, where minimising the cost and weight of spares carried mitigates against minimising the risk of non-achievement of availability targets, but both can easily be transformed into probability distributions of cost.

However, such balancing analyses are now sometimes carried out. For example, NASA has recently described a decision process for their "Faster-Better-Cheaper" projects (Dillon and Pate-Cornell 2001). This process recognises the move towards increasing complexity and shrinking lead times that we identified in Chapter 4, but identified with this a requirement for increasingly reliable systems. Thus there is a need for risk trade-offs between time/cost and reliability within the project. The process they describe:

- starts with identifying the lowest cost design for each functional configuration;
- optimises the design for each configuration and budget allocation;
- optimises the risk mitigation strategy for each configuration, including all aspects of risk strategy; then
- selects the optimal design to minimise the expect cost of failure states.

Of course, this is for a single, well-defined, success criterion, which can be costed fairly straightforwardly. But in principle a similar decision process can be undergone for multi-criteria performance measures, so long as there is some mapping in to a cost function.

As a final step in the analysis, we must remember that "cost" isn't just "cost"—in many projects it means cash flow. This means that sometimes, rather than studying cost, we will want to study the Net Present Value (NPV). Essentially, that's little different as far as simulating the model is concerned. What it does do is add an extra dimension of management decision-making. There is a considerable literature on optimising deterministic networks by NPV, and there is no room here for a proper discussion of this topic. See instead Yang *et al.* (1993) who set start and finish dates using Integer Programming to maximise NPV; Padman and Smith-Daniels (1993) who again maximise NPV, but allow earliness too; and Russell (1986) who puts cash flow considerations into resource-constrained networks. But once the network becomes stochastic, little work has been done in calculating how to schedule the project to optimise NPV (although Schtub (1986) tries to maximise NPV by trading off late start of activities with the probability of the project as a whole being late.)

There is one other area of projects for which cash flow takes on a new significance. This is where the project contractor also owns the facility, either permanently or for a predefined period of time. In many domains, rather than simply building a facility, or designing and building it, contractors are taking responsibility either for maintaining and operating it for a fixed period (e.g. DBOM: Design, Build, Operate and Maintain), or even for complete ownership, with transfer back to the client after a fixed period (e.g. BOOT: Build, Own, Operate, Transfer). In this case, we are interested not only in the cost of the project over the build phase but the (discounted) through-life cost (or at least, cost over the fixed period).

Conclusion

This chapter has described modelling for projects where we can take individual items or individual aspects and model them separately. There are lots of issues we haven't covered here: to start with, we haven't discussed how to collect data for these models, nor how to model "softer", human aspects, nor what happens when there are systemic combinations of effects. Crucially, we also haven't considered what happens when management start reacting to the behaviour of the project—all of these models simply look at the effects of impacts on a project, without considering how project management will react. All of these factors are covered in forthcoming chapters. But this chapter has given us the basis for creating models of projects that can be useful to understand what is happening in large and complex projects.

6   Discrete effects: collecting data

Introduction

Everything we talked about in Chapter 5 depends on data that has to be collected for each project. Since, by definition, projects are novel one-off ventures, the data generally don't exist—so we rely on forecasting, subjective analysis and extrapolation. To begin with, this is difficult. It is here that models can lose credibility—it's often not the models themselves that are questioned but the data that goes into them ("Garbage In—Garbage Out").

This chapter will discuss a few aspects of collecting data for the types of models covered in Chapter 5. Two caveats need to be made. First, it's a big subject, which we started to discuss in Chapter 3; there are general principles on collecting data for management science models which also apply here, and we do not have space to do full justice to the subject. So only a few topics will be covered, which are those that the author has found to be helpful in his experience of modelling projects. The second caveat is that the ideas here only cover data for the models described in Chapter 5. Later on, we'll revisit this subject when data is needed on other variables in models, such as the "softer" effects in projects. And here we'll meet a number of ideas, in particular the idea of cognitive mapping, which helps managers to express their mental models and helps to build up quantitative models. This can be developed in causal maps.

This chapter will first look at some well-established general principles. Then it will look at two particular topics. The first is how data is estimated and probability distributions chosen for simple activity-duration models. Second, when estimates have been made and plans established for a project, those in themselves affect the behaviour of the project, and the last section looks at this issue. Before we start, it is assumed that basic, deterministic planning data for a project is available: a WBS, a high-level network, a responsibility matrix, and so on. Now how do we gain data to be able to model uncertainties, risk and "what-ifs"?

Since, as we've said, each project is a unique one-off enterprise, there are essentially only two ways to gather data: either take historical data from past projects and extrapolate that into the future, or depend on the judgement of those who know about the domain of the project. Of course, in practice the data is a mixture of the two, since on the one hand extrapolation into the future is informed by expert judgement, and on the other hand subjective judgements are informed by the past. But it's helpful in discussion to look at the two separately.

We won't say much in this chapter about using historical data on past projects. There are a number of problems in practice, the main one being a lack of data. In the past, surprisingly few organisations have collected data on project performance. It's often been found that, when trying to look back at past projects, while there are personal memories, often there is no formal database of project success or failure. Some domains are more successful at data collection. Oil companies tend to have well-developed databases, (although they are also secretive), particularly as two of their main areas of uncertainty—weather and geology—are particularly amenable to collecting empirical data and carrying out statistical analyses. A second domain which ought to be good at this is defence, since as each nation has a single main customer carrying out risky development projects. In fact, for the UK, there is surprisingly little available summary data, although there is a great wealth of anecdotes which give valuable insights into the success or failure of defence projects (e.g. Bryson 1982, 1986). The turning point in effective UK defence project management was the Downey Report (Ministry of Technology 1969), which stated that

> The need throughout the Ministry of Aviation for systemically recorded information on past projects has been recognised for some time, but our investigations have disclosed that unfortunately much of the information required is not readily available, and where it exists is not suitably recorded. Moreover, little progress has been made towards devising a suitable system of recording . . . It is true that in the Controllerate of Aircraft, the Project Time & Cost Analysis Branch (PTC(An)), formed from the old Technical Development Plans, can provide some information about airframe development, but this is not in a form in which comparisons can easily be made . . ..

Developing just this area of work in PTC(An), Pugh (1987) describes a database of military aircraft (and guided weapons) project out-turns and discusses the results on timescale out-turns. (For example, he shows that time- and cost- overruns are not highly correlated.) But even in this domain, data is very sketchy.

In recent years, this lack has been recognised, and databases of risks are being built up. Two early examples of databases of project risks are Niwa and Okuma (1982), who describe a well-structured database (with a structure reminiscent of a Risk Register) in use at Hitachi, and its value for knowledge transfer on project risk; and Ashley (1987), who describes a number of examples of expert systems based on risk knowledge. Some software vendors will now sell databases specially structured to store Project Risk Registers from one project to the next.

Of course, even when historical data is available, the interpretation of it for use in forecasting is rarely obvious. Pugh (1987), for example, gives an example of plotting the duration of military aircraft development projects over time, which gives two quite different answers depending on whether the plot is by start of development (which implies a small but steady increase in project durations, 1950–1980) or by end of development (which shows a rapid rise in project durations, starting again with very short-duration projects and again rapidly rising—this hiatus being due to a fundamental change in aircraft technology). Even where the meaning of past data is clear, how much this can be extrapolated into the future remains a question of expert judgement.

So let's turn now to how to elicit judgements about uncertainty and risk from domain experts.

Collecting subjective data: identification

The first stage in establishing the risk to a project is to identify those elements which are causing risk. There are a series of techniques discussed in the standard industry handbook, the PRAM Guide (Simon *et al.* 1997), also discussed in Chapman and Ward 1997. These include:

- *Assumptions analysis.* All project planning is based on assumptions. If those assumptions prove to be wrong, then the project might not proceed as planned; therefore, consideration of the assumptions in a project plan or bid is likely to reveal risks. Typically, such assumptions will cover external interfaces such as performance of suppliers and sub-contractors, or the behaviour of the client. Internal assumptions might include productivity and learning rates, staff availability and so on. Simple projects will be planned with implicit assumptions; these plans must then be scrutinised, perhaps based around the WBS, to identify those assumptions. In the planning of complex projects, an assumptions database is sometimes used, and this provides a valuable source of data for the risk analyst. In either case, a brainstorming session is often useful to draw out those assumptions which have still to be made explicit.

Having identified each assumption, the project team must then estimate the likelihood that it proves to be false and the effect on the project if that is the case (usually initially as "High", "Medium", "Low" or "Nil"—see Chapter 5). This then provides a direct input into the Project Risk Register.

- *Checklists*. These are simply *aide-mémoires*, usually taken from experience of previous projects. Many companies develop their own checklists, although Hiltz (1999) has now published a vast handbook of checklists. Again, checklists are often structured around the WBS, although this can often miss out the most important risks, which are either systemic or external (e.g. the client behaving in an unexpected way). Figure 6.1 shows the start of a typical example.
- *Prompt lists* are similar, allowing more open-ended questions for a brainstorm. Such lists need to be multi-dimensional in order to provide as exhaustive an analysis as possible, so one part of the list could treat aspects of the project, and another part could look at project phases (or use the WBS) (see Figure 6.2).
- *Brainstorming*. This is well-known, and comes in a variety of unstructured or more more structured (i.e. prompted) formats. The key to the technique is the encouragement of all contributions, and the subsequent building of ideas on top of previous contributions.
- *Interviews*, which are self-explanatory!

Area	Keyword	Question	Yes/No/NA	Action
Client	Previous work	Have we worked with this client before?		
	Knowledge	Is the client experienced in this field?		
	………			
Requirement	Clarity	Do we understand the requirement?		
	Definition	Is the requirement well defined?		
	Client interfaces	Are the interfaces with the client risky?		
	………			
Contract	Fixed-price	If fixed-price, is the work bounded?		
	………			

Figure 6.1—Start of typical checklist

Aspects	Phases	Requirements
Technical	Conceptual design	Internal resources
Commercial	Detailed design	Sub-contractors
Legal/contractual	Construction	Information
Financial	Testing	Client agreements
Political	Commissioning	Permissions
Environmental	....	....
....	....	....
....	....	....

Figure 6.2—Typical prompt list

More advanced techniques use mapping techniques, particularly those invented by Ackermann and Eden, which will be mentioned later in this book.

Collecting subjective data: general principles of quantification

Identifying where risks will arise in itself provides a project with useful benefits, as discussed in Chapter 5: it identifies where we need to take management action to avoid or reduce risks, it prompts management to consider insuring against particular risks, and it helps management draw up a suitable contract, with ownership of risk shared in the most appropriate way. But in order to make quantitative decisions or forecasts, we need to model the project, and for this we need quantitative estimates of the likelihood and impact of each risk. Estimates of the impact are usually fairly straightforward, sometimes even being given by definition of the risk. "Impacts" are difficult to discuss generally anyway, so we'll concentrate on the elicitation of probabilities in this section—many of the general principles also apply to elicitation of impacts.

There is a whole body of knowledge on what subjective probability is, and how you can get an expert to quantify his subjective feelings about probability in a robust, coherent way. Wright and Ayton (1994) have written a set of papers describing the current considerations of subjective probability, and discuss the type of biases that can occur when trying to elicit probability. There is no scope here to discuss the philosophy of subjective probability (although it isn't always obvious: for example, if I ask you to estimate the probability that I vote for the UK Labour party, what are you estimating? Either I am or I'm not—it isn't a probabilistic statement, you're measuring a "degree of belief").

If we take as read for now the existence of mental concepts of probability, a literature of formal methods to elicit subjective probabilities to ensure consistency and uniformity has built up: for a review, see Kahneman *et al.* (1986) or Keeney and Winterfeldt (1989), but the classic paper is by Merkhover (1987). In certain risk analyses, where the number of probability distributions is fairly small and the decisions to be taken are very important, it is worth putting a lot of effort into getting an expert to specify one probability distribution (getting experts to specify or quantify risks is generally known as "elicitation"). The best-known methodology for doing this is *SRI encoding process*, and this is described in Merkhofer's paper. This is a six-stage process, and Merkhofer's paper has been summarised below. It should be stressed that in project risk management *it is very rarely worth carrying out this methodology in full.* Generally, we have a lot of distributions or probabilities to quantify, and just enough time to get a good estimate. But the methodology is summarised here because it highlights the main biases that can occur in such elicitation. It is these biases that we have to watch out for when we are quantifying our models.

Stage 1: Motivating the subject

The first stage is to establish a rapport with the subject. First, the aim of the exercise is explained: namely to measure the subject's knowledge and best judgement concerning the quantity; not to predict the quantity. This distinction may be very important if the analyst detects in the subject either *management bias* or *expert bias*. The first of these is when the subject views the quantity as a goal rather than an uncertainty—"if the boss wants me to minimise cost, I'll estimate it as low as I possibly can". The second, expert bias, is where the subject feels that as an "expert" he should down-play his uncertainty—a question such as "you're the expert in estimating this parameter, what is the uncertainty in its forecast?" is likely to result in an underestimate of the possible deviation. An important goal at this stage is also to explore the potential for *motivational bias*—that is, for a conscious or unconscious adjustment in the subject's probability assignments motivated by a perceived system of personal rewards.

Stage 2: Structuring the variable

The second stage has two purposes. The first is to structure the uncertain quantity into one or more logically related, well-defined variables suitable for quantification. The second is to explore how the subject thinks about the quantity, which helps to indicate the likelihood of various *cognitive* biases (distortions associated with the simplified rules that research suggests people use to reduce the complex task of assigning probabilities to events). First, the elements are precisely defined so as to remove all possible ambiguities in definition (otherwise questioner and answerer might have different understandings of the variable in question). Then the analyst explores the usefulness of disaggregating the variable into more basic variables (which can help to combat motivational bias by producing a level of detail that disguises the connection between the subject's judgements and personal interests). The final step is to list all the assumptions the subject is making in thinking about the variable.

Stage 3: Conditioning the subject

The third stage aims to draw out into the subject's immediate consciousness all relevant knowledge relating to the uncertain variable. This is to avoid technical errors in judgement that are commonly found to occur, such as underweighting distribution information and regression toward the mean. Then the analyst seeks to counteract *anchoring bias* (the tendency to produce estimates by starting with an initial value) and *availability bias* (giving a higher probability to occasions that are easier to recall).

Stage 4: Encoding the judgement

This stage quantifies the uncertainty. There are various methods available, most related to presenting the subject with choices which are given probabilities, or choices which are equated in probability (e.g. by using a "probability wheel"). These are described by Merkhover.

Stage 5: Verifying the result

Following encoding, the judgements obtained are tested to see whether they agree with what the subject really believes, by checking that the subject is comfortable with certain aspects, such as shape or implied results.

Stage 6: Resolving expert differences

Finally, it is often desirable to obtain probabilistic judgements from more than one individual. Merkhover discusses how these might be aggregated into a single distribution.

Collecting subjective data: simple activity-duration models

So we've had some pointers about types of bias we should avoid when we try to estimate probabilities. But let's consider our particular circumstances. We're generally trying to:

- make many estimates in a short time;
- generally with scarce data;
- initially estimate probability distributions of expenditure or activity durations (we'll concentrate on the latter to be specific, but the considerations also apply to the former).

Encoding distributions directly using, for example, the SRI method under these circumstances is generally impractical for all but a few activities in a network, because of the length of time the process takes; and even if encoding is used, generally an *a priori* distribution is fitted (e.g. the Beta). So we'll generally need activity durations to be given *a priori* probability distributions, and then estimate parameters. There has been a lot of debate about which *a priori* distribution to use (e.g. Golenko–Ginzburg 1988a and a new distribution proposed by Berny in 1989). For many years the Beta was used, and PERT made simple assumptions to analyse the network, but this has been shown by a number of authors to be incorrect (see the discussion in Golenko–Ginzburg 1988a). This section will discuss the number and choice of parameters, and the choice of distributions, for activity durations, and their use in practice, to support the types of model discussed in Chapter 5.

To define an activity-duration distribution, five parameters generally need to be specified, either explicitly or implicitly: (1) a parameter expressing position; (2) a parameter expressing spread; (3) a parameter expressing skew; (4) a minimum (which might be zero); (5) a maximum (which might be infinite). In thinking about parameter estimation, three questions need to be considered: (1) How many parameters should be estimated? (2) What default or generic information can be used? and (3) Which parameters should be estimated, and how are they to be estimated in practice?

First, the number of activity parameters to be estimated must be decided. For example, distributions requiring estimation of four parameters (e.g. Berny 1989) may be impractical if only two are accessible, but if information is available it should be used. Five factors need to be considered: (1) *The project status*. At the feasibility stage, even the project structure itself is ill-defined (at the earliest stage, only qualitative analysis may be possible, but quantification is important as soon as practical). At this stage, generally only "one and a half" parameters are available for each activity, at best: a position parameter, and some perhaps less quantified feel for spread. In such cases, we can often make an initial definition of the position parameter (see below), and use generic data to aid quantification of the spread (also see below). In later stages, activities are better defined, so more parameters may be available; however, a well-managed project will have established its ongoing Project Risk Analysis/Management early on, with later analyses updating earlier analyses rather than starting afresh. (2) *Historical data*. In some cases, previous projects might give indications of shapes or types of distribution (e.g.the PTC(An) work referred to above). Parametric methods might be of value, in a similar way to parametric costing methods. (3) *Planners who are giving advice*. Planners who are able to advise on activity duration and uncertainties and durations might not be able to supply more sophisticated parameters, such as "the probability of falling below a nominal minimum" (Berny 1989). (4) *Time available*. As we've already said, if there are many activities and time is limited, it may only be possible to estimate two parameters per activity. Even with a more manageable network, four parameters per activity might prove more than the available expertise is able or willing to estimate. (5) *Ease of analysis*. The objective of the modelling is to provide an analysis of the whole network. More general distributions might obscure the overall results. The modelling principle of parsimony suggests that as few parameters as necessary should be used.

Rather than estimate each individual parameter, default or generic rules can be used. Such rules arise from either (a) a general appreciation of project activities or (b) analysis of previous projects or activities of a generic type. We've already said that the original PERT assumption, from category (a), that duration standard deviation is one-sixth of the range, is now considered unacceptable (and anyway assumes that the "range" is between two particular percentiles—see the discussion in method of moments in Chapter 5). Two simple rules of thumb are often of value when looking for the set {position, spread, skew} in an ill-defined project:

- In category (a), to estimate skew and thus reduce estimation from three parameters to two, we can observe that durations generally tend to have a 2:1 skew (the mode being 1/3 along the range); this has also been proposed separately by Golenzo–Ginzburg (1988a). While not applying to all activities, this can act as a useful default when no indication suggests an alternative shape.
- In category (b), to further reduce estimation from two parameters to "one and a half" where there is only a "feel" for spread, levels of uncertainty have been suggested for different activity types, with descriptions giving guidance as to categorisation (this has been developed by Bowers (1994) in practical work with Pugh of PTC(An). Each class is given a "generic factor", equal to the Standard Deviation/Duration Position Parameter (which is the Coefficient of Variation if the mean is used as the position parameter). An example might be as shown in Table 6.1:

Table 6.1—Example uncertainty levels

Uncertainty Level	Generic activity type	Generic factor
0	Deterministic	0
1	Low variability	Manufacture	0.2
2	Medium variability	Full development	0.3
3	High variability	Project definition	0.4
4	Very high variability	Trials	0.6

In deciding the parameters to estimate, the most important is the position. This is generally a recognised parameter, such as the mean, mode, median or "target". It is the position parameter that project managers tend to have a "feel" for, so deriving it from other parameters loses the best source of estimates. Estimation will be influenced by the question asked, but it is important to establish which parameter corresponds to project managers' innate mode of thought. Bowers (unpublished, quoted in Williams 1992b) has suggested that this is the mean, since if the mode is estimated (assuming a positively skewed distribution), few projects would complete by the planned end-date, and history would force estimators to revise their methods. This author's personal view is that project managers generally estimate modes for individual activities, but add a safety margin when estimating total project durations, perhaps intuitively recognising the probability combination. This can be contrasted with the idea of disaggregation, that experts combine probabilistic events wrongly, so cognitive biases need to be removed by estimating event probabilities individually (Tverksy and Kahneman 1974).

The remaining four parameters—spread, skew and upper and lower limits—are interrelated, since most distributions do not have five degrees of freedom. The best set for managers to estimate needs to be found. All of these parameters pose problems for subjective estimation, since they do not correspond to parameters that managers readily envisage. Five criteria can be applied when choosing parameters to estimate:

1. The parameters and the assumptions involved must be *easily understood* by the estimator. This must be one of the most important considerations: if the project manager does not understand or cannot subjectively envisage the parameters, no sensible estimates can ensue. "Mode", "Optimistic value" and so on are readily understood; "Certainty of minimum" perhaps less so. A position parameter is generally more easy to understand.
2. The parameters should be *easily estimated*. If the project manager understands the nature of a parameter but its estimation is not natural, the quality of the estimates will be degraded.
3. It is helpful if information such as percentiles is *easily calculated*, implying that the manager can readily see the implications of choosing a particular parameter.
4. The applicability of lower and upper *limits* to the distribution needs to be considered.
5. *Particular considerations,* such as *a priori* assumptions, historical data, or the need to be compatible with other projects, should be taken into account.

Some risk analysts use the uncertainty levels described above, and illustrate them (having assumed a distribution and 1/3 skew) by giving 10% and 90% points, showing the "probable minimum" and "probable maximum". This set of parameters, (most likely or mean) and (probable limits or uncertainty level), is a natural set for a manager to estimate at relatively early stages of a project, and also gets around the difficult questions of "absolute" maxima and minima. (Berny's "minimum" and "probability of falling short of the minimum", for example (1989), appear considerably less natural—and we've already noted the problems with estimating "absolute" maxima in our discussion of the method of moments in Chapter 5).

All of the comments above, of course, must be tempered by the general principles for eliciting uncertainty discussed in the previous section.

Which distribution should be chosen? The uniform distribution is

applicable only in special cases. The normal distribution has problems due
to the probability of being negative. There are thus three main candidates:
beta, triangular, and gamma.

1. The beta distribution is often not understood by practitioners, nor are
    its parameters easily estimated. If the distribution should be unlimited it
    is not applicable, but where it can be limited, the beta fails on its under-
    standability (as far as project managers are concerned). Also, its four
    degrees of freedom are a nuisance in practical application.
2. The triangular distribution offers comprehensibility to the project-
    planner. Williams (1992b) has found that project planners are happy to
    accept this distribution, and the use of the 10% and 90% points and the
    "levels of uncertainty" described above have eased the process of uncer-
    tainty elicitation. The use of the "probability of exceeding the mode"
    can sometimes be meaningful if the skew is to be estimated. Williams
    (1992b) also gives the ratio between the tails of triangular distributions
    and beta and gamma distributions to show how close a triangular
    approximation is. Figure 6.3 shows some of the equations required to fit
    a triangular distribution. However, it does have the problem of absolute
    upper limits.
3. The gamma distribution is of additional value where an upper limit is
    specifically not wanted. However, the calculations involved are not

Triangular distribution:

$$f(x) = \frac{2x/bc}{} \quad 0 \le x \le b \quad \text{(minimum: zero)}$$

p.d.f. f(x)	=	$2x/bc$	$0 \le x \le b$ (minimum: zero)
	=	$\frac{2(c-x)}{c(c-b)}$	$b \le x \le c$

Mean	$(b + c)/3$
Variance	$(b^2 - bc + c^2)/18$
Mode	b
P (x > mode)	$1 - b/c$
10% point	$\sqrt{[0.1bc]}$
90%	$c - \sqrt{[0.1c(b-c)]}$

To fit a triangular distribution with minimum A, mode A + b and maximum A + c,
given a mean μ, variance σ^2 and mode M:

$$c = \sqrt{[24\sigma^2 - 3(M - \mu)^2]}$$
$$b = (c + 3M - 3\mu)/2$$
$$A = M - b$$

Figure 6.3—Results for triangular distribution

Gamma distribution:

p.d.f. $f(x)$	$=$	$(x/b)^{c-1}e^{-xb}/b\Gamma(c)$	(minimum: zero)
Mean	bc		
Variance	b^2c		
Mode	$b(c-1)$		

$P\,(x >$ mode) and 10% and 90% points require calculation of incomplete gamma functions.

To fit a gamma distribution with minimum A and parameters b and c, given a mean μ, variance σ^2 and mode M:

$b = \mu - M$

$c = \sigma^2/b^2$

$A = \mu - bc$

Figure 6.4—Results for gamma distribution

simple (see Figure 6.4), and require the use of tables or simple computer algorithms.

Where there are dependencies between activities, various methods have been used, from estimation of correlation coefficients between activity pairs, to complex use of joint distributions. The simplest method is to model the independent and common-cause elements of the durations separately, providing a number of independent variables, then to combine them either additively or using more complex construction. This facilitates modelling of effects over a large number of activities. Of course, the questions of which distribution to use, and which parameters to estimate, must be addressed again for the common-cause effects. Now, however, more abstract concepts are generally being dealt with (e.g. "'effectiveness of project definition", "success of system X design", political factors, etc.), so the difficulties of elicitation are exacerbated, and the justification for sophisticated distributions weakened. Many modellers find a simple and direct distribution (such as the triangular) most acceptable for these factors.

Effect of targets

In the previous section, and in all work in estimating parameters for network analyses, it has been accepted that the meaning of these estimates is known and understood. Not only that, but certain assumptions are implicit in the stochastic calculations, such as that if the duration of one activity falls below the central estimate, then the succeeding activity can draw upon the spare time with no penalty, and the establishment of the estimates will not affect the actual duration that occurs. Following chapters will look at some of the softer effects in projects, such as the relationship between targets and participants' attitudes, but before we've looked at these more sophisticated models, we should first question some of the basic network assumptions and, where necessary, modify our models.

We can note three issues from recent literature which suggest that the nature of network estimates, in particular the central estimate, might not in fact be well understood.

1. Adding uncertainty to activity durations always increases the expected project duration, since nodes take the maximum of preceding finish-times. It has been observed that since most project planning is now and has in the past been done deterministically, estimates of project durations should in the past have been consistently too low (e.g. Bowers, quoted in Williams 1992b). While it is a generally accepted opinion that projects take an inadequate view of risk, we don't often see straight-forward projects with aleatoric uncertainties amenable to estimation being consistently highly underestimated (with no learning from experi-ence by project managers) being reported in the literature as observed in practice.

2. It has been established that there is a relationship between setting (deterministic or central) PERT estimates and setting targets. In par-ticular, Littlefield and Randolph (1987) compare PERT with Manage-ment by Objectives (MBO). They conclude that "there are definite similarities in the way PERT activity time-estimates and the way MBO objectives are developed . . . The main reasons for PERT's success seems to have been the process of estimating activity times rather than the estimates themselves . . . The mathematics of PERT are of secondary importance, and the real value of PERT is the estimating process itself."

3. A natural consequence of the idea of the PERT estimate as a target is the observation that the actual duration is rarely less than the target. To some extent, this is due to the idea that activity durations tend to be skewed—as we have said, often regarded as skewed twice as much to the right of the mode as to the left. However, the main cause that has been discussed recently is *Parkinson's effect* (Parkinson 1957). Gutierrez and Kouvelis (1991) attempt to define some models in which the duration of an activity is dependent upon the allocated duration; this includes mathematical statements of "expect all activities to be late",

and "it is the busiest man who has time to spare", and goes on to derive lessons for management, such as setting initial targets for each of a set of serial activities, and a single initial target for parallel activities.

So what data are available when a risk analysis is carried out? Let's suppose, following the last section, that there is one set of "official" estimates for the project duration: a set is usually given to a risk analyst and provided as part of an official project plan; this is generally the set the corporation is happy to "go public" on and on which they base their bid or project budget. This provides the central estimate for activity durations. When carrying out a risk analysis, and setting estimates for the distribution of the activities, it becomes clear, following the three points above, that:

1. For any single activity, that there is often a high probability of achieving this central estimate (that is, of the activity duration being less than or equal to the estimate). This probability is much greater, say, than the typical 33% of achieving the mode (noted above); in one project I analysed, this probability was felt by the company to be 80%, which appears to be not dissimilar to other projects. (Of course, the experience within other domains might differ.)
2. These central estimates influence the activities themselves, since they are treated as targets to which the project works.
3. Therefore, Parkinson's law comes into play; if an activity turns out to be faster then expected, the work slows down, with the degree of slowing greater the quicker the activity (otherwise) turns out to be.

These points obviously influence the *a priori* distribution that should be used in the risk analysis. When the first point applies, this means that the "central" estimate m is likely to be a certain percentile, an $100C\%$-ile, with C being quite high (eg a $C = 0.8$ (80%)). Furthermore, it is probable that taking C as constant over the activities is likely to be an appropriate first approximation, at least if a homogeneous corporate culture is in operation across all of the estimating parties. The third point implies that the probability distribution of completion time below m is likely to be "squashed up" towards m—that is, if the cumulative distribution of completion time without any influence from the target date were known to be $F(x)$, then Parkinson's effect would give $F'(x)$, where $F'(x) \leq F(x)$ for all $x \leq$ m. The second point could suggest that the probability distribution of completion time above M is also likely to be "squashed up" towards M—if the cumulative distribution of completion time without any influence from the target date is $F(x)$, then the target effect would give $F'(x)$, where $F'(x) \geq F(x)$ for all $x \geq$ m.

It can be concluded, therefore, that where the above experiences apply, temporal risk analyses have tended to use cumulative probabilities for the central estimate, that are too low, and deviations from the estimate, that are too high. This perhaps explains one reason why risk analyses have so often given unrealistically low probabilities of on-time completion and unrealistically broad percentiles for the *a priori* distribution of completion time, which have caused them considerable credibility problems in recent years. (Another reason we shall see is that simulations do not reflect the actions that management would take to bring late-running projects under control—we'll deal with this in Chapter 9.)

In choosing an *a priori* activity-time distribution shape, no account has been taken of the effect of target completion date. It follows from the above that the distribution may well be discontinuous about the central estimate, a possible shape being shown in Figure 6.5. In one major development project analysed by the author as project risk co-ordinator, in the absence of other information he used an approximation to Figure 6.5, a modified triangular distribution was used (as shown in Figure 6.6) given by the equations:

$$f(x) = \begin{array}{ll} 2\,C \times m^{-2} & x < m \\ 2\,(1 - C)(1 - x)(1 - m)^{-2} & x > m \end{array}$$

where for convenience and without loss of generality the minimum and maximum are taken as 0 and 1 respectively. This can be described as follows: 100C% (in this case, 80%) of the distribution is below m, with decreasing triangular distributions towards the minimum and maximum (with a discontinuity at m). For the sake of clarity and replicability, it is this explicit distribution that is analysed throughout the discussion below.

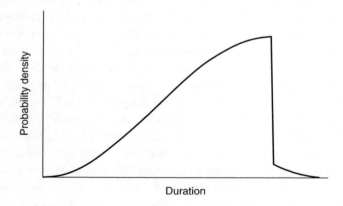

Figure 6.5—Possible activity-duration distribution

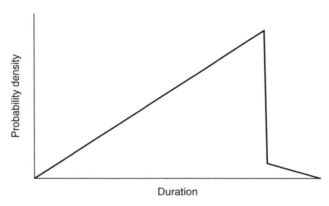

Figure 6.6—Triangular approximation to Figure 6.5

If it is the case that the "central estimate" and distribution are as described above, what does that mean about the estimation of whole projects? If the estimate m is used in a deterministic calculation, how does this compare with a stochastic calculation based on this distribution? If it is similar, does this explain issue (1) above, namely that projects have not been consistently highly underestimated in practice? Williams (1995b) studies the behaviour of this distribution by looking first at sets of serial, then sets of parallel, activities. Briefly, if N identically distributed random variables, each with the distribution shown in Figure 6.6, are added together, representing the duration of N activities in series, then the total distribution can be found by numerical simulation to have a $100C\%$-ile generally slightly below that which would be estimated in a straightforward deterministic calculation (namely Nm). Similarly, if the maximum of N similar identically distributed random variables is taken, representing the duration of N activities in parallel, then the total distribution can be found by numerical simulation to have (for typical values of parameters) a $100C\%$-ile generally around 50% above that which would be estimated in a straightforward deterministic calculation (namely m). Put together, these two effects tend to cancel themselves in projects: the degree of safety built up by serial runs of activities roughly balances the generally forgotten about risk implicit in high levels of parallelism. This can be seen intuitively, with the degree of error depending on the shape of project networks found in a particular organisation; it can also be shown by experimentation. Williams (1995b) gives a numerical example, showing that where the culture of the organisation is to estimate activity target-durations at the $100C_0\%$ level, the project duration calculated deterministically from the activity target-durations is a good estimate for the $100C_0\%$-ile of the project duration distribution.

So, there are two points to this brief chapter. The first is to stimulate thought on what is really estimated when PERT activity parameters are estimated, bearing in mind Parkinson's law, the relationship with Management by Objectives, and the historical basis on which these estimates are made. The second is to suggest an underlying distribution that follows from these points, both a general shape and a pragmatic approximation, which can be shown to reflect behaviour found in practice, and which has been used in the practical analysis of a large development project.

Conclusion

This chapter has described some issues we need to consider when populating models built on the lines of those described in Chapter 5. The comments are designed for the usual situation of building models quickly with a paucity of data, and we've suggested how we might populate a whole network simulation model with only "one and a half" parameters for each activity. However, we've also discussed the SRI method which, as well as giving general principles, also allows more careful estimation of subjective probabilities. We've also identified some problem areas and proposed some quick fixes, such as the existence of Parkinson's law. This means that we can now make a start on some modelling. However, we'll need to revisit this subject when we start looking at the "softer" project issues that we need to model.

7 The soft effects

Introduction

Anyone who has experienced a number of actual, large projects will have read Chapter 5—and indeed many books on project management techniques—and said, "but real life's not like that". So far, we've only dealt with the absolute, clearly defined aspects of a project—what must be done, in what time, under what circumstances, at what cost and so on. But the problems and issues that arise in real-life projects are often much harder to define and specify: these are the "softer" aspects of a project, and are to do with how humans operate and react, whether they are clients, project managers or the project team. But although they're harder to define and quantify, they are still important and can even be crucial to project performance. This chapter will try to define some of these, and discuss how they can be modelled.

But can such things be modelled? Is there any point looking at such factors if they aren't amenable to modelling? Well, modelling here is more demanding than it is for easy to define objective factors. By definition, "soft" factors are difficult to define and measure, but there are three issues which justify this chapter, which should become clear as the chapter progresses.

1. As we've already said, experience shows that often these are the critical aspects that explain how projects behave—indeed, they often determine whether projects are successes or failures. Some of the examples we quote will illustrate some of these issues—but already our discussions of projects have made frequent references to, say, the characters of the main players (the architect of the Sydney Opera House, the political driving forces behind the Calcutta Metro, . . .). In fact, a concern with "softer" factors has increased within operational research/management science generally. In the UK, we have come to appreciate this rather quicker than in the USA—only in 1998 a leading US operational

researcher wrote, "Our current models are concerned with tangibles . . .
It seems to me that the field would make a vast creative step if it were to
look seriously into models that handle intangibles and their measurement, because most of our problems deal with such factors" (Saaty
1998).

2. While these aspects are difficult to model, we'll mostly be looking at the
effects caused by the aspects, and in particular at the effects of changes or
perturbations in the aspects, so we won't need to define absolute
measures (which in general would be very challenging) but, instead,
relative measures and models of relationships between these measures.
Saaty, quoted above, goes on to say that, "The measurement of intangibles cannot be done on an absolute scale with an arbitrary unit of
measurement. It must be done in relative terms. An intangible, by definition, has no scale with a unit. Thus, it must be evaluated by comparing it
with other intangibles in the context of a property or a goal." Well, that's
true until the intangible starts to affect tangibles, which will be the case in
this chapter. For example, studying "morale" is interesting in itself, but
here we are especially interested in the effects of other influences upon
"morale", be they tangible (say, quantity of design changes) or intangible
(say, client hostility), and the effects of "morale" on other influences,
especially tangible (productivity, staff turnover, error generation) but
also intangible (say, effectiveness of relationship with client).

3. Finally, difficulty in defining and measuring a variable does not imply
that that variable should not be included in a model. I can't put it any
better than Jay Forrester, who said almost 40 years ago:

> There seems to be a general misunderstanding to the effect that a mathematical
> model cannot be undertaken until every constant and functional relationship is
> known to high accuracy. This often leads to the omission of admittedly highly
> significant factors (most of the "intangible" influences on decisions) because
> these are unmeasured or unmeasurable. To omit such variables is equivalent to
> saying they have zero effect . . . probably the only value that is known to be
> wrong.

He goes on to say "A mathematical model should be based on the best
information that is readily available but the design of a model should
not be postponed until all pertinent parameters have been accurately
measured. That day will never come" (Forrester 1961).

So let's have a look at some of these aspects, and how we might model
them. In fact, while we'll discuss some models of individual aspects, we'll
find that it's not so much the individual aspects themselves that are important, but chains of aspects (where a change or effect in one aspect causes

something else to happen, and so on), particularly when you take into account managers' responses. So perhaps the most important role of this chapter is to list the individual items that will be discussed in the next chapter, on systemic effects in projects, and the following chapter, which looks at one particular method for modelling such behaviour, System Dynamics.

We could look at several aspects of this. We'll look at some of the most important, taking the three players mentioned above (clients, project managers and the project team) in turn. After a brief note on a few key characteristics of the project, the chapter will look at:

- client behaviour, and similar external effects on the project;
- certain aspects of project management decision-making, particularly as a result of changes and perturbations in the project;
- the results of one particular important aspect of project management decision-making, namely project manning (determining the size of the project team);
- effects within the project team, and their reactions to the effects from the previous sections.

Some key project characteristics

As we discuss the soft aspects within a project, and in particular the effects on project behaviour of changes and perturbations, we'll need to talk about, and measure and model, some key project characteristics. While these would be constant in a static, problem-free environment (if you can imagine such a thing), changes in the project will imply changes in these characteristics, which will be important in understanding the behaviour of the project.

The first characteristic is project *size*. "Size" can be characterized in a number of ways. Studies have looked at the overall size of a project and drawn conclusions—for example, Schwarztkopf (1995) quotes a study of electrical construction projects giving the relationship

$$(S_x/S_y)^{0.6} = D_x/D_y$$

where S_x is the size of project x measured in man-hours, and D_x its duration.

But these overall conclusions derive in the main from project *complexity*, a

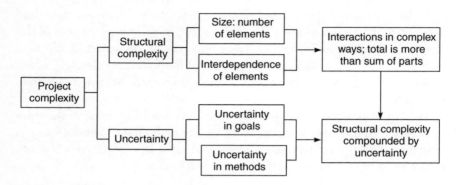

Figure 7.1—Dimensions of project complexity

subject discussed at length in Chapter 4. We summarised project complexity by Figure 7.1.

These dimensions clearly affect the degree to which human factors impact on the project, so they will crop up through this chapter. Increasing the size element of structural complexity will increase the "communications overhead" on a project (i.e. the proportion of time needed for communication across the project team) . Increasing the interdependence element of structural complexity will imply increasing cross-impact (since effects on one element will affect interdependent elements) and mean that effects in one part of the system "ripple through" the rest of the system more. Uncertainties in goals will cause unexpected client behaviour, which will have a multitude of effects. Uncertainties in methods will affect engineer behaviour, as they react to internal hesitations and changes.

Client behaviour and external effects on the project

The behaviour of the customer/client is generally key to the behaviour of a project. Understanding and predicting how the customer will behave is a key element to bidding for and managing a project. Even when a project is governed by a fixed-price arm's-length contractual arrangement such as "EPC" (Equipment Procurement and Construction) or "EPIC" (Equipment Procurement, Installation and Construction), where the project is supposed to be carried out essentially independently of the customer, experience shows that how the customer behaves can make or break a project. While there isn't space here to do full justice to any of these aspects, let's look at five ways in which customer behaviour can affect a project—these will form the original causes for many of the effects discussed later in this chapter.

Scope changes

Where there is the Uncertainty in Goals element of project complexity, the customer is likely to require changes to the scope of work or the specification of the work during the project. This can either take the form of substitution—changes to a design to give a product of an equivalent value (changing a green car to specify a blue car) or addition—increasing the value (changing a Ford to specify a Rolls Royce). It can be couched in terms of a contract change, in which case the client accepts responsibility and the contractor has to cost the change; or, it can be simply "preferential engineering", where the client expresses a preference despite being given a design fit for purpose, in which case the contractor has, as well as costing the effects of the change, also to submit a claim for the extra cost. In any case, the cost of a mid-project change to the project definition or scope will nearly always be higher than if the change had been made before the project started.

The costs of a change to the specification are many, and range from those that are clear-cut and easy to specify and calculate to those that are soft and ill-defined. There is the cost of:

- the additional work;
- deleting and redoing any design work;
- retro-fit of any items already manufactured;

So far so good—these can initially be estimated as the original project was estimated:

- where the project is structurally complex, there is the effect on other interdependent items, and the ripple-out effect: secondary or tertiary cross-impacts, etc.;
- where the items have already started to be manufactured, there is the effect on the learning curve (again, see below);
- there is the compounding effect when there are many changes, which we'll come to shortly;
- there is the subjective effect on the designers (again, which we'll discuss below);

- and there could be other "Delay and Disruption" effects (Eden *et al.* 2000).

Because of all of these effects there is also:

- the effect on the project duration—either a time extension or project acceleration (which we'll discuss below in Management decisions).

Because of these non-primary effects, unexpected change orders are usually—perhaps nearly always, although I know of no empirical evidence for this—undercosted. Examples of the wide effects of scope changes in the projects listed in Chapter 2 are manifold, but I will only quote one here. In Engineering Project Y, a large number (many hundreds) of external aero-nautical parts were being designed and manufactured. Midway through the project, the client changed the aerodynamic lines of the parts very slightly—which meant that many parts which previously came in identical pairs were now to be left- and right-handed pairs. The actual change in terms of the first three bullet points above was fairly small. But look at the six bullet points above: there was cross-impact throughout the product; the single learning curve became an interlinked pair of learning curves; the designers now had to deal with twice as much paperwork and configuration control; the manufacturers now had two assembly lines of very similar-looking parts which had to be kept separate as they were crucially different; and unless the project duration was extended to take account of all this, there had to be management acceleration as well. All this, from one very small and simple design change!

Another example, which we'll follow in Chapters 8 and 9, is the naval ship life extension project, described in Williams (1997b). This project was the life extension of an old naval support ship, involving the insertion of an additional mid-section and a complete refit. The contract specification required compliance with the regulatory and statutory regulations in force at the date of signature but, mid-project, the 92 SOLAS (Safety Of Life At Sea) safety regulations were ratified, and shortly afterwards the client decided that this ship should be subject to those regulations. The effects of the changes caused by these regulations were various, but of particular rel-evance were (a) the air conditioning (HVAC) system had to be redesigned and enhanced, and subsequent changes caused the HVAC line to be rerouted and related services adjusted; and (b) the deck head spaces (thus the space available within the ceilings) had to be reduced. But upgrading the HVAC would have caused deckhead space to be very tight and the routing of services very complex anyway; reducing deck head spaces exacerbated these problems, and indeed in a few cases made design infeasible without contravening the specification. The effects of this change mid-design were catastrophic, and by Chapter 9 we will have demonstrated why this was so.

Multiplicity of scope changes

The effect of scope changes is seen particularly when there are many scope changes. These can lead to further delays in client approvals; multiple changes to cross-impacting elements (which can of course be contradictory, such as a demand to increase redundancy followed by another to reduce weight); changes can increase product complexity, producing increasing cross-relations between parallel activities developing cross-related parts of the product; then this implies increasing difficulty in providing a system freeze. Also, redesign causes disruption to the design schedule; this often means that system elements are designed without having full specifications of the necessary interfaces; the workforce sometimes has to be increased which, as we shall see below, has multiple effects; the design staff can be disincentivised, as they are working with unclear parameters. Plus, when a concurrent manufacturing phase is considered, there are additional effects, both because design activities finish later and thus increase concurrency, but also because items begin manufacture and are then changed, which leads to retrofit and degradation of manufacture learning, and also because the products are no longer Designed For Manufacture (DFM), a key element of Concurrent Engineering (Syan and Menon 1994).

We are already starting to see the systemic impacts that can come from these effects, and it is this that will form the basis of Chapters 8 and 9. But we can see that many of the effects triggered are subjective and "soft", and it is these we will discuss in this chapter.

Many examples of continuous specification change are provided by the requirement to satisfy ever-changing safety regulations. One such domain is, of course, the field of nuclear technology, which is subject to strict regulatory bodies. In the UK, Morris and Hough (1987) describe the UK Advanced Gas-Cooled Reactor (AGR) programme up to 1986. In particular, they describe the Hinckley Point B station project, estimated in 1966 at £96mn, which overspent by £48mn (£14mn of which was due to inflation): £19mn (40%) of the over-spend was ascribed to "modification and development needed to bring the basic plant design to revised standards". However, writing in 1987, they also state that the philosophy of safety cases adopted by the Nuclear Installation Inspectorate had led to less "regulatory ratchetting than in the United States (where the Nuclear

Regulatory Commission wrote and promulgated regulations)." They quote Canaday (1980), who analysed 35 US nuclear power plan projects, which had resulted in up to 400% cost overruns, highlighting increased safety requirements as one of the causes. Kharbanda and Pinto (1996) devote a whole chapter of their book to such projects, quoting, for example, the Marble Hill Plant, which is thought to be the most expensive nuclear plant project that has been abandoned, because "the cost of complying with additional regulatory safeguards simply became prohibitively expensive". Another such domain is the field of transport, which is an obvious area in which products are the object of national and international safety regulations; those regulations are subject to unexpected change (particularly resulting from transport disasters); and the regulations are rigorously enforced. This domain provides the naval ship life extension project above, and also the shuttle wagons project, which was subject to continuous changes as the safety regime kept shifting. But this latter example also included customer delays, so let's look at this idea next.

Delays

External factors such as safety regulations give a good example of the potential for delays within a project. The shuttle wagons project, for example, was undertaken by a contractor for TML. A number of aspects of the design, construction and operation of the Channel Tunnel required approval from the Intergovernmental Commission (IGC), a body of British and French civil servants. During the development phase of the project, their major focus was on safety, defence, security and environmental issues (as described by the Major Projects Association 1992). It became clear partway through the project that design changes required by the IGC were not only causing delays, but that work was having to proceed prior to gaining IGC approval, with subsequent changes and rework when IGC decisions turned out not to be favourable. It is instructive to read a newspaper report from 1991 (the concession had been granted in 1986, and UK Parliamentary Approval gained in 1987):

> [Eurotunnel] said delays were expected because of changes in the design of fire doors separating rail shuttle wagons to meet strict safety guidelines. The [IGC] has insisted that fire doors between wagons carrying passenger vehicles be widened by at least 10cm to allow easier access . . . [Eurotunnel] warned yesterday that changes in the design of fire doors were likely to lead to a delay of up to 6 months . . . Eurotunnel was discussing the possibility of introducing bonus payments to encourage the shuttle wagon manufacturers to make up any lost

time caused by the design change . . . The [IGC] also warned that the design of semi-open-sided wagons to carry heavy goods vehicles would be unacceptable in its present form . . . discussions were continuing with the Commission . . . The need to complete the project as quickly as possible to start earning revenue to repay bank borrowings meant that design had to be completed and contracts placed before the [IGC] completed its deliberations. (Taylor 1991)

But a client can himself impose delays at various stages to the project. If the client has obligations within the contract to comment upon or approve documents, or to supply equipment, there is the potential for delay. And even where strict obligations are placed on a client to avoid delay, he can use tactics to delay matters: for example, if a client has to approve or comment upon documents within a certain time, he can simply send the document back with spurious comments or questions, to remain con-tractually compliant. Often the delays are difficult to pin down when documents are "in limbo", as a client thinks about proposals or goes into extensive discussions or requires "studies" (see below); this again causes the effects above, but also leaves the project particularly susceptible to changes to the design late in the design process, and also inhibits the release of work from design to construction. As in scope changes, delays can build up and compound each other—and we shall demonstrate some of these effects over the next few chapters.

Extra supporting work

One particular type of delay, worth a particular mention, is when the client forms part of the design approval process and requires unreasonable or over-extensive validation or supporting evidence for proposals. Such requirements might come under the headings of:

- *unreasonable comments* on design documents; while reasonable comments are expected during the design process, excessive and unreasonable comments can significantly delay the early stages of a project (Williams *et al.* 1995 shows a model including this on the shuttle wagons claim);
- *excessive design-proving* or *benchmarking*: an inexpert client might not feel assured that a design is optimum, or would achieve its requirements, so can ask for further proof, or for the design to be benchmarked against other extant constructions. This can also cause considerable delays, especially benchmarking against constructions which are scattered worldwide and which need to be visited;
- *studies*, where further-ranging studies of design options are required.

These delays are particularly significant, since they come early in the project and during the conceptual design phase.

Interference

There are other ways in which the client can interfere directly with the project, particularly the design phase. Indeed, an analysis by Kaming *et al.* (1998) of a sample of projects lists "interference" as the most important impact upon productivity. Such interference can take place at all stages of the project: "breathing down the necks" of designers (so reducing productivity, although there are well-recognised benefits to having contiguous contractor and client design teams), changes to designs late in the design process, changes to test procedures, and so on. When we claim that a client has "interfered", we must characterise that interference by these specific types of actions, then they can be quantified, even if subjectively ("engineers' productivity was reduced by 5% because of having client engineers present . . . 3% of agreed conceptual design documents were later changed because the client changed his mind . . .").

Trust

Much of what is described above is symptomatic of the amount of trust that client and contractor have in each other. While characterising "trust" as a variable and quantifying it would be very challenging, by identifying the types of variables we've discussed in this section, and quantifying them, we are able to model the effects of a lack of (or the benefits of the existence of) client-contractor trust. There isn't scope to explore this area in this book, but it is a new area of study in which research is being undertaken (Hartman 1999) and new developments expected.

Management decisions

As we shall see in Chapter 8, client actions or external events are, in themselves, not sufficient to explain effects upon projects. When the external environment acts unexpectedly or changes (whether this is caused by the client or another element of the external environment), the project's management will have to take decisions in response. The overall effect on the project comes from the combination of external impulses and management responses. Indeed, we said that this was the problem with much of the work done using the type of network simulations described in Chapter 5: that such work frequently gives rise to very wide probability distributions, so is deemed not credible, largely because the simulations do not reflect the actions that management would take to bring late-running projects under control. Such actions are difficult to include in models, not because the actions themselves are complex, but because the effects of those actions are not well understood. We'll look at some of these actions here, then model some of their effects in the following chapters.

Before we look at particular actions, we need to make the point that project management make decisions based on the information they have. This means that, in our models, we will have to include the information flows, including delays, misperceptions and errors, in order to understand the behaviour of the project. So, for example, where management make decisions based on engineers' assessments of activity completion, we must include the effects of those engineers' perceptions in our model, such as the "90% syndrome" (which we'll discuss in Chapter 9).

The key actions that management take are in response to project slippage, such as that caused by client delays. In these circumstances, management will either adjust the schedule, or will attempt to accelerate or compress the timescale or, frequently, aim for a balance between these. Various actions can be taken to compress a project, and these are increasingly common in today's world of tight deadlines and heavy Liquidated Damages. Whether these actions are actually efficacious is another matter, and we will return to this once we have modelled the actions and can evaluate their effects.

There are two obvious ways of compressing a project. The first is to make individual activities shorter (in the planning phase, this is traditionally called "crashing"). The most obvious way to do this is by increasing available manpower, which we'll discuss in the next section, but there might be other ways of shortening an activity, perhaps by buying in more of a support resource. The second way is to carry out activities earlier than would be expected from the planning network. Such policies could include:

- design management working on items for which the surrounding system is not yet frozen—items on which they would not normally wish to work;
- increasing the use of parallel activities (such as designing related parts in parallel rather than in series, or increasing design/construction concurrency);
- starting to commissioning work that is not yet completed.

Of course, such actions increase the cross-impacts between parts of the project, and thus the structural complexity of the project, and this is one of the effects of the actions that we shall have to include in our models. Over the remainder of this chapter and the next two chapters, we'll explore in detail some of the effects of such actions and their modelling, which can often be counter-intuitive (Howick and Eden 2001).

Let's look at a couple of examples of these actions. The first is the London Ambulance Service project. There was a two-month delay in starting the programming while the system design specification was written, and a further delay due to the late delivery of the radio interface system specification. Mid-project, a new systems manager was recruited, and (despite not being directly involved in this particular project) he carried out a review of progress and insisted that the implementation date be kept as it was in order to maintain pressure on the suppliers. Lateness continued, and there was a decision to implement a partial solution at the target start-up date. It was this partial solution that caused many of the problems. The issue of "maintaining pressure" within a project we'll come back to in the section on subjective effects in a project, below. But the decision to compress the project led to the need to implement the partial solution, which had a small error in it, hence the resulting debacle. Furthermore, it meant that the system was implemented piecemeal across different divisions over an extended period, during which the system was never stable, frequently having changes and enhancements made to the software and system.

One example in which the results of management actions can be seen and measured more easily than in most domains involves software quality. In the KDCOM project, software design quality was critically important. The company had a design review process, but it was suggested that this could be replaced by a more thorough novel inspections technique. But this latter was very time- and effort-consuming—so was it worth it? Rodrigues (2001) describes a model allowing either the existing or the novel quality regime, with the critical direct impacts of using the novel inspections included and quantified (e.g. by improving the defect detection efficiency, by reduced overlap of defects detected by different reviewers, and links to parent and related documents).

While there are sometimes such directly measurable technical results from management actions, the more interesting effects, the modelling of which is not obvious, are the effects on the project behaviour. One set of management actions which lead to particularly interesting effects is that involving adjustment of project manning. We'll therefore look first at actions concerning project manning, and then we'll look at the "softer" resulting effects on the project team.

Project staffing

The immediate reaction of many managers when a project is slipping is to put more staff on to the project. In some circumstances, for some work, there is a direct relationship of duration = work/manpower (the old school maths problem: "if it takes three men one day to dig a hole x feet deep, then . . ."). In some circumstances, of course, duration is independent of staff numbers (such as the old—rather sexist—adage about one woman being able to produce a baby in nine months, but nine women cannot produce a baby in one month). But most real project instances are, of course, not that simple. It is natural to think that putting on more staff will reduce project duration, and it is easy to fall into the mistake of thinking that the reduction will be linear, but there are often more complex effects at work. This section will look at some of the effects of increasing project staffing. These results will be taken further in the following section and the next two chapters, until we find that some results can be completely counter-intuitive.

At a gross level, it is recognised that taking a team of workers above the natural limit produces a less effective workforce simply due to overcrowding. The US Army Corps of Engineers' Modification Impact Evaluation Guide 1979 (quoted in Schwartzkopf 1995) provides graphs for determining the effect of overcrowding, as shown in Figure 7.2.

Here, overcrowding is defined as (actual manpower/scheduled manpower – 100%), but it seems more justifiable to assume that it ought to be actual divided by some reasonable limit. Similar graphs are given in Schwartzkopf (1995) for the relationship between square footage available

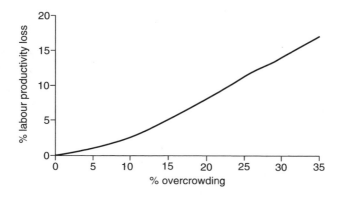

Figure 7.2—Gross effect of overcrowding, from Schwartzkopf (1995) Schwartzkopf, W. (1995) *Calculating Lost Labour Productivity in Construction,* John Wiley & Sons, New York. Reproduced by permission of Aspen Publishers.

to a worker and his efficiency, taken from oil companies and other similar corporations. But these graphs are highly domain-specific, depending heavily on the complexity of the product being constructed, so that, for example, very few workers can be crowded into a section of a submarine under construction, while a larger number can be accommodated on an open construction site where little has been constructed.

But gross overcrowding is obviously only one effect. Our discussion of project complexity has already said that as inter-element dependencies increase, then project complexity must also increase. Where the increase in project staffing is simply increasing the size of a homogenous set of essentially identical entities (modern examples are hard to imagine—perhaps slave labour building an ancient pyramid) then perhaps there are no inter-element dependencies. Generally, however, there is a communication overhead as elements need to interact with each other, and this means that the increase in output does not linearly increase with manpower. Again, the software industry is able to measure this effect better than most, and a number of experiments have been undertaken to demonstrate the effect. Early simulation experiments in this area were undertaken by Scott and Simmons (1975), modelling the communication overhead within a software development project. They provide a useful model that can describe productivity as a function of the number of programmers and the team's communication structure (characterised by a matrix of probabilities of interaction, much like the cross-impact matrix in Chapter 4). This also reveals a productivity that declines exponentially with the number of programmers, concluding that "there is an upper limit to the number of programmers that can effectively add to the total group productivity"—an early form of Cooper (1994)'s "$2000 hour" effect. Brooks (1978) says that human communication in a software development project is the most significant cause of overhead [meaning slowdowns and obstacles], and since everyone must communicate with everyone else, this overhead expands in an n^2 rule: "Oversimplifying outrageously, we state Brooks' Law: adding manpower to a late software project makes it later." (Note, by the way, that his law applies to a *late* project, not to a project running on time: the effects discussed here and particularly in the next section apply when management start to overload or overcompress a project.) Shooman (1983) gives a similar n^2 rule.

But there are other effects, such as those outlined in Eden *et al.* (2000). Two, in particular, are important:

- It will be some time before new staff are acquainted with the company and with the project, during which time they are less productive. During this time existing staff will also become less productive as they take time to train the new staff.

- As the workforce changes, the project team is "churned": staff are reallocated from one job to another, they lose the value of the learning they have gained, and begin a task with less expertise and thus lower productivity. This is particularly noticeable on a production line, where learning curves are generally carefully tracked: we will revisit this topic in more detail in Chapter 9.

Modelling these effects within a project assumes that we have a model to determine when the manpower will increase or decrease—i.e. (generally) how management makes decisions to increase or decrease the labour force. As we move into Chapter 9, we shall see that this will prove the most challenging aspect of these models.

Subjective effects within the project

The effects we have discussed so far involve variables that are generally clearly measurable. However, many of the aspects we will consider in Chapters 8 and 9 are not so easily measurable, but form an essential part in the chains of effects that build up in a project.

When a project is running late, or is disrupted, or management decide to try to achieve "early delivery" bonuses, they often try to get their team to work faster—that is, they apply *schedule pressure*. To a certain extent, there is often slack within a project, and sometimes workers can work harder. Boehm (1981a, b) showed that computer programmers normally work at around 60% efficiency—that is, in an eight-hour day, they put in 4.8 hours of effective work (the remainder he called "slack time"). He looked at the effect of schedule pressure (i.e. the understanding that there isn't enough time to finish the job) and found a relationship that could up to double the amount of effective work per day (i.e. by using overtime). But applying pressure brings a number of other effects, and we shall see in Chapter 8 that this particular management action can have much reduced—sometimes even contrary—effects.

The first device often used to increase the amount of output from a project team is *overtime*. This leads to an obvious increase in available man-hours but also, over an extended period of time, to fatigue or exhaustion. Schwartzkopf (1995) again provides tables and graphs of the overall effect of periods of overtime. As expected, working for isolated or sporadic periods of time leads only to a limited loss of productivity (one data source suggesting a single day extended from 8 to 12 hours would be 92% productive). However, Schwartzkopf quotes some (fairly limited) data for the construction industry from the Business Roundtable, indicating that extended periods of *n* weeks working a 50-hour week resulted in productivity of around $(100 - 3n)\%$ up to $n = 9$ weeks, where the effect levels off; similarly, extended periods of $n > 2$ weeks working a 60-hour week resulted in productivity of around $(105 - 5n)\%$ up to $n = 7$ weeks, with the rate of decline thence slowing to around 64% productive time after 12 weeks. An alternative or additional policy is to move to *two-* or *three-shift working* and if necessary to extend the shift-lengths. Again, Schwartzkopf (1995) provides graphs of the overall effect of different extended shift patterns.

Abdel-Hamid and Madnick (1991) use a straightforward relationship relating the *rate of increase in exhaustion* to the *actual fraction of a man-day worked on a project*—that is, using Boehm's (1981a, b) norm (quoted above) that computer programmers normally spend 0.6 of the day on a project, they take a variable

$$X = \frac{(1 - \text{actual fraction of a man-day worked on a project})}{(1 - \text{nominal fraction of a man-day worked on a project})}$$

and set *the rate of increase in exhaustion level* (i.e. the rate at which a limit on tiredness is reached) as a function of X, linear for $X > 0$ and more steeply linear as X $(\rightarrow)$ -0.5 (an arbitrary lower limit, representing double the normal amount of effective work per day). Such models will clearly be specific to the particular industry and domain of the project being modelled, but their form can be adapted to most circumstances.

As well as the effects of fatigue and exhaustion from simply working more hours, schedule pressure causes other, less easily definable, subjective effects on staff. Cooper (1997) discusses modelling the "unwanted side-effects [of staff overtime]. The quality impact (the later need to do it again) is far less visible, but no less real. Equally real are longer-term impacts of sustained pressures. Every experienced manager has seen the considerable morale impacts when the staff is pressured from all sides to improve not only on the schedule, but also the costs and the quality as well. . .[This effect] though often acknowledged in spirit, is consistently underestimated." The effect of schedule pressure on worker motivation, morale and stress must be taken into account in modelling, as the effects of accelerating a project cannot be judged without some sort of model of these effects.

But of course it is not only schedule pressure that has such effects. Client changes, and increased project uncertainty complexity (either uncertainty in goals or uncertainty in methods) will lessen engineers' ability to plan properly and effectively, leading to a piecemeal and inefficient approach to the work. Furthermore, it will disincentivise design staff as they work with unclear parameters and knowing that their work may turn out to be pointless. All of these elements will affect productivity, as well as other parameters such as error rate, scheduling and so on, and we will try to model some of these effects in Chapters 8 and 9. Such models were used, for example, in the shuttle wagons project (Williams *et al.* 1995b) as the team attempted to explain the effect of a continuous stream of design changes from the client.

The attitudes and feelings of a project team of course depend not on their actual circumstances but on their *perceptions*. We have already said in Chapter 3 that managers rely on their measurements and perceptions, and it is on these that their decision making is based. As we said in Chapter 3, we don't need to take the epistemologic line of denying the existence of an objective reality, but we must understand that our data will always represent some particular perception of reality. Indeed, the models in Abdel-Hamid and Madnick (1991) use a lot of variables representing management perceptions of the values of parameters: "perceived job size", "estimate of days left", and so on.

These perceptions in turn influence the behaviour of the project. Abdel-Hamid and Madnick (1991) state that "a different estimate creates a different project", since management and workers will react in different ways to different estimates and different perceptions of schedule pressure. This complexity is exacerbated by the difficulty in many domains of estimating how much of a task is left to do. For example, in the software world, it is well known that estimates of "proportion of activity completed", at least in the early stages of an activity, are made simply by dividing resources expended by budgeted resources (De Marco (1982), Baber (1982)). This is a major contributor to the "90% syndrome".

One final subjective area which has to be taken into account in modelling a project concerns activities that depend on creativity or inspiration in the project team. Obviously, estimating time and effort for such activities is very difficult, and the actuality will depend upon all these factors we have discussed. To take just one of our project examples, in the Sydney 2000 Olympic Games, as noted in Chapter 5, "Certain [activities] are based on inspirations. The time dimension of inspirations is quite difficult to anticipate. Allowing sufficient time for inspirations to prosper, while necessary, will severely restrict the possible lead times on these programs. . ." (Cleland *et al.* 1998).

Summary and looking forward

These are some of the main subjective effects that we need to be able to model within our project. This chapter has listed the main variables and some simple relationships whereby they could be incorporated into models of the type we discussed in Chapter 5: discrete, decomposition-based models. However, even for these types of models we've noted some of the problems of quantifying, measuring and validating these variables and relationships. But, in practice, many of these aspects can be allowed for as experienced project managers assess their projects—they allow for a certain loss of productivity when using overtime; they understand the communication overhead as a team is expanded. Where the problems go beyond such straightforward analysis is where the aspects combine, in particular where they produce feedback. There is much research which says that our mental analysis and decision-making is poorer with such systemic effects, and particularly in circumstances of dynamic feedback (e.g. Diehl and Sterman 1995). So now we'll move on to looking at how the various tangible and subjective aspects that we've been discussing combine to produce project behaviour. We'll look at their inter-relationships in Chapter 8, and at one particular type of modelling in Chapter 9, System Dynamics. Using System Dynamics to model project behaviour, though, will have its own problems, and Chapter 10 discusses combining this method with more standard Chapter 5 methods.

8   Systemic effects

The effects

In Chapters 5 and 6 we dealt with the main physical and tangible effects we wanted to model in projects. As we moved through Chapter 7, we captured some of the "softer", less tangible effects that experience shows are important in determining the behaviour of projects. So we've now got an, if not exhaustive, at least well-rounded picture of all of the effects? Well, yes and no. It is true that we have discussed many of the important individual effects. But anyone reading this who has experienced projects will certainly feel that there is a certain something that hasn't been captured—something which means that project life isn't as simple as it might seem from the foregoing chapters.

That something, of course, as we discussed right back in Chapter 4, is that the effects are not individual, isolated influences which can each be studied independently, but that they combine together to produce what we called "complex" behaviour—in particular, we haven't captured structural complexity. Two particular manifestations of that are important, and will form the discussion in part of this chapter.

The first of these is the compounding of influences that is sometimes called the *portfolio effect* (Eden *et al.* 2000). Frequently, effects combine together to give an effect greater than the sum of their individual effects. To some extent, this can already be recognised in our decomposition models. For example, a number of small delays can push a project into a period in which a large delay is incurred, such as missing a weather window—an example here would be the North Sea oil platform project discussed in Chapter 5: as small delays impact, the project gets moved back into the window, and all the weather-dependent activities become longer, until completion of the project within the year becomes infeasible. However, many examples are harder to model simply, and the portfolio effect is not so obvious: for example, a succession of Change Orders on a project (Eden *et al.* 2000), which collide and, as management try to deal with them, their effects compound each other.

The second is the combination of effects into *feedback loops*. A frequent type of relationship between effects is when a causal chain is produced where effect A causes or exacerbates or promotes effect B, which causes or exacerbates or promotes effect C, and so on. This can be captured by the decomposition methods, so long as the chain does not return and form a loop. However, where effect A leads to effect B leads to effect C leads back to effect A, we have a feedback loop. These loops can be either positive, so each effect tends to increase itself and the project spirals (these are called "vicious circles" if the effect is unwanted, or "virtuous circles" if the effect is a good one); or negative loops, in which increases in an effect produce a balancing or controlling effect by which the effect is brought back towards its original value. These loops are fundamental to the understanding of the behaviour of projects. It is well known that managers make decisions particularly poorly for problems involving feedback mechanisms, and it is these loops that often produce counter-intuitive behaviour within projects. Some of the loops which we will be discussing have been identified as fundamental building blocks of project behaviour, such as the re-work loop (Cooper 1993, 1994, 1997), the Delay and Disruption effects (Eden *et al.* 2000) and the effects from project compression (Howick and Eden 2001).

The counter-intuitive nature of these relationships is described by Cooper (1997) who cites three hypothetical examples:

- of non-linear behaviour: a customer requires several design changes— virtually no adverse impact on project performance is visible, but when more changes follow, these produce big delays and extra costs;
- of time-delayed effects: a manager, faced with a project behind schedule, gets the staff to work overtime; progress improves, so overtime continues; within a few months, the pace of work has slowed more than ever;
- causal feedback: a manager hires new staff when the project falls behind schedule; progress does not improve quickly enough, and more new people are brought in; work progress remains slow, or even declines.

The relationships described in this chapter and the next will begin to explain these apparently counter-intuitive behaviours.

To demonstrate and illustrate these effects, it's best to first describe a simple language for describing the relationships between effects, so we'll now discuss just such a language—in fact, what could be called a qualitative modelling technique—known as cause mapping. Then we'll use that to look at the portfolios and feedback mechanisms in some of our examples. Finally, we'll touch upon the issues involved in quantifying some of these models, looking forward to one particular quantitative modelling technique to be used in Chapter 9—System Dynamics.

Which aspects of our modelling will these considerations affect? Well, all aspects, when we are dealing with complex projects. Let's take one example—the management of risk that we discussed in Chapter 5. This set up a structure of management (illustrated in Figure 5.1), based around the Project Risk Register (PRR). However, this was all predicated on the assumption that risks in the PRR are independent (as well as all-inclusive). As our discussion above (and the remainder of this chapter) will show, this is very rarely so—some risks will be directly implied by other risks (and there might even be whole cascades of implied risks), and some risks will be more subtly interconnected (e.g. the risk of an unsuccessful engine development and that of an unsuccessful gearbox development might both depend on the risk of an inadequate definition phase). Thus, effects such as portfolios and feedback loops will be set up. In practice, of course, when carrying out a risk analysis these effects are (or should be!) taken into account—but in the past these have had to be researched as a separate exercise. We will see during this chapter that, in the presence of these sort of effects, the PRR is inadequate and needs to be taken further, because it does not contain the inter-relationships between risks and the systematic structure of these inter-relationships. This makes it, first, an inadequate tool for the capture and representation of risks, so it often fails to perform a useful function (and is seen as such). It also makes it inadequate for acting as the basis of analysis and decision-making, because it lacks knowledge of the systemic relationships. Therefore, some have suggested replacing the PRR by, or enhancing it with, *causal mapping* representations that can represent these relationships (see, for example, Williams *et al.* 1997).

A brief introduction to cause mapping

An important technique used to interview managers and subsequently model their explanations for situations in a wide variety of domains is *cognitive mapping* (see Eden 1988). This structures the way in which humans construe and make sense of their experiences by developing a map consisting of elements, or concepts, joined by links showing relationships between elements. This is a useful technique to help elicit the underlying structure of causes in a "messy" problem (in the sense of Chapter 3), and results in a "cognitive map" of the various causes and effects, with arrows or lines showing inter-relationships between the elements. Where the concepts are sufficiently well defined, and the links between them can all be given a direction of causality (so that A and B are not simply "related in some way" but A is a cause or promoter of B), then we have a *cause map*. The maps are drawn simply as concepts in boxes, linked with arrows showing the direction of causality (see Figure 8.1).

Figure 8.1—Elements of causal maps

Such maps are often drawn by the managers in a group, helped by an expert facilitator. Often software such as Decision Explorer (Banxia 1999; based on the ideas of Eden and Ackermann) is used, so that the map can be stored, discussed, analysed and whose complexity can be managed (Williams *et al.* 1997). The technique is widely used in strategic analysis, and Eden and Ackermann (1999) is the seminal work on this subject. In project-modelling, there are many benefits claimed for simply drawing up such a map, such as (Williams *et al.* 1997) revealing and dealing with duplications or inconsistencies, helping to spark off new thoughts on important influences and their relationships, and particular benefits when used with a group of managers with a well-defined, methodologically sound facilitation process. However, our interest, of course, is the particular aid it can give to our modelling. Causal mapping is a valuable aid in structuring and understanding the problem. Causal maps are also amenable to a wide variety of qualitative analyses (Eden *et al.* 1992), in particular the identification of feedback loops. Of particular interest is their development into the systems dynamics models that we shall see as we reach Chapter 9.

Rather than look at examples of maps here, we'll look at examples of portfolio effects and feedback in the next two sections.

Qualitative modelling: simple compounding

The portfolio effect occurs where two or more influences come together, but their combined influence is significantly more than the sum of the individual influences—the "2 + 2 = 5" effect. Clearly, this sort of effect will be greater as we add in other interconnecting links, especially as feedback comes in. But let's look at some examples where feedback does *not* come into consideration, then we shall see these effects greatly exacerbated in the next section, where we do consider feedback. The simpler examples here could, of course, be modelled using decomposition methods, but the combinations of influences shown in the bigger models would be complex to model in this way, and—once we start to include feedback—impossible. Causal mapping will also help us to structure and understand the problem in order to begin the modelling.

Let's look at some of the influences in Construction Project X. This is typical of work to design and construct a large piece of plant, such as a power plant or process plant. The study performed for this project identified a considerable number of effects, combined in a network of influences. But let's look at just a few now. First, it was claimed that the client had delayed the design process by dithering over design approvals. He had also interfered with the designers during their work, in a variety of ways. This led to a delay in design (Figure 8.2).

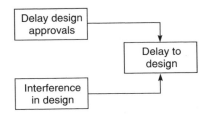

Figure 8.2—Construction project X: map (i)

The delay in design caused the construction work to be late, which meant both that workers were carrying out unplanned work in winter and also that work had to be compressed, so that the site became over-crowded with workers (Figure 8.3).

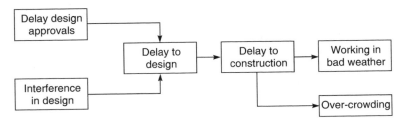

Figure 8.3—Construction project X: map (ii)

Since the delay to design was not uniform across the whole design process, some elements were heavily delayed while others were hardly delayed at all, so some drawings could be completed while other, more fundamental, drawings couldn't—so we have drawings and plans going to construction in the wrong order, which exacerbates the decrease in construction workers' productivity (Figure 8.4).

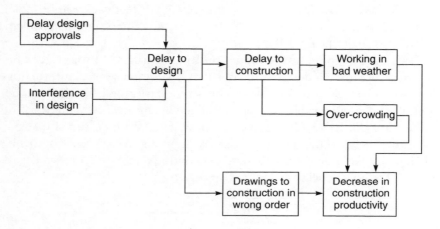

Figure 8.4—Construction project X: map (iii)

What is the effect of construction productivity declining when the end-date is fixed? Well, the delay to construction is increased, so we have a feedback loop (Figure 8.5).

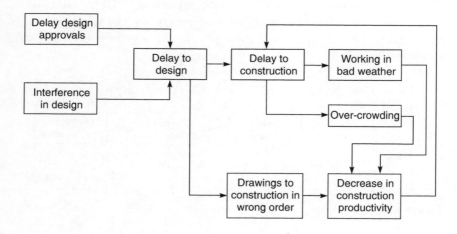

Figure 8.5—Construction project X: map (iv)

It seems sensible now to move immediately on to discussing the recognition, and modelling, of feedback loops.

Qualitative modelling: loops

We talked about the "2 + 2 = 5" effect in the previous section; but when we start to find positive feedback loops, this effect becomes a "2 + 2 = 6, 7 or even 8" effect, as effects cause themselves to increase in vicious/virtuous circles.

Let's look at the two examples we looked at in Chapter 7: the naval ship life extension project and the shuttle wagons project. Problems in both of these projects arose from the mid-project injection of changes into the design process. The effect of such changes on the progress of a project can be traced back to the initial impacts, which are generally two-fold:

1. Additional requirements or additions to the scope of work are required during the course of the project (thus not envisaged or planned for); these not only increase the time required to carry out the design work but also might have cross-impacts on other parts of the system;
2. If design changes are being considered, there will normally be delays— often extensive delays—to the approval process. While individual delays can be measured and sometimes their implications assessed, the cumulative impact of a number of delays is very difficult to assess.

These primary effects then cause a number of secondary effects:

- The changes are systemic (within the product), so often a number of project elements must be redesigned simultaneously. As each element is reworked mid-design, in a design process where design of cross-related parts of the product is occurring in parallel, each activity has to take cognisance of the others, and cross-impacts between elements mean there are secondary redesigns. Indeed, cross-impacts can be more complicated, with sequences of interactions and even feedbacks when a change to system A changes system B which changes system C. . ., which changes system A.
- Most such changes increase product complexity, producing increasing cross-relations between parallel activities developing cross-related parts of the product. This implies increasing difficulty in providing a system freeze, since changes in one component will increasingly cross-impact other components, creating a ripple effect across the system.

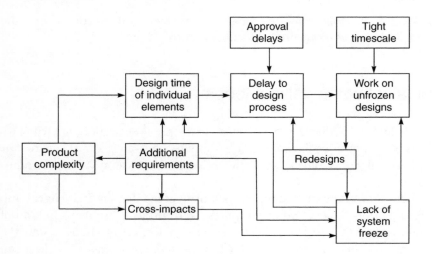

Figure 8.6—Causal map of the project, with feedback loops

- Additionally, or alternatively, this redesign causes disruption to the design schedule, which means that system elements are often being designed without having full specifications of necessary interfaces, because the lack of system freeze, combined with a tight time constraint, forces management to work on project elements for which the surrounding system is not yet frozen, and the design of such items will have to be reworked if there are changes in the as-yet-unfrozen surrounding system.

Already, these effects are beginning to display the elements of feedback. For example, a causal map could be drawn of the effects described in this section, as shown in Figure 8.6.

This map could be used to describe some of the fundamental effects in either of these projects, and it will be used as the foundation of the quantitative models in Chapter 9. This is quite a complicated map, and there are already three interlinked feedback loops generated, all positive:

- clearly, delay to the design process leads to more work on unfrozen designs, which leads to more redesigns, which will cause more delay to the design process. This is the classic rework cycle;
- this is exacerbated because redesigns inhibit the system freeze, which increases the design times of individual elements, thus delaying the design process more;

- both of the feedback loops are exacerbated by the lack of system freeze, leading to management having to decide to work on unfrozen elements, thus increasing the need for redesigns.

Each of these loops is a positive, "vicious circle" loop. Each on its own would therefore tend to bring in non-linear, time-delayed causal feedback. Where all three combine, these effects compound with each other to produce even more non-linear, dynamic behaviour.

Here, we have only dealt with basic effects. As we add additional, interlinked effects, more feedback loops can be seen. For example, consider one of the "softer" techniques we talked about in Chapter 7: loss of engineer morale. Engineers will lose motivation when they have to keep redoing their work (redesigns). Indeed, they'll lose motivation if they're trying to work with guesswork on a system which has not yet been defined, and which they know could change in the future. So this concept could be added to the right-hand side of Figure 8.6, as shown in Figure 8.7.

What is the effect of this concept? Well (among other things), the engineers, being demotivated, work more slowly and less effectively, giving us a link forming a feedback loop back into the structure, shown in Figure 8.8.

Then we can add in the effect of the use of overtime: increased project complexity; the increased probability of downstream errors, and so on.

Quantitative modelling

Clearly we could go on adding these effects for some time, producing bigger and bigger maps. But while the techniques described above allow us

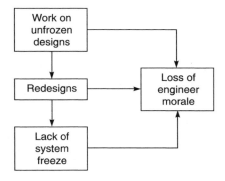

Figure 8.7—Adding "loss of engineer morale" to Figure 8.6

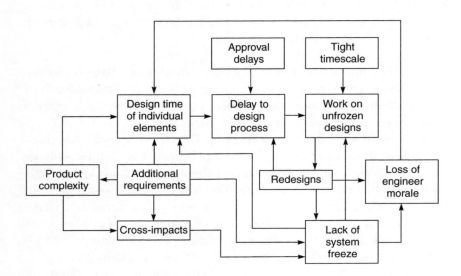

Figure 8.8—Extended map of project

to explain the various effects taking place in our projects, the feedback effects need to be quantified. We need to provide practical assistance to planners and analysts or, in the two litigation cases described above, the effects needed to be quantified to support a legal claim. Readers who have stayed with us so far will see that relying on standard network analysis alone is insufficient; indeed, it can be misleading because the analysis can incorrectly suggest satisfactory progress and adequate planning. This is not because the network techniques are no use but, as the feedback loops take effect, we need to be aware that the network structure itself changes: activities become longer, and therefore more and more concurrent, and the inter-relationships between activities change.

So we must look for a simulation method that can capture these changes. There are two relevant methodologies for constructing simulation models. The first is *discrete event simulation*, which is well-known and which we used in Chapter 5. Models here are constructed based on events at discrete points in time, with the attributes of the model entities, which describe the state of the entities, changing at the event points. Events are generated using probabilistic variables, sampling from the whole to produce typical profiles of the system, and running the model many times to provide a good replication of likely system behaviour patterns. The second method is known as *System Dynamics* modelling, and follows naturally from the use of qualitative mapping techniques. It is particularly suitable for situations exhibiting dynamic behaviour such as feedback, and is geared towards modelling the information flows and softer effects that we have been discussing in the last two chapters. We shall discuss System Dynamics in the next chapter—including how to develop quantitative maps in parallel with, and flowing from, the qualitative maps of this chapter.

9 System Dynamics modelling

Introduction to System Dynamics

The modelling method we're going to concentrate on in this chapter is known as System Dynamics, or SD. SD was developed in the late 1950s by Jay Forrester of the Sloan School of Management at Massachusetts Institute of Technology (Forrester 1961) and, since then, the method has been applied to a wide variety of situations, and a whole body of knowledge has built up around it. This book will not give a complete description of this technique: interested readers should read the very good textbook by Sterman (2000), or that by Wolstenholme (1990), which give good overviews of the current state of the art.

SD can be thought of as being predicated on four premises (e.g. Abdel-Hamid and Madnick 1991):

1. The behaviour of an organisational entity over time is principally caused by its structure, including not only physical aspects but also the policies and procedures that dominate decision-making.
2. Managerial decision-making takes place in an information–feedback framework.
3. Our intuitive judgement is unreliable about how systems within such frameworks change with time, even when we understand the individual parts of the system.
4. Model experimentation can indicate the way in which the parts of the system interact to produce possibly unexpected overall system results.

The first two of these show that this method is exactly aligned with the type of feedback systems we were starting to discuss in the previous chapter. The latter two indicate that we can use SD simulation to explore the behaviour of systems.

SD simulation can be distinguished from discrete-event simulation in three ways: it is concerned with the state of the system and rates of change, it uses pseudo-continuous modelling (people often think of these models in terms of flow of fluids in and out of tanks), and the details of discrete events are not included. Despite the advantages of using this method, the latter property will be a flaw in our application to projects, as we will have difficulty in distinguishing operational detail within the models; we will discuss this further in Chapter 10.

The modelling approach focuses on an understanding of feedback and feedforward relationships, so it is particularly appropriate when we have the sort of effects that we have been discussing in Chapter 8. It is based on a holistic perspective of managerial problems, and focuses on "soft" as well as "hard" aspects of a system's behaviour and information flows; it is therefore natural for modelling some of the problems we have described in the last two chapters, and it has a number of uses in the project management world (Rodrigues and Bowers (1996a, 1996b) give useful reviews). One other key issue for us here is that causal maps are a natural predecessor to System Dynamics models, and SD models can be built directly from causal maps built up using the methods discussed in Chapter 8. We'll discuss this further later in this chapter.

SD models are usually prepared using a computer package based on a diagrammatic interface. Model construction requires the analyst to construct the relationships between the variables, with equations for these relationships being embedded within the variables on the diagram. Three packages are in popular use: Stella/iThink (High Performance Systems Inc. 1996), Powersim (Modeldata AS, Bergen, Norway, 1993 and later) and Vensim (Ventane Systems Inc. 1988 and later). But all of these use the same SD logic, using three types of variable. Their actual representation on diagrams depends on the package used: the diagrams used here will use either Stella or Powersim pictures.

The first type of variable is often called a "stock" or "reservoir" and is generally shown diagrammatically as a rectangular "tank". Such variables represent "stocks" of material which characterise the fundamental state of the system at any one time. They are, then, those things that could be counted if the system stood still—for example, in a plant the number of people working on site can be counted, the extent of completion of a construction can be evaluated, and these can be used to determine whether extra staff should be hired. If staff are to be hired or fired, then the staff level will subsequently change and can be counted again later. Flows between the stocks are represented by "rate" variables, usually shown as a symbol resembling a valve; these show the rate at which the stock variables are changing. All other calculations are undertaken by the third type of variable, which is called an "auxiliary variable", and is generally represented by a circle (or a diamond for a constant). (Note, too, that in the Powersim figures shown in this chapter, the variable icon might also have a "?" in the centre (showing that the variable is as yet undefined) or an ▦ icon (showing that a delayed variable is involved—see below).)

In a model entered into one of these packages, all relationships between the variables have to be shown by arrows: it is this explicit representation of the intramodel relationships that makes such models so transparent. And of course arrows between variables are equivalent to, and can in a general sense be derived from, the arrows drawn in the causal maps in Chapter 8.

Let's look at some examples. Let's suppose that there was design work to do on a project. That work could be represented as a reservoir of work waiting to be done. Since the work was done at a certain rate, work would flow out of this reservoir into a tank of design work that had been performed. This would be drawn as two stocks and a flow, which in Stella/iThink would be shown as in Figure 9.1.

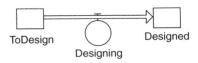

Figure 9.1—Stella stocks and flow

However, the rate of design would not be constant: rather, it would depend on the number of designers involved, productivity rates, the stage of the project and so on. A modeller might represent the design rate as an auxiliary variable, and the relationship would be shown as in Figure 9.2: this is a Powersim diagram, and it can be seen that the diagrammatic representation is almost the same as in Stella/iThink.

Drawing such diagrams—which of course can be very large in practice—specifies the logic of the relationships between the variables. It doesn't, of course, quantify these relationships, and this has to be done

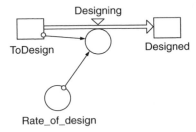

Figure 9.2—Powersim variables

Reproduced from Powersim business-simulation software. For more information on Powersim visit www.powersim.com

separately by defining equations within each variable (stock, flow and auxiliary). The packages will not allow variables that have not been linked by an arrow to be used within these equations, providing the transparency of logic that we mentioned above.

Of course, there are many more facilities available to SD modellers than these building blocks. These include:

- Delays in links (shown in Powersim by an arrow with two small "crossing-out" bars, as below)

- Packages such as Stella/iThink have several specialist kinds of stocks, such as conveyors, queues, ovens and so on, each with specialised attributes; packages that don't have these (such as Powersim) can generally create identical functionality using the various variables and functions available in that package.
- Output facilities, in particular time graphs to show the dynamic behaviour of a model over time, and tables with numerical time-based records of behaviour.

But the basic concepts give us the language with which to start modelling some of the effects we have identified in Chapters 7 and 8.

SD's track record of use in explaining and modelling the systemic effects in complex projects daily from 1964. It has been used notably by Pugh-Roberts Associates (part of PA Consulting)—see Cooper (1994, 1997) and Cooper and Mullen (1993) for some details. A number of successful applications have also been reported at NASA (see Rodrigues and Bowers 1996b). Perhaps its most straightforward application makes use of its explanatory power, in the post-mortem analysis of projects. In particular, it has been used in litigation to explain complex effects (such as Delay and Disruption; see e.g. Eden *et al.* 2000). The first major success at this was the Ingalls Shipbuilding case against the US Navy in the 1970s, in which an SD model was used to quantify the cost of disruption stemming from Navy-responsible delays and design changes; the total settlement was finally $447mn, and Cooper (1993) claims that the model was the basis for at least $200–300mn of this. Since this major legal precedent, the method has been used for a number of such disputes, key being the shuttle wagons case, some aspects of which are discussed in this book (Williams *et al.* 1995; Ackermann *et al.* 1997).

Using System Dynamics with mapping

We have already looked at the usefulness of causal maps for modelling the complexities we find in projects. A key reason for using System Dynamics for quantifying this type of modelling is that it can be thought of as naturally following on from causal mapping.

The first step in modelling a project is to consider how the project *should* flow, to plan out the stocks and flows of work and materials. We'll look at some basic models of this type in the next section. Then we will consider the influences and causal relationships that may cause problems or perturbations within the project, including any important information links. These are complex and interlinked, which is why we used causal mapping in the last chapter. The obvious thing to do, then, is to take the causal map and impose it upon a simple "as planned" model.

As an example of both these steps, let's return to Figure 9.2 (see page 169) and try to develop a simple "as planned" model. Let's think what this "design rate" might be. First of all, we have to define some sort of unit for what it is that is flowing through the diagram. Let us simplify a design project for now, and suppose that there are 1000 drawings that have to be designed, and there are some logical predefined rules on the order in which they must be worked upon. Therefore, the initial value of "ToDesign" will be 1000, and "Designed" will be 0. The project is complete when all 1000 drawings have been completed, and let us suppose that the time unit we are dealing in is weeks.

To begin with, we can define the number of hours it takes a designer to complete a drawing (on average—and we shall see later that one problem with this type of modelling is that it deals with averages) and the number of hours a designer works per week. If we then take into account the size of the work-force, then we get Figure 9.3.

Of course, if you run this model (having somehow put a value into the "Number of designers", to which we'll return), it will do all the work very quickly—we haven't taken into account the ordering of designs, in which some need to be done before others can be done. We could model this by dividing the designs into two subsets—some of which are ready to be worked upon and others which need some of the first set to be completed before they can be worked upon. This would lead to a flow that looks like that in Figure 9.4.

The relationship "Pass to designers", in which some drawings that cannot be worked upon are freed up by the completion of others, is not trivial to calculate and depends upon the inter-relationships between drawings, which would give a relationship with the "Designed" stock. The flow in Figure 9.4 can thus replace that shown in Figure 9.3. It then remains

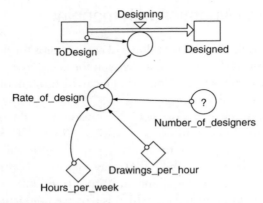

Figure 9.3—Simple model extended

Reproduced from Powersim business-simulation software. For more information on Powersim visit
www.powersim.com

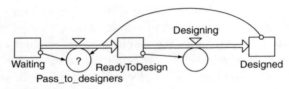

Figure 9.4—Extended flow

Reproduced from Powersim business-simulation software. For more information on Powersim visit
www.powersim.com

to define a variable giving the number of designers working on the project.
The simplest such rule would be simply to look at the numbers of drawings
ready to design and ensuring that enough designers are available to
complete the work in a fixed time (say, 8 or 12 weeks). This is a very
simplistic rule (and, even so, cannot be implemented directly, since without
a delay function the SD model will display instabilities). In practice, workers cannot be taken on or off a project at will, and modelling the decision
rules that determine the size of the workforce is often a crucial element of
the project modelling. But, with this simple rule, the model becomes as
shown in Figure 9.5.

   Finally, let's suppose that the designs have to be approved by the client,
who will take a certain amount of time to carry out this operation. This
would give Figure 9.6 (note that "Pass_to_designers" depends on the total
designs completed, which must now be calculated as the sum of two stocks).

   Running this through a Powersim simulation would show how long all
the drawings would take to complete, as shown in the "original model" line

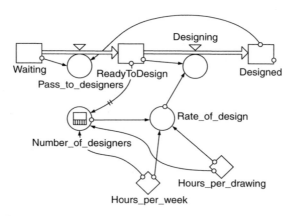

Figure 9.5—Design model

Reproduced from Powersim business-simulation software. For more information on Powersim visit www.powersim.com

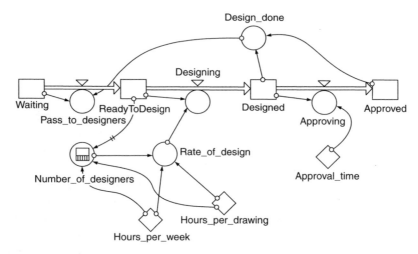

Figure 9.6—Design model

Reproduced from Powersim business-simulation software. For more information on Powersim visit www.powersim.com

of Figure 9.8. Now let us look at some of the issues described in Chapter 8. Let's take the simplest example, as shown in Figure 8.2 (part of Construction Project X), where design approvals can be delayed, and where design can suffer from interferences. First of all we would need to put a delay into the design approval process. Obviously, in practice this could be due to many factors which would need to be modelled, but for now we'll just put in a simple delay (in the model below we've called it "DELAY_

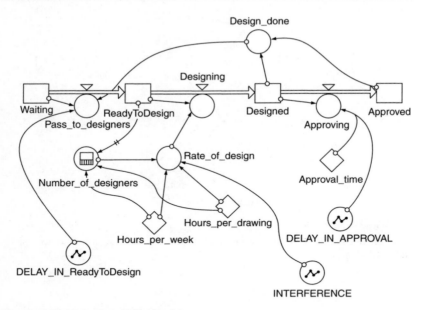

Figure 9.7—Complete design model

Reproduced from Powersim business-simulation software. For more information on Powersim visit www.powersim.com

IN_ APPROVAL", and it's been time-phased, hence the graphical ⊗ symbol). Now we need to put in "interference in design" and in particular, its causing of "delay to design". Here we see one of the advantages of having to model in a structured, quantitative way, as we are now forced to address questions such as "what do we mean by interference in design? In what way does this delay the design process?" There are various answers we could come up with in different situations, but two possible explanations which we've shown in the Figure 9.7 are: "DELAY_IN_ReadyToDesign", a type of disruption or interference causing delay in being able to start designing (i.e. a delay in completed drawings releasing further drawings to be worked upon), and "INTERFERENCE", a type of interference causing designers to work more slowly (i.e. a decline in productivity—we'll come to such issues later). Again, such effects could well be in a long line of causal explanation, but for now we've shown them simply as individual effects. Figure 9.7 then shows the complete model, with the three added effects shown in capitals.

If we were to run the two models shown in Figures 9.6 and 9.7 (with entirely hypothetical data), then the time at which drawings arrive in the "Approved" stock is shown in Figure 9.8, which illustrates the combined effect of the delaying variables.

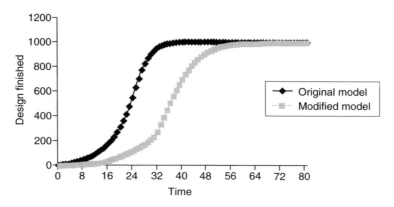

Figure 9.8—Results of running the Powersim model

While the ability to model a causal map appears simple on paper, in practice it is not a simple one-way process. Indeed, we've just seen how modelling an effect on the causal map which appears to be self-explanatory becomes ill-defined when faced with the rigours of quantitative modelling. So the process is often two-way, with inconsistencies or insufficiencies in the causal map being identified in the System Dynamics modelling, resolved within the causal map modelling and then remodelled in System Dynamics. Papers such as Williams *et al.* (2002) or Rodrigues (2001) give various structures of cognitive maps, causal maps and SD models.

One particularly useful feature of these structures is their ability to handle a high degree of complexity in the models. A modeller working with SD on its own can often get lost in the maze of his own model. Newer SD packages such as Vensim help the modeller because they can trace causal chains, and so on. But the causal map/SD combination, when causal map software such as Decision Explorer is used (from Banxia Software; see References), can be a powerful aid in keeping track of, and analysing, complex multiple chains of effects.

Elements of models

All projects, by definition, are new ventures. Having said that, part of the point of this book is that we can draw lessons from one project to use on later projects. This tension is similarly found when system dynamicists come to build models of projects. As we have already indicated, writers such as Eden, Ackermann, Williams and Howick (Eden *et al.* 2000, Williams *et al.*

2002) develop models from the causal map "from the ground up", although they use experience of elements and sub-structures that commonly recur (which will be discussed in this chapter). Others use models as archetypes (Senge *et al.* 1994, Richardson 1996) and, rather than build models individually for each particular project, would use a generic model to represent projects generally (Cooper 1997). However, whichever route is followed, it is clear that common structures are used, and there are certain types of building blocks which commonly recur. The following two sections will cover these elements.

Rodrigues (e.g. Rodrigues and Williams 1998) considers two parallel processes within a project: the engineering process, in which the development of the task output occurs, and the management process. The latter he divides into progress monitoring (estimating work performed, effort spent, productivity, etc.) and replanning (manpower availability and allocation etc.). Abdel-Hamid and Madnick (1991) use a very similar structure, but divide their management process more explicitly. They use a four-part structure called "Human Resource Management", "Planning", "Controlling" and "production" (in this case, of software). We will thus look at these parts separately, starting with (in Abdel-Hamid and Madnick's terms) the production element, then make a few comments about human resource management/planning, and finally controlling.

Production elements

The structure

This section describes the flow of the main product of the process. We are taking "production" to mean the main flow of work as opposed to the management process—"production" here could include the production of design drawings, lines of software code, and/or a physical product. The word "production" is therefore not limited to physical production (compared, say, to a design phase) but to the flow of work producing the main project output.

Ford and Sterman (1998) describe a generic development process model which looks like that shown in Figure 9.9.

In this structure, showing what they describe as "circular iteration", tasks start in the Tasks_not_Completed stock; as tasks are completed they move into the Tasks_Completed_not_Checked stock; if the tasks need no change (e.g. they pass quality inspection) they pass into Tasks_approved and are subsequently released to Tasks_released, which represents deliver-

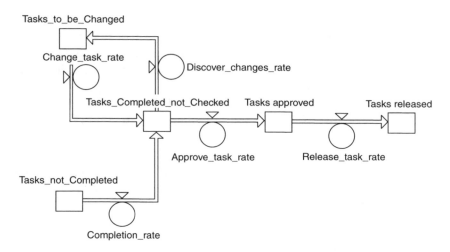

Figure 9.9—Ford and Sterman's development process model. Adapted from Ford, D N and Sterman, J D (1998) Dynamics modelling of product development processes. *System Dynamics Review* **14**(1): 31–68. Reproduced by permission of John Wiley & Sons, Ltd. All rights reserved.

ing tasks to managers of downstream phases or to managers. If tasks do require changes, they pass to the Tasks_to_be_Changed stock, where they flow back to Tasks_Completed_Not_Checked as changes are carried out.

In Ford and Sterman's model, rather than using individual sets of activities, as would occur in a PERT/CPM chart, the inter-relationships between tasks are available in what they call "Internal Process Concurrence", which seeks to capture the degree of sequentiality of concurrence of the tasks aggregated together in a phase. Ford and Sterman then use this structure as the building block in multiple development phases.

A key assumption we've made here is that it is "tasks" that are flowing through the structure. Perhaps the most important step in drawing up a System Dynamics model of a project is to define *what* flows through the stock/flow diagrams. Cooper (1997) says that any project work can flow through, "be it feet of cable, tons of steel, lines of code, design drawings". However, in practice the identification of an appropriate unit is not that simple, since it is vital that the unit:

- can be understood and related to by the modeller's audience. So if a construction project was measured simply by "% of the construction work", the project team might find it difficult to see how the different activities can be combined into a simple metric like this, and not be sure what "30% of the total construction" means.

- can be supported by measurements. "Lines of code" in an IT project (Abdel-Hamid and Madnick 1991), or "number of design drawings" (Williams *et al.* 1995), can be seen physically, and can be counted.
- as in all modelling, sufficiently represents what is being modelled—the added complication here being that a continuous homogenous variable is being used to model a flow of discrete and clearly heterogenous items (lines of code may be similar to each other, but "design drawings" are clearly very different from each other in size, complexity and impact).

Now, the structure as drawn in Figure 9.9 has a number of elements, and it is worth looking at three of them in more detail, as they recur frequently in project models:

- productivity;
- the rework cycle;
- changes in the size of the task, or changes in the description of the task.

Worker productivity

The first element, and perhaps most difficult to quantify, is worker productivity. Assume that you assign a value of 100% to the maximum amount of work you could get from a group of workers under optimum conditions (where this is sensibly defined—not "perfect" conditions but conditions it would be reasonable that you could come close to achieving). Then, within a complex project, there are multiple reasons why 100% productivity might not be achieved—we'll just look at some of the most common reasons here. Of course, the important thing to remember within this modelling is that this an *endogenous* and *time-dependent* variable. That is, these effects on the value of productivity come from within the project and will be determined by other factors within the model; and furthermore, these factors vary over the time of the project, and it may well be that your model shows high productivity during some project stages and low productivity during other stages.

The first set of reasons for productivity being lower can be seen by looking at *the individual worker*. Three common reasons are:

- the use of overtime. Indeed, law-texts such as Schwartzkopf (1995) give standard curves for productivity after certain periods of either spot-overtime or extended periods of overtime. Thus productivity can be quantified as a recognised function of the working week. Perhaps the best-known table, quoted in Schwartzkopf (1995), is that given by the

Bureau of Labor Statistics (US) (1947); this assumes a normal week of five eight-hour days, then gives figures for the productivity lost (as a percentage) if prolonged overtime is used in a five-day week of (8 + n) hours which can be summarised as $0.2 + 4.5n - 0.3n^2$ (i.e. for prolonged use of an 11-hour day, productivity lost is $0.2 + 4.5 \times 3 - 0.3 \times 9 = 11\%$, thus achieving 89% "normal" productivity). Figures are also given for six-day weeks (which are, interestingly, different from a five-day week with the same number of hours), where the use of a six-day week of (8 + n) hours gives a loss of $3.2 + 9 \times 4n - n^2$.

- Schedule pressure by management. This is a slightly more difficult relationship to quantify. It is certainly true that, as management perceives a project to be slipping, they will impose pressure upon their workers to finish earlier. This may cause some loss of productivity (or, arguably, some gain in productivity).

- Morale. This is an even more difficult relationship to quantify. Abdel-Hamid and Madnick (1991) explain that many morale or motivation issues are a function of the overall organisational setting and can be assumed to be a constant for a project, so can be included in the definition of 100% productivity we made above. However, it is undoubtedly the case that certain effects within a project will lead to a loss of worker morale, and thus a loss of productivity. For example, a difficult client who keeps changing the work (so work has to be continuously undone and redone) will decrease the commitment workers feel towards the work, and lower productivity. Interference from the client, disempowering by the management, and external impacts can all decrease morale. While this might seem impossible to measure as a variable, the key point to remember is that it is the inputs and the effects on the outputs that need to be measured, and the variable "morale" need only be a modelling device. As a very simplistic example, consider that when a client makes no changes to a project there is no effect on productivity, but 10 changes a week leads to a 1% drop in productivity (solely due to loss of morale) and 20 changes leads to a 2% drop in productivity. It is thus reasonable to multiply "productivity" by a variable "morale" which is defined as $(1 - 0.001 \times$ [Changes per week]$)$.

If we look beyond the individual, the *number in the worker group* is important. Two obvious reasons for that are:

- Overcrowding. In the projects quoted in Chapter 2, this featured in a number of projects, notably Construction Project X and the Montreal Olympics 1976. Again, texts such as Schwartzkopf (1995) give standard curves for productivity loss when the area of construction is overcrowded. In particular, as we saw in Figure 7.2 he quotes a US Army Corps of Engineers (1979) study giving a percentage loss of productivity as a function of "% crowding" (defined as $100 \times$ ([actual-manpower/scheduled manpower] $- 1$)) (call this C), where these graphs can be summarised as $0.256 \times C + 0.00775 \times C^2$ (where $0 < C < 35$).

- A larger group will also be more difficult to manage, and there will be communication losses. Abdel-Hamid and Madnick (1991) quote research in the software development field indicating that the communication overhead (i.e. loss in productivity) increases in proportion to the square of the size of the team. So in their example, while a single programmer will spend 4.8 hours per day in useful work, in a team of 30, 2.4 hours of this time will be lost in verbal and written communication, extra interfaces, etc.

Third, beyond the mere size of the group, we need to consider *changes within the group*. Two areas in particular are well-known areas for loss of productivity:

- New staff. If new staff have to join the team, there will always be a training period, whether they are
  - new to the discipline, i.e. they've never done this type of work at all before—there are projects that get so large (beyond what was foreseen) that they have to take on workers who have no experience in that type of work at all;
  - new to the domain, i.e. they've done this type of work but not in this industry (so when the supply of experienced automotive structural engineers is exhausted, then structural engineers from other industries might be taken on and trained);
  - new to the company—who will still need training in company practices, systems, software and so on; or
  - new to the project—who will need familiarisation with the project's own idiosyncracies and practices.
  It is worth noting that, of the projects described in Chapter 2, both the Montreal Olympics 1976 and the shuttle wagons exhausted the number of appropriate workers in the geographic region.
- Reassignment of existing staff within the project will also lead to losses of productivity from stop-start and loss-of-learning effects.

Finally, *management actions* on the activities within the project can lead to losses of productivity. As discussed in Chapter 7 there are two common such actions:

- Bringing an activity forward. For example, a lack of system freeze, combined with a tight time constraint, might force management to work on project elements for which the surrounding system is not yet frozen. As well as decreasing productivity, this will, more importantly, lead to the sort of feedback loops discussed in this section including, for example, increased rework and increased delays, leading to more parallelism and thus increased cross-relations between activities, hindering a system freeze and hence exacerbating the feedback.
- Reducing an activity's duration, or "crashing". This idea of "crashing" activities is well known, but the downstream effects of crashing are often not understood. They are caused by immediate impacts such as
  - using more manpower, as we have already discussed. Brooks" law was formulated in the 1970s as "adding manpower to a late software project makes it later" (Brooks 1978). Cooper (1994), referring to this law and trying to explicate it, discusses the feedback loops involved when extra personnel are brought in to reduce activity times to result in the "$2000-hour" effect.
  - decreased quality. Cooper (1993) uses "quality" as a critical metric, and defines this as the fraction of work being executed that will not require subsequent rework. Rodrigues and Williams (1998) similarly discuss the effects of reducing an activity's length (based on work in the software development domain), showing that it leads to more downstream problems due to quality problems (errors in code), and leads to more problems in parallel activities due to increased parallelism between activities.

Even having identified the different effects, there are three issues that need to be considered before a single equation can be defined for "productivity":

- There might be effects that are time-dependent. In Construction Project X, productivity was heavily dependent upon the weather until the project was weather-proof, thus productivity was a function both of the endogenous progress on the project and the exogenous temperature. Either a warm winter or on-time completion of the project up to a weather-proof building would have minimised this effect; it was the combination of cold and lateness which caused the problem and again set up feedback loops (since this lowered productivity caused more lateness, etc.).
- While the individual effects can perhaps be quantified, the interaction between them is not clear, and caution must be exercised in defining the overall equation. Schwartzkopf (1995) says that, "Although many

studies have been done to determine, or measure, the effects of specific factors (such as temperature, overtime, crowding, and learning curves) upon productivity, there has not been significant research for measuring how various effects interact . . . Because of the interaction of different factors upon labour productivity, the prediction of lost productivity is at best a range of losses that can be anticipated rather than a single lost productivity value."

- Finally, all of the above has defined productivity as a slower rate of working. It is important to be clear what is included in *your* definition of productivity, since some authors will include various levels of this metric:
  - a slower rate of working, as above;
  - periods of time during which work is non-existent, and catching up on such periods—idle-time, or stop-start effects;
  - unproductive work—doing activities that will not benefit the project (researching ideas which are abandoned, pointless or unnecessary documentation); or
  - rework to correct errors, or to deal with client changes.

The first two of these are taken into account in the discussion on productivity above. The last of these should *not* be included in an all-in productivity definition, since it is important that rework is modelled separately to include its (sometimes unintuitive) downstream effects (Cooper 1993, 1997). Similarly, the third point above can be included in the definition of productivity if there is no need for it to be modelled separately; however, if the influence-diagram analysis showing that taking engineers away to do extra research or documentation affected the project, then this might need to be modelled explicitly.

Rework

Ford and Sterman (1998)"'s diagram, shown in Figure 9.9, described "changes" where work did not pass a quality test, and where the need to do rework is very important to project behaviour. In Kaming *et al.* (1998)'s analysis of a sample of projects, which we mentioned in Chapter 7, "repeat work" was listed as the fourth most important impact upon productivity. To writers in the Cooper/Pugh-Roberts school, the rework cycle is fundamental to project behaviour. As described in Cooper (1993), the Rework Cycle structure portrays flows of project work, which again could be lines of code or design drawings—just as in the figures above. As previously, at the start all work is in a stock called "Work_to_be_done" then, as the project progresses, changing levels of effort means that work is gradually done (Figure 9.10).

Figure 9.10—Flow of work

Reproduced from Powersim business-simulation software. For more information on Powersim visit www.powersim.com

But in parallel to this line of work, Cooper identifies that work is executed at varying, but usually less than perfect, quality. Thus,

> a fraction that potentially ranges from 0 to 1.0, the value of quality . . . depends on many variable conditions in the project and company. The fractional value of quality determines the portion of the work being done that will enter the pool of "work_really_done", which will never again need redoing. The rest will subsequently need some rework, but for a (sometimes substantial) period of time the rework remains in a pool of "undiscovered_rework"—work that contains as-yet-undetected errors, and is therefore *perceived* as being done. Errors are detected by "downstream" efforts or testing; this rework discovery may occur months or even years later, during which time dependent work has incorporated these errors, or technical derivations thereof. Once discovered, the Known Rework demands the application of people, beyond those needed for completing the original work . . . (Cooper 1997)

Thus, using his own drawing conventions, we have a model that looks like that shown in Figure 9.11.

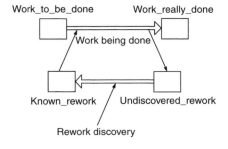

Figure 9.11—Cooper's rework cycle

These ideas of Undiscovered Rework, work "really done" being different to that "perceived done" and the Rework Cycle are fundamental to Cooper/ PA models. Of course, errors are only one reason why rework takes place.

Frequently there are changes to the project specification, and it is often very difficult to understand the impact of those changes to the project behaviour. Where these changes ask for a like-for-like replacement, this could also be termed "rework". However, this is *not* a case of items intrinsically containing "undiscovered rework" as in Cooper's model above, but a case where "work really done" is defined (by the redefinition of the project scope) to need rework. In this case, and particularly where (as often is the case) improvements are made, or the work increases in complexity or volume, it can come under the heading of "scope change".

Scope change

Mid-project changes to the scope or definition of a product can come from a variety of sources. Sometimes, a client will make changes for no clear reason other than preference ("Preferential Engineering"). It is important to be able to model the impacts all of these changes would have on the behaviour of the project.

Two common reasons for mid-project changes are an advance in relevant technology (see, for example, the Sydney 2000 Olympic Games project) and the increasing imposition of safety requirements. As an example of a change in project scope in the latter category, let us look at the Naval ship life extension (Williams 1997c) project which was described in Chapter 7. In this project new regulations (SOLAS 92) had been imposed, mid-project, over a period of time which meant that the air-conditioning (HVAC) system had to be redesigned and enhanced, and the deck head spaces (thus the space available within the ceilings) had to be reduced. Chapter 7 describes how these two changes complicated each other. The extra work caused directly by the introduction of SOLAS 92 was straightforward to evaluate. However, the extra work caused a number of additional effects, as described in Chapter 7 and briefly below:

- *Rework* and *cross-impact*: all the work was inter-related, so that when items had to be redesigned, other items had to be redesigned as a consequence, which had the effect of further changing other parts of the system. And all of these subsequent changes caused secondary effects on the work modelled.
- *Loss of productivity*: the design process was less efficient because much more work had to be done while still trying to keep within the schedule in order to avoid delay to the overall project (e.g. more workers, the introduction of three-shift working).

- *Additional complexity*: the redesign was much more complex than the original design because there was less space to fit in more services, causing extra management attention, and making follow-on work more complex.

And of course these effects are interdependent, each exacerbating the others. Thus, the extra time pressure caused less efficient working, which caused more delay, which added to the time pressure; design feedbacks and cross-impacts produced more redesign work, which caused more delays and exacerbated this feedback loop, and so on. Furthermore, the changes were not immediately well defined, but time had to be taken by both the project and external agencies to consider the full definition of the changes. This also caused delays to the redesign, exacerbating the time pressure and the need for secondary and tertiary redesign, etc. Again, these factors compound each other.

So let's try to model this. We dealt with loss of productivity in the example above, but the rework cycle can be seen at its simplest in the Figure 9.12.

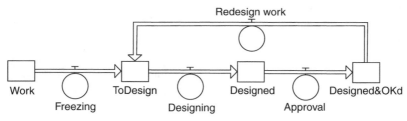

Figure 9.12—Naval ship life extension basic model

Reproduced from Powersim business-simulation software. For more information on Powersim visit www.powersim.com

Here, work that can be begun (i.e. the surrounding system is sufficiently frozen) is designed as fast as the available manpower and its productivity will allow, and these designs are approved. In an ideal world, that is all that happens (this would represent the project as originally conceived and budgeted for) but, in case of changes, work can be extracted from the state of being "Designed and OK'd" and moved back to be reworked. There are two mechanisms controlling this flow. The first is the flow of changes caused by SOLAS, represented by another set of stocks and flows, as shown in Figure 9.13.

The SOLAS changes are released at a certain time, then some are delayed while external agencies and the design office consider all their implications, then gradually all the changes flow until they are done.

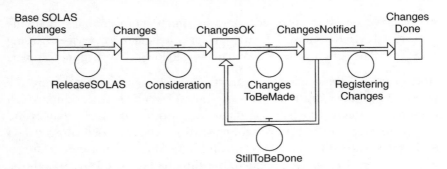

Figure 9.13—Naval ship life extension basic model: SOLAS changes

Reproduced from Powersim business-simulation software. For more information on Powersim visit www.powersim.com

Changes here cause redesign work in the main flow by affecting the variable "Redesign_work" in the main flow shown in Figure 9.12.

The second mechanism is the management of manpower. A set of auxiliary variables controls the addition and removal of manpower to the project, and the transfer on to and off the three-shifts regime. This is controlled by simple logical rules depending on the progress of the work compared to the original plan. We will look at such models in the next section.

There are a number of other issues that need to be considered. Let us turn now to modelling changes. Three in particular are as follows:

- the additional effects that arise from a multiplicity of changes, as discussed in Chapter 7.
- the effect of changes on construction learning curves. This is a subject slightly beyond the scope of this book, although fundamental to projects involving medium-length runs of production. Eden *et al.* (1997) describe how mid-production changes to a product cause interruptions to the learning curve, as workers have to start again with a piece of a product. Thus, the normal logarithmic learning curve, which is well established in industry, is interrupted, as part of the project has to be relearned. Figure 9.14 shows a "perfect" learning curve together with an interrupted curve.
- There is the problem of a client spending time thinking about and discussing designs rather than instantly accepting or rejecting them. While this might appear to a client to make little difference to the project, it will cause considerable compression, as the stock of approved design work will not grow as quickly as planned. This could be modelled

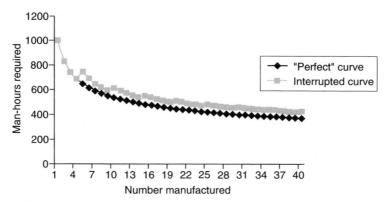

Figure 9.14—An interrupted learning curve

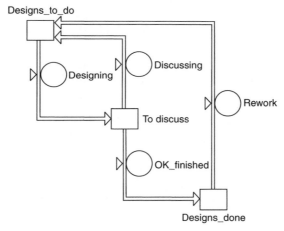

Figure 9.15—Designs being considered

Reproduced from Powersim business-simulation software. For more information on Powersim visit www.powersim.com

in the sort of model shown in Figure 9.15 (which shows part of Construction Project X).

Of course, the whole issue of change control is part of standard project management, and in a perfect world the contractual devices used to control projects would reflect the requirements of that project. In practice, however, there are many projects of a fixed-price or "EPC" (US) or "EPIC" (UK) type, under which client changes should not occur, but where there is major disruption caused by such client behaviour. Having a transparent model to evaluate these effects is important for understanding and controlling these problems.

Other elements

Abdel-Hamid and Madnick (1991)'s four-part structure described in Elements of models (above) had three more elements.

One of these elements was referred to as Management of Human Resources. This covers, in particular, taking on (and letting go) personnel and structuring those teams. We've already noted the issues involved in identifying the effects of these decisions—such as overcrowding and the need to train new staff. A model will often have to model the decisions made by management for taking on and releasing workers from the project, based on the perceived amount of work remaining and due to come. Abdel-Hamid and Madnick have rules giving the Workforce Level Needed, as a function of how much work required to be done within the scheduled completion time, while seeking to retain stability in the workforce, and so on. As you can see, in building System Dynamics models, once you try building even the simplest elements of such decisions, modelling becomes difficult. To include the intelligence to avoid the pitfalls of too many (or the wrong number of) workers is getting beyond the capabilities of a simple SD model. Again, the ideas of requisite modelling apply here—if the rules are sufficient to show how the project will (or did) behave for the purposes for which the modelling is being done, then they are sufficient. However, as we'll see in the next section, this area can be problematic in building SD models.

The second area is that of "Control", which Abdel-Hamid and Madnick characterise as consisting of measurement, evaluation and communication. The last of these is often modelled (if at all) simply by a device such as a delay. Evaluation is usually a comparison of actual occurrence compared to some prespecified (exogenously input) plan. Measurement, though, can be problematic. What is actually measured in a project are perceptions— perceptions of the amount of progress made or the number of resources being consumed. Often, particularly on progress or remaining rework, perceptions can be wrong, and it is only by developing a model, such as a System Dynamics model, that the underlying processes can be revealed and thus the bias in progress reporting explained. The best-known example of this is the "90% syndrome" problem, described by De Marco (1982).

McComb and Smith (1991) give the 90% syndrome as one of 15 reasons for "runaway" IT projects. Indeed, Abdel-Hamid and Madnick (1991) devote a whole chapter to the 90% syndrome in their book, quoting Baber (1982)'s description of the problem (". . . estimates of the fraction of work completed (increase) as originally planned until a level of about 80–90% is reached . . . individual estimates then increase only very slowly until the task is actually completed"). They also include the syndrome in their model and look at the dysfunctional consequences. Control of a project depends crucially on the metrics used to measure and evaluate progress, and these metrics need to be tied to the underlying processes. The benefits from good metrics collection programs are well recognised (see, for example, Grady and Caswell 1987). Often when teams such as the Eden team start to model a project (e.g. Williams *et al.* 1995), a major problem is that the key elements of the project have not been measured at all, and metrics have to be constructed retrospectively.

Managerial actions

We've already discussed, in the context of Human Resource Management, the difficulty of modelling decisions made by management—in that case, it was for taking on and releasing workers from the project, based on the perceived amount of work remaining and due to come. We saw, that in building System Dynamics models, once you try building even the simplest elements of such decisions, modelling becomes difficult. But the decisions taken by management are absolutely fundamental to the behaviour of the project. If it were the case that external shocks occurred to the project but management ignored them, then analysing the effects of those shocks would generally be straightforward. The difficulty—and the need for our models—is that management react to those shocks. As an obvious example, if something happened to delay a project by a month (say, a client holding up design-freeze), if management didn't do anything then the project would be delayed by one month; but in practice management could take any of a wide range of actions to work around the situation (e.g. working on construction "at risk" of the design changing, compressing the project once design freeze is approved, and so on; Eden *et al.* 2000); thus the impact in practice would be a delay of something less than a month but at an increased cost—but evaluating this delay and this cost requires some model of the management actions and their effect on the project.

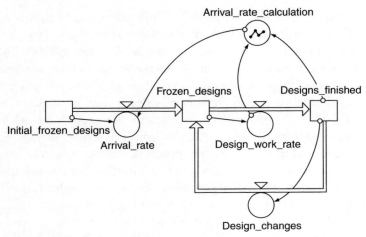

Figure 9.16—Simplified design cycle

Reproduced from Powersim business-simulation software. For more information on Powersim visit www.powersim.com

Figure 9.17—Extract from causal map

In these simple models, we have been able to include straightforward, simple decision rules. We have discussed the need to take actions to bring an activity forward, or to "crash" an activity, or to work on designs out of order. Let's look at the system shown in Figure 9.16, which shows a very simplified design cycle.

Now let us suppose management decides to work on designs out of order as a reaction to the lateness of design (Figure 9.17).

To model this by a simple decision rule, it is first necessary to:

- characterise the delay to the design process as a single variable; this can be simply done by taking the stock of completed design and comparing it with some exogenously defined "plan" of completion to give, say, the number of weeks late, or the shortfall in percentage complete.
- characterise the variable "work on designs out of order".
- define the relationship between these two variables.

The first of these is fairly straightforward: taking the stock of completed designs and comparing it with some exogenously defined plan will give

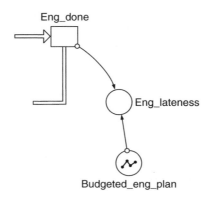

Eng_done

Eng_lateness

Budgeted_eng_plan

Figure 9.18—Extract from design

"lateness", whether defined in terms of weeks late or the percentage short-fall—Figure 9.18 uses the latter, where eng_lateness = budgeted_eng_plan − Eng_done (a negative value denoting "early"). The second requires a variable to be defined—let us say the variable "out_of_order" denotes "the proportion of work remaining that should not (optimally) be worked upon that it is decided to work upon out of order". Then, this decision rule will need to be quantified by discussion with managers to derive an equation appropriate to this particular project. The variable "out_of_order" will then operate on the ability to start designs—that is, the variable "arrival_rate_calculation"—and of course it will also have deleterious effects, such as an increase in the amount of rework necessary as assumptions made prove to be false (i.e. it will affect the variable "design_changes") and it will usually also affect productivity (since working on designs out of order is more difficult than working in the correct manner). These effects will only come into play when the ability to work on designs is inhibited in some fashion. Thus we get a system which modifies the design cycle in Figure 9.16 to that shown in Figure 9.19.

When run with the "Inhibitors" (i.e. the external effects) slowing the arrival rate, adding the "out_of_order" will then show designs finishing earlier but at a higher cost, and demonstrate the effect of this decision rule. Of course, management might well take this decision based on the immediate (speeding-up) effect without due regard to the negative effects—but this is simply an illustration that the response of such complex systems cannot be intuitively forecast by the unaided human brain.

This is clearly a very simple decision rule. There are many such decisions that need to be modelled to represent the behaviour of a whole

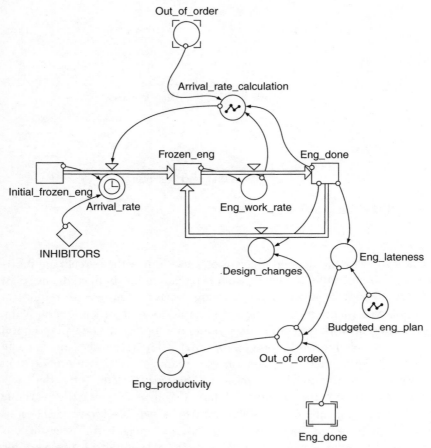

Figure 9.19—Modified design cycle

Reproduced from Powersim business-simulation software. For more information on Powersim visit
www.powersim.com

project. Some of these can be represented in the manner of this simple
rule—particularly straightforward individual parameter changes based on
project lateness. But many will be much more complex, such as manpower
bring-on and -off rules, and we will need to consider further in Chapter 10
whether more powerful decision modelling can be used.

Before we leave this subject, it is worth noting that the project management team is not the only decision-makers affecting the project. In
particular, the client can affect the project in the way the approval process
is carried out, design changes demanded, quality assurance is monitored,
and so on. Thus the modelling of behaviour is central to System Dynamics

modelling of projects, but it is also perhaps the most difficult element to model effectively.

How effects compound

We discussed above how effects combine, exacerbating each other's feedback loops, so that the combination of two effects is often considerably greater than the sum of the two individual effects. One of the advantages of systemic modelling is that it can show this compounding of effects.

Chapter 7 described the effects in the shuttle wagons project, and it is instructive to show the results of this model as an example to illustrate this compounding (these results are taken from Williams *et al.* 1995). Obviously, the results for the actual shuttle wagons are confidential but, for the purposes of illustration, the model was run with closely approximating numbers, and the resulting number of man-hours scaled to a proportion of the original budget. The model built was run under a variety of circumstances: first, the project as originally anticipated, then varying the levels of three variables to see their differential effect:

1. Increasing the average time for a document to gain client approval/ comment from the level contractually agreed (the "Low" level) to a level nearer to that experienced in the project (the "High" level).
2. Increasing the proportion of documents the client commented upon (without requiring extra-contractual modifications to the product) from a "Low" level to a "High" level.
3. Increasing the proportion of documents the client required extra-contractual work on, either unjustifiable changes or enhancements to the product.

The results of the eight runs carried out, with the three variables each at two levels, were as shown in Figure 9.20, where the last column shows the number of man-hours of designers used, normalised to 100 at the base case where all factors are Low. The first run corresponds to the anticipated case (i.e. as budgeted) and the last corresponds to the actual case. The actual results found were not identical to those below, but they were similar.

The compounding effect is clearly seen in these figures. If you want the compounding effect quantified, suppose the total man-hours used (T) is 100 multiplied by parameters depending on which factor is there (an analysis-of-variance-type approach). Thus, the first experiment results in a T of 100;

(1) Average approval time	(2) Proportion Comments	(3) Proportion Extra work	Total Man-hours used
Low	Low	Low	100.0
Low	Low	High	192.0
Low	High	Low	111.8
Low	High	High	267.9
High	Low	Low	100.4
High	Low	High	190.3
High	High	Low	113.1
High	High	High	325.7

Figure 9.20—Results of model runs

the second in a T of $100 \times X_3$, where X_3 is the effect due to (3); the fourth has two factors applied, so $T = 100 \times X_2 \times X_3 \times X_{23}$, where X_{23} is the compounding effect of having both (2) and (3) applied together; and the last has 100 multiplied by seven multiplicative parameters, the three single-factor parameters, three double-factor parameters, and one triple-factor parameter, X_{123}. Solving for the X_i's gives:

$$
\begin{aligned}
X_1 &= 1.004 \\
X_2 &= 1.118 \\
X_3 &= 1.920 \\
X_{12} &= 1.008 \\
X_{13} &= 0.986 \\
X_{23} &= 1.248 \\
X_{123} &= 1.218
\end{aligned}
$$

The actual size of the base effects is, to a certain extent, determined by the size of the High factors chosen in this study. However, the compounding effect of the factors can be seen. When comments increase (factor (2)), they add a certain proportion to the cost of a slack project (11.8%); however, when extra work is put into the system (factor (3)) and the comments increase *as well*, their combined multiplicative effect is bigger than the two individual factors combined (24.8% (X_{23}) bigger). If, to this, you then add in approval delays, which have little effect on a slack project, there is an effect 21.8% beyond what is explained simply by the additional multiplication. In fact, the effect of all three factors together is equal to the individual factors multiplied by $1.008 \times 0.986 \times 1.248 \times 1.218$ of the individual factors, or an extra 51%.

So when effects combine, their effect is much greater than the sum of their individual effects. Even at a simple level, we saw in Construction Project X that the effect of the weather, which was not particularly large in itself, became greatly magnified when other effects made the project late. Such compounding is difficult to predict quantitatively without some sort of modelling, and System Dynamics modelling is one useful way of doing this.

Validation

Finally, the resulting model has to be validated. Validation comes in two forms—the individual equations each need to be related to the data collected and validated, and then the model as an entirety (or subsets of the model) has to be validated.

In terms of the individual equations, we discussed some aspects of this in the preceding individual sections. There are obvious and clear problems in measuring "soft" aspects such as morale, but so long as we can measure and validate the relationships within which morale lies then we have by inference measured the effect of morale (e.g. if design changes affect morale, which affects productivity, so long as we can measure the relationship between design changes and productivity, "morale" simply becomes a step between these two (measurable) variables).

Measuring and validating the decision rules is clearly much more difficult. Some decisions are obvious and can be modelled easily. But the majority need some sort of rational evidence and, as we discussed in the previous section, this can be difficult. One suggestion (Williams 1996b) is to use interactive models as management "flight simulators", in which management can make decisions while "playing the management game", and mini-expert systems can be built from those observations, which can then be inserted into the model to emulate the management decision-maker. This will be revisited in Chapter 10.

To validate our final model, we can use various aspects discussed in Chapter 3. But the System Dynamics world has developed its own sets of validation tests for SD models. A structured framework of such tests has been available for some time, given by Forrester and Senge (1980). A more formal approach is described in Barlas (1996), who uses direct structure tests (a direct qualitative comparison of each equation with what is known about the real system), structure-oriented behaviour tests (running a simulation and assessing behaviour against the behaviour of the real system) and, finally, behaviour accuracy tests. Barlas' approach is subsumed in the approach used by Rodrigues (2001), who gives a much fuller structured set of validity tests divided into structure validity, tests of the model structure and tests of the model behaviour. Further useful discussion of these tests as used for models of design processes is given by Ford and Sterman (1998)— these include behaviour-reproduction tests in which data was collected for actual occurrences and compared to simulation outputs, which requires careful and sophisticated statistical analysis. Study of these specialised validity tests is outwith the scope of this book, and the reader is recommended to look at the above references for more information.

Conclusion

So, we have been able to model using these elements that other techniques cannot model. "Softer" aspects of projects can be included in the analysis; mismatches between perceptions and reality can be included (the "90% syndrome", or hidden rework); we can include chains of causality; we can include feedback and rework; we can include management decision-making (a key flaw in network modelling—Omsen (1992) said that "most project managers, when audited, do not actually manage their projects in the work sequences originally planned"). Crucially, these models can explain phenomena that cannot be easily explained using more conventional methods—such as Brooks' law or the big overspends resulting from positive feedback loops.

But there are problems with the method. Its lack of general acceptance by practising project managers is probably partly due to its lack of operational detail—while this detail can be seen clearly in WBS and CPM networks, an SD model can be seen as very aggregated, and the entities flowing through the model are homogeneous, rather than the attribute-tagged heterogeneous entities that would be found in a conventional discrete-event simulation (and also those "entities" are not discrete entities in SD, but a continuous flow, which can also cause modelling problems). For risk analysis purposes, too, SD is an essentially deterministic analysis, not immediately amenable to probabilistic extension. Furthermore, while SD avoids the problems in conventional analysis of not including managerial decision-making, it brings the extra problem of how to characterise, analyse and model that decision-making, implying the need for sophisticated reasoning to be built in to the models. The next chapter, therefore, will discuss hybrids of these models, as we seek to bring together the benefits of different methods.

10 Hybrid methods: the way forward?

Introduction

We saw at the end of Chapter 6 that conventional modelling techniques were inadequate for a variety of reasons: in particular, they did not capture system-wide effects, they did not consider "soft" effects, and they did not properly allow for decision-making within the project. We therefore developed the ideas of System Dynamics (SD) modelling. However, we finished Chapter 9 by saying that there were a number of problems with SD; in particular its lack of operational detail (including its use of homogeneous entities); its essentially deterministic nature; and its generally simplistic modelling of managerial decision-making. Effectively, we are saying that SD is good at capturing the systemic and non-intuitive nature of complexity, but that if we consider our original definition of complexity in Chapter 4 (see for example Figure 4.5), then SD models in practice (respectively) do not consider Structural Complexity sufficiently; barely consider Uncertainty at all; and do not sufficiently model the actions of management in response to Uncertainty and Structural Complexity. This chapter will therefore start by considering each of these problems in turn, to see how the benefits of SD can be used in tandem with other methods to lessen the effects of its shortcomings.

We'll concentrate on the first of these: the insufficient consideration of Structural Complexity. One of the reasons that the System Dynamics models described in this book have not gained a great deal of acceptance in the project management world is that practitioners can see that they do not capture the operational detail of ordinary project management models. The project management world has standardised sets of (highly detailed) tools (in particular, the PMBOK; Project Management Institute 1987, 2000) and System Dynamics does not really fit with these. In order to reap the benefits of systemic models in practice, therefore, we first need to consider whether these two ways of working can be brought closer together. In the next three sections we'll suggest a few ways of doing this, although it is only the last of these sections that discusses hybrid models.

The following two sections will go on to look at the second and third issues above: extending SD to include, for example, Uncertainty, and the need to model management actions.

Adapting standard models using lessons learned from SD

There are important generic lessons that conventional modellers can learn from the results of our SD models. The most straightforward way of bringing the conventional approach and the SD approach together, therefore, is simply to modify conventional techniques in the light of these lessons. In particular, let's revisit the techniques we studied in Chapter 5, where we looked at network simulation. Under the heading Management decisions we said that simulation outputs often give very wide distributions because they simply carry through each simulation run in an unintelligent fashion, rather than including actions that real management would take to control a project going out of control; and this has significantly weakened the credibility of the time-risk analyses used in practice. And those few authors we quoted who did recognise the need to incorporate management control into the models used very simple control actions that had very simple results, whereas in practice, as discussed in Chapter 9, the effects of management actions are more subtle.

Let's look here at some typical management actions. There are two generic types of action which appear to be most important, as discussed in the section on worker productivity in Chapter 9:

1. Bringing an activity forward. If activity i has a standard finish-start dependency (or dependencies) as shown in Figure 10.1a, this action would start activity i earlier than would normally be the case, resulting (theoretically) in the dependency shown in Figure 10.1b—but of course we need to look at systemic models to see the effects of this action.
2. Reducing an activity's duration: thus if activity i has duration t_i, this action would change its duration to λt_i (where λ is a "crashing" proportion, such that $0 < \lambda < 1$). Of course, this idea of crashing activity durations is well-known, and there is a fair amount of literature on finding the optimum project duration when each of a subset of activities

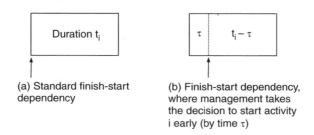

(a) Standard finish-start
dependency

(b) Finish-start dependency,
where management takes
the decision to start activity
i early (by time τ)

Figure 10.1—Modifying start-finish dependencies

independently has crashing potential. However, this is a hypothetical situation, and it is not clear to what extent the ideas are used in practice: Kamburowski (1995) describes an optimum algorithm, but in the subsequent discussion Chapman (1995) comments that "work on the properties of exact project scheduling network models is . . . of little practical interest". One reason for this is because the downstream effects of crashing one activity are not included in the model; again, we can look to System Dynamics to gain insight into these effects.

Chapter 9 discussed the effects of these actions. We described a series of interlinked feedback loops where bringing activities forward (thus doing work before engineering judgement said it should be done) increased rework, which increased delays, which led to more parallelism and thus increased cross-relations between activities, hindering a system freeze, and hence more work is done before it should be done, and so on. We referred to Cooper's work (1994) (see also Brooks 1978) which discussed the feedback loops involved when extra personnel are brought in to reduce activity times, leading to increased durations and increased costs. We also referred to Rodrigues and Williams (1998), who discussed the effects of reducing an activity's length in software projects, bringing downstream problems due to quality aspects and increased activity parallelism.

How should such indications be modelled in our network simulations? Looking at the two management actions above, simple models could include the following, where activity i has nominal duration t_i and cost c_i:

1. Bringing activity i forward by τ (where $0 < \tau < t_i$) will have the effect that:
   - even being optimistic, the remaining activity duration after the dependency, theoretically $t_i - \tau$, will in fact be a figure greater than that, say $t_i - \alpha\tau$ where α is a factor such that $0 \leq \alpha < 1$;

- the new cost, rather than c_i will be $c_i/(1 - \beta(\tau))$ where β is a function of τ such that $0 < \beta(\tau) < 1$;
- both parallel and downstream activities will have their nominal durations increased from t_j to $t_j(1 + \delta(j, \tau))$, where $\delta(j, \tau)$ is a non-negative function of τ (which we could expect to decrease as activity j moves towards the end of the project).

2. Reducing an activity's duration from t_i to λt_i:
   - the work described above gives a crashing time-cost function more realistic than a simple linear function, where the cost is divided by λ^k;
   - parallel activities j will be affected: that is, their durations will become $t_j(1 + \gamma(\lambda))$ (where $\gamma(\lambda)$ is a non-negative function of λ);
   - downstream activities will have their nominal durations increased from t_j to $t_j(1 + \epsilon(j,\lambda))$, where again $\epsilon(j, \tau)$ is a non-negative function of λ which decreases exponentially as activity j moves towards the end of the project.

Furthermore, these new lengthened activities will in general themselves be crashed, to stop them becoming critical, so their costs will increase, and the effects described above will be repeated in a secondary wave of knock-on effects.

Let's look at the simplest possible example, to indicate the type of model and the type of result. Suppose that a project has an important mid-point milestone; we will combine all of the activities before this point into a single activity, A. Suppose further that there is a subsequent activity, B, that management can control. We will combine all of the other activities into two: activity C, which represents activities parallel to B, and activity D, representing downstream activities. The resulting simple network is shown in Figure 10.2.

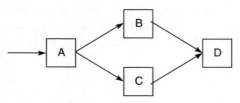

Figure 10.2—A simple example network

Suppose the activity durations have distributions as shown in Table 10.1.

Table 10.1—Distributions of activity durations (in months)

Activity	Distribution	Minimum	Mean	Maximum
A	Beta	15	20	30
B	Beta	5	6	10
C	Beta	2	3	6
D	Beta	4	5	8

Assuming the activities are independent, this is simple to simulate. Suppose that the final date for completion of the project (beyond which liquidated damages are payable) is 35 months; simulation shows a 90.2% probability of achieving this. But suppose that the milestone by which A is supposed to be finished is month 23, and management knows that if this slips, the final target date of 35 months is unlikely to be met. If activity A slipped, then management would take two actions:

- If activity A completed after month 23, part of activity B would be brought forward, so that (say) two months' work would be done in parallel to A. Figure 10.2 represents the original plan, but management often has the option of bringing forward part of an activity if the project is running late, e.g. setting engineers to work on designs even though the concept has not been finalised, or beginning construction on the basis of detailed designs that are not fully completed. However, due to the effects we've discussed, let us suppose that:
  - the remaining duration of activity B would only be reduced by 1.5 months (i.e. $\alpha = 0.75$);
  - the cost of activity B would be increased by 6.5/6;
  - activity C (parallel to B) would be increased by 0.5 months;
  - activity D (downstream from B) would be increased by 0.5 months.
- If activity A completed after month 24, activity B (that element which was not brought forward to before the milestone) would be crashed, so that its length would be reduced by 20%. However, again suppose that:
  - the cost would be increased by 25% (i.e. $k = 1$)
  - the duration of activity C would be divided by 0.9;
  - the duration of activity D would be divided by 0.95.

This network has been simulated 1000 times using the @RISK package, both the initial version (with no management control) and the latter version. Figure 10.3 shows the probability of the total project duration exceeding certain times for both the crude simulation and this latter "controlled" version; the controlled version now has a 95.2% chance of achieving the deadline of 35 months (as compared to the crude simulation which only had

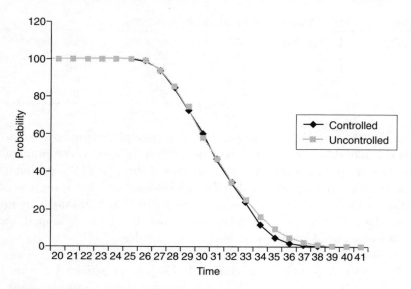

Figure 10.3—Results of the simple example

a 90.2% chance). (Furthermore, the cruciality—as discussed in Chapter 5—of activity A is reduced from 95% to 93% in going from the crude to the controlled version, showing that management can take some action to reduce the effect of activity overrun, but cannot catch up completely. This implies a deterministic project duration and thus a cruciality index of zero.)

Thus this example shows:

- the effects of management control, restricting the longer project durations;
- the resulting project duration, which is less optimistic than might be first thought of by management, since the time saved by bringing an activity forward or crashing it is lost to a certain degree by the effects of the project dynamics;
- additional costs: since the first of the above actions occurred in 14.9% of iterations, and the second in 8.7% of iterations, the cost of activity B was increased by 3.2%.

In conclusion, then, the first proposal is to take the lessons of SD and try to wind them into our network simulation models. Currently, network simulation models are rarely regarded as credible, partly because of the resulting wide probability distributions, because the models do not reflect the actions that management would take to bring late-running projects under control, and the dynamic results of these actions. By including generic lessons from SD we may be able to can bring additional realism to probabilistic network modelling. However, estimating the parameters represented by the Greek characters above would not be an easy task, and much more empirical work is needed here.

Using conventional tools to generate SD models

One key problem with SD is that SD models are not attractive to project managers, who do not see the operational detail within them. The previous section approached this question by not using SD models with managers at all, but using lessons learned from these models to inform a conventional method. However, another option could be to take the operational plans within the conventional methods and use them to produce the base SD model, which would then be more familiar, recognisable—and perhaps more acceptable—to project managers.

Project risk analyses usually start from a very high-level network (which could include as few as 20 activities, and generally includes less than 100 activities). If you have such a network with, say, 20 activities, this can be modelled as an SD model. Take, for example, a simple three-activity activity-on-the-arrow network, as shown in Figure 10.4.

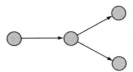

Figure 10.4—A simple activity-on-the-arrow network

This can immediately be simply modelled in System Dynamics by representing each activity as a stock-flow-stock triple, shown in Figure 10.5.

This allows us, then, to impose all the SD effects that we modelled in Chapter 9. The difference here is that the activities will be recognisable to project management, and the stocks and flows have an obvious meaning to which they can relate. Obviously, this can only be done with a small initial network, but this is true of a lot of high-level conventional studies. It also means that the size of the final SD model is larger than an SD modeller would wish, and does require care, since many of the project-wide effects

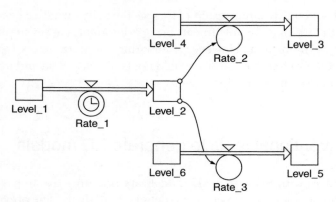

Figure 10.5—SD version of the simple activity-on-the-arrow network

Reproduced from Powersim business-simulation software. For more information on Powersim visit www.powersim.com

we wish to model will affect many or all of the activities, which can lead to a very repetitive and highly linked model. For example, the same resources may be undertaking many of the activities, so the rate variables on the stock-flow-stock triples modelling each of these activities might have to be linked to each of a set of resource variables. However, this can be a helpful start to the modelling, and can overcome some of the initial scepticism many project managers, used to conventional methods, feel towards SD.

Using SD and conventional models to inform each other

In our first proposal we looked at SD informing conventional methods. The second, which we've just looked at, considered conventional methods informing SD. The natural alternative to these two, as we suggested in our introduction, is the idea of using SD and conventional models to inform each other—and this can be done not only at the start of the project, but dynamically as the project proceeds.

A good example of this is Rodrigues (Rodrigues 2001, Rodrigues and Williams 1997, 1998), used on the KDCOM project. This uses an SD model of the project, divided into the engineering process of physical product development and the management process of project control. It then links this SD model to the operational project management models in an integrated scheme for managing a project. The idea here is that in planning, a network plan is developed as traditionally, but the project manager uses the SD project model to test the likely outcome of that plan (having first calibrated the SD model by the network). Similarly, in monitoring, metrics are collected, and the SD model is calibrated to reproduce past behaviour. This thus represents a robust project model with which to experiment and plan. The SD models are linked to the project network models with formal data- and structure-links, including a more general hierarchical version of the ideas in the section above on using conventional tools to generate SD models. Figure 10.6 illustrates the bare essentials of this scheme, although a great deal more richness is described in Rodrigues (2001) and Rodrigues and Williams (1997, 1998).

One area where SD can make a significant difference to the operation of conventional methods (not particularly covered by Rodrigues' work) is where the project uses Earned Value Analysis. The idea of Earned Value (see Chapter 2, section on Basic project management techniques) is to measure the baseline and planned costs of work scheduled and complete, and come to judgements about lateness and overspend based on how much work has actually been completed. The discussion we have had about the problems of metrics collection using only traditional methods, and the 90% syndrome in particular, clearly has implications here. Of course, if the work completed has been significantly overestimated, or if processes underlying the project tell you that significant extra work or rework is going to happen downstream, then Earned Value calculations will be useless or, worse, misleading. So a project making significant use of Earned Value can be helped tremendously if a model describing the systemic effects within the project is available, either to give indications of possible issues (as in the

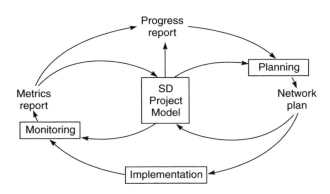

Figure 10.6—Summary of Rodrigues' (2001) combined SD/project management model

above section on Adapting standard models using lessons learned from SD) or formally linked to the Earned Value models, as in Rodrigues' type of system above. A systemic model can give estimates of cost and duration at completion, which can be a valuable triangulation with the Earned Value estimates and, where these significantly differ, the types of causal model we described in Chapters 7–9 can help to explain the differences.

This coming together of SD and traditional tactical decision aids within the management decision-making cycle is very promising, and helps both to bring some of the results of the systemic analysis into tactical decision-making, and some of the implications of Structural Complexity recognised by the tactical methods into the system analysis. However, it must be said that there is as yet little empirical support for it and it remains to be fully proven in practice.

Extending SD: discrete events and stochastic SD

The ideas above all fall under the umbrella of System Dynamics modelling. However, the nature of projects means that we need to be prepared to go beyond what the SD community has traditionally regarded as "proper" SD, especially in two ways.

First, System Dynamics has been distinguished from traditional discrete event simulation in that its effects are continuous, discontinuities generally being identified as errors in the modelling. Furthermore, the "material" within the stock/flow system is regarded as homogenous—as compared to discrete event simulation which expects the (discrete) entities flowing through the system to be tagged and identifiable and thus allows for them to be differentiated. By definition, projects with a tangible outcome are normally concerned with producing a small number n of items—when large quantities are produced, then we move into the operations-oriented environment which we contrasted with project management in Chapter 2. Sometimes, n is equal to 1, as in building the Channel Tunnel. For other projects, however, we are manufacturing small quantities—such as a subset of the Channel Tunnel project, the shuttle wagons project, where a few hundred wagons were built of a few different types, and a model had to be able to distinguish which type of wagon was being referred to at any one time, using various modelling artefacts. Even more particularly for modelling projects, Chapter 5 discussed the effects of different types of shock on a project—and often these shocks will come in the form of a single one-off effect; for example, in the naval ship life extension project, a sudden one-off change came in the environment, and the system had to adjust to it. Modelling these types of discrete events is not natural within System Dynamics, and the pure form of SD has to be pragmatically adapted. There is a long history of such work, dating back at least to Wolsteholme and Coyle (1980) and Coyle (1985), and it is now commonly recognised that, where such effects need to be modelled, the methods can be adapted, and the most modern SD packages allow some elements of discrete events to be included.

The second extension to System Dynamics comes in the need to model the probabilistic nature of many of our effects. At the very simplest level, we have really only considered average values of project disturbances rather than the distributions. For instance, the examples discussed in Chapter 9's section on how effects compound only considered the average approval time, although in real life it is not only the average but also the distribution of approval time that has an effect, since a small number of crucial documents held up for a very long time have the effect of stopping much of the system being frozen; this was for simplicity, but also because averages are much easier to consider in standard SD systems.

But more than this, the requirement to model events that might or might not take place—risks—was the topic of Chapter 5. The objective of modelling risks is to understand the combined effect of the various combinations of risks. Being now able to represent systemic relationships, we can better understand the interrelationships between the risks and the combination of effects; there is then a need to feed this into our probabilistic understanding. This, of course, is no trivial numerical task. If the project model has n independent exogenous parameters $e_1, \ldots, e_n$ as inputs, each of which has epistemic uncertainty characterised by a probability density function $f_i(e_i)$, and a single output $C(e_1, \ldots, e_n)$, then it is necessary to carry out multiple simulation runs of the models in order to gain a numerical estimate of the resulting distribution of C. This will be further complicated when there are dependencies between the e_i's, so that distributions are dependent upon the other parameter values: $f_i(e_i \mid e_j, j = 1 \ldots n, j \neq i)$. Morgan and Henrion (1990) give full details of the equations to derive confidence intervals for quartiles and so on, and also discuss in detail ways to reduce the computational burden of this task, although more work is still needed to make this task less onerous.

Alternatively, of course, the most modern SD packages have a Monte Carlo extension by which inputs can be given distributions and then standard Monte Carlo simulation runs carried out. This is a useful additional feature, although it is worth noting that:

- Monte Carlo simulation is really for looking at the likely overall effect from the combinations of aleatoric uncertainties (with epistemic uncer-

tainties, where we are looking at the effects of our lack of knowledge rather than subjective probability, we are as interested in the envelope of likely results);
- deriving the pattern of effects over time (rather than single-value esti-mates) is one of the most informative outputs from SD, and the best way of interpreting this under a Monte Carlo regime is not clear;
- this only allows multiple "what if" runs of the model, and does not incorporate probability distributions into the running of the model itself.

This is a new area, and with Palisade's new Powersim Studio Expert, one which will grow in importance.

The need for intelligence

One ongoing issue for all such modelling is the need to represent within the model the monitoring and control actions that management would carry out within each scenario. We said at the start of this chapter that models which do not adequately represent management responses to progress on the project are significantly flawed and give results that are neither realistic nor credible.

Clearly within project management there are a range of well-defined decisions that need to be modelled; not only the two described above (bringing an activity forward and "crashing" an activity) but also various other decisions mentioned in Chapter 9, including:

- starting work earlier than intended based, say, on incomplete or un-confirmed information;
- bringing workers on or off a project;
- moving to overtime or multiple shifts;
- opening up a new production line or rebalancing an existing line;

and so on. To effectively model the behaviour of a project, it is essential that the model is able to mimic management decision-making on such problems.

SD lends itself to modelling information flows within the project, so that the information can be represented for the modeller just as it would be for the human decision-maker within the project. However, with the current state of modelling, it is worrying that the decision rules used are in some cases crude, and not nearly sufficiently representative of the decision-making procedure. Much more work is required here to represent the intelligent manager within the models. Single decision rules in SD models can sometimes suffice, but the robustness of the model to errors in such rules must be checked. In particular, models can be very sensitive to continuous decision-making rules (e.g. bringing workers on or off a project, as opposed to one-off decisions such as opening a new production line), setting up oscillatory or erratic behaviour.

We could of course use a human to drive the simulation, but this means that results are non-replicable and lose statistical significance. We would thus like to have some intelligence embedded within the model. But how to carry out such embedding is more difficult. Russell *et al.* (1992) say that, "unfortunately, there seem to be almost as many solutions to the problem of integrating simulation and artificial intelligence as there are investigators into the problem. However, there is one point of agreement . . . the need for some intelligent agent to control the behaviour of the simulation."

One possible approach (developed in a different domain in Williams 1996b) uses a sequence of methods, which combines the benefits of simulation and expert systems. First, a simulation is made into a "management flight simulator" or "Visual Interactive Simulation" in order that an intelligent user can control it; then archetypal user decisions are defined so that a user can simulate a reasonable period of time without having to model every action. Expert user(s) are observed and their knowledge of the task captured, which enables an expert system to be created, which is then embedded in the simulation to provide an intelligent, automatically-running simulation. Schematically, this can be shown as follows:

Completely user-driven Visual Interactive Simulation:
→ Visual Interactive Simulation with archetypal user decisions
→ Knowledge acquisition
→ Expert system
→ Automatic intelligent simulation

This method therefore has three stages, each of which has extra benefits:

- *Elicitation*: (the first two steps above). During elicitation, problems are identified, clarified and structured (including the definition of archetypal decisions), forcing decision-makers to think. This gives the benefits of providing structure to the problem and adding to the domain knowledge;
- *Emulation*: building an "expert system" which could also be used by itself; for example, the system could be used as an aid in the implementation of the project, or perhaps as a training aid;
- *Embedding*: providing a realistic simulation.

This is a powerful technique, although the requirement "define archetypal user decisions" is clearly much more complex than the simple statement suggests. However, as far as I know, the technique hasn't been used in full for project management, although the first two steps have been done in a number of projects (see e.g. Williams *et al.* (1996), which describes an SD model in a Visual Basic environment providing a management "game" through which senior managers can learn about feedback within projects and the effects of particular management actions).

This is perhaps the key area for further research we must make our simulations mimic real projects by making them mimic the decisions of human managers in the system, otherwise we severely limit the scope of problem we can address.

Conclusion

We ended Chapter 9 with a toolbox of techniques, some traditional project management techniques (WBS, CPM, organisational breakdown structure, C/SCSC, and so on), with probabilistic additions to these (the ideas of Chapter 5 allowing extra effects to be modelled, analysis of criticality/ cruciality, etc.), ideas of "soft" effects that had to be modelled to properly represent the project; methods for qualitative causal mapping, and System Dynamics modelling to represent the complex webs of causality and their combined effects on a project. However, each of these methods, while good for attacking particular aspects of projects, has flaws, some of which the other methods try to address.

It would have been nice to have come, at this point, to a unified modelling method where we could provide one single technique that brings together all of these ideas. But management modelling is not like that—and if it were, we would have less need for skilled modellers. The first thing to say is that the modeller needs each of these techniques and an under- standing of their flaws to apply the right tool at the right time. But more than that, with our knowledge at its current stage, the modeller must be prepared to mix and match methods, and to hybridise and develop them further. Each project is unique; each modelling situation is different, and each modeller must make the best of his toolbox. While a purist might object to muddling different methods with clearly different underlying paradigms, the practising modeller must seek the best combination of tech- niques for the job. So I'd like to encourage you to experiment with the techniques—and the use of more than one technique to aid in triangulation. Perhaps, as we develop these tools together, more formally defined hybrid or combination techniques might be defined and find common use in practice, and be developed to model sufficiently the situations we meet in our profession.

11 The role of the modeller

Introduction

We said at the start of this book that we were going to discuss how to model the behaviour of complex projects, as a modeller helps to advise and inform a project team or senior management. So far, we've been looking at how the modeller can construct his models. But he has to fit in with a real project and a real project team. What *is* the role of the modeller in the management of a project? What contribution does he make, how does that contribution change over the life-cycle of a project, and how does he relate to the rest of the project management team?

In this chapter, after discussing the importance of the modeller within a project management team, and what makes a good modeller, we'll look at the stages at which the project modeller can play a role in a project, and how that role varies over the course of the project: before, at the start, during and after the project.

Project management

A project operates at three fundamental levels (Morris 1979): (1) the integrative, (2) the strategic, and (3) the tactical level. As a project team manages the objectives of the project, at level 1 they must define how the project contributes to the aims and objectives of the business, and as they execute the project at level 1 they must integrate it into the context of the business. At level 2, strategies are defined for how to achieve the objectives of the project, and these are worked out in tactical level 3. Traditionally, these levels continue to be broken down further in structures such as the Work Breakdown Structure, Organisational Breakdown Structure, Product Breakdown Structure or C/SCSC. However, our understanding of complex projects (as we have stated throughout this book) is that the behaviour of the projects is not adequately explained by easy, linear, breakdowns such as these and, indeed, projects can respond counter-intuitively to actions taken by the project team. This means that, particu-larly at levels 2 and 3, a project team needs advice on how the project is likely to behave, in order to make rational decisions. This chapter will mainly be concerned with modelling at these levels.

Furthermore, many traditional texts view the project manager as one person who superhumanly makes all the decisions in a project; they talk about "project organisation" but don't talk about the organisation of project *decision-making*. However, most major projects have multiple levels of decision-making, with no single person making all the decisions. So the modeller has to fit into a project *team*. Indeed, Tampoe (1989) says that the effectiveness of the project team is the heart of successful project manage-ment. But some of his indicators of team effectiveness require the support of a modeller, for example: high commitment to goal achievement (but you must understand the results of your actions to achieve your goals); search-ing for real solutions and analytical problem-solving (which needs the tools of a modeller), and so on.

Similarly, the role of the project manager himself in a complex project requires analytical support. Turner (1993a, based on Fayol 1949) describes five functions of management:

- planning the work to be done to achieve the defined objectives;
- organising the team of people to do the work;
- implementing by assigning work to people;
- controlling progress;
- leading the team of people.

In a complex project, in at least the first, second and fourth of these, basing decisions on intuition and breakdown structures runs the risk of inefficient or even counter-productive plans.

This all means that, in order for the project team to carry out rational, coherent decision-making, a modeller is important to allow the conse-quences of decisions to be understood, the current status of the project to be comprehended, and sensible forecasting to be carried out. The area where this is perhaps best-recognised currently is in risk management, since this is such a fundamental part of the project team's role. There is some wise advice about the risk analyst as modeller in the PRAM Guide (Simon *et al.* 1997) some of which we'll look at below. Risk analysts/managers are clearly becoming a more integral part of the project team; Williams (1993c) says that in the future he will be:

- integrated into the project structure: in the past the risk manager or modeller has often been an outside expert unfamiliar with the project or even the project domain. The requirement for a modeller to be expert in modelling (or in this case, specifically risk management) will remain, and he is quite likely to be found within a vertical "risk" component of the matrix structure, but increasingly he is becoming established within project domains as the necessary techniques, knowledge and attitudes are being disseminated;

- high-profile, providing top-level visibility and understanding of the overall project behaviour and project risk, and enabling the key decision-makers in a project to make coherent decisions based on a valid view of the overall expected project behaviour/risk. The modeller's role is increasingly seen as providing support to the highest level of a project. It is true that in the past the risk manager has sometimes been given a formal position near the top of project management "organigrams", as an outward show of acknowledging the importance of the role, but this formal position is gradually becoming consolidated into one of the more important inputs to the project management decision-making process.

What makes a good modeller?

What makes a good modeller within a project management context is to a large extent the same as what makes a good management science modeller generally. Thus, advice given in management science textbooks (for a good, simple textbook, see Mitchell 1993) apply equally well here, and we looked at some of these issues in Chapter 3. Modern management science modelling isn't run on the old lines where a consultant took a problem, modelled it, solved the model and appeared to a client with a solution grasped in his hand which the client would welcome with delight—or, as often happened, put on a shelf and ignored (the traditional process originally devised by the pioneering work of Ackoff—see Churchman *et al.* 1957 —and continued by many others). Management science has developed with the work of many authors (particularly Eden—for example, Eden and Sims (1979), Eden (1982, 1987)) into a much more client-centred approach, where the client forms part of the problem-structuring, search for alternatives, implementation and monitoring. In our case, of course, the "client" is the project team, specifically, the project manager, and it is essential that modeller and project team work together to develop understanding and facilitate the decision-making process.

A key attribute of the modeller is the perception of neutrality: he is seen to be objective and bringing no preconceptions or partiality to the decison-making process. The PRAM Guide (Simons *et al.* 1997) gives useful advice to the risk analyst—but which is equally true for any modeller advising or forming part of a project team: the modeller needs to be able "to elicit and capture data about risk in an impartial manner, and to reflect information in a controlled and structured way. In reality, the risk analyst's relationship with the project team can have a major bearing on the outcome of the PRAM [Project Risk Analysis & Management] process. The project team will need to trust the risk analyst's judgement and take his/her guidance during the PRAM exercise."

It then goes on to highlight four aspects of the relationship between a modeller in a project context and the project team. One is the problem caused when modellers have a dual role, also holding an authoritative position on the team so that his neutrality is called into question. Another is the previous relationship between the modeller and the team. The other two points are worthy of more discussion:

- Domain knowledge: the management science literature does not guide us definitively on whether a modeller should have knowledge of the domain in which he is operating; and indeed, it is well accepted that many project management skills are generic and can be transferred from one domain to another. However, the PRAM Guide says that, "It is unlikely, for instance, that a risk analyst fundamentally trained in software engin-eering will be readily accepted by a team who are building a bridge." A modeller does not need to be an expert in the project work—and much of his data come from eliciting the expert opinions of others. However, in my experience some domain experience is important in order for a modeller to gain and maintain credibility with the project team—and, without credibility, the results of the modelling and the advice will be ignored. At the very least, the modeller needs experience in a closely related domain: building chemical plants and oil refineries might have similarities; building an IT system is fundamentally different in project characteristics and even project management techniques.

- Interpersonal skills of the modellers; that is, "their abilities to develop sound and trusting relationships with individuals within the project, are crucial to the effective implementation" of any modelling process. This is a key requirement; a modeller who likes to stay in a back room would find it difficult to operate in any management science field. Within the project context, where teamwork and application are so highly prized, such an analyst could not operate at all.

Stages of project modelling

The modeller has an important role throughout the project life-cycle. This continuing role is essential in giving continuity to the models developed. We can identify four stages of the project, in which the role of the modeller can be distinguished.

1. Before the project

Before the project starts, the modeller has a variety of roles, but *estimating* and *risk analysis* are two of the more important. The supporting role to the estimators is fairly clear, and we have dealt with some of the techniques involved in previous chapters. But what about the risk analysis role?

Before the project starts, risk analysis has a variety of functions, but there are two worthy of note here. First, it provides a firm basis for the project bid, taking into account the (correlated) distributions of all cost uncertainties and liquidated damages or other underachievement penalties. And note that the bid is not a single figure, but must include analysis of the cash-flow out (i.e. spend) and in (i.e. stage payments: for example, Elmaghraby (1990) suggests a very simple model using the time to, and cost to, Key Events).

Second, as we discussed in Chapter 5, risk analysis must also inform the contract. Obviously, changing the contract does not change the actual risks involved but "a prime function of any contract is to identify, assess and allocate risk" (National Economic Development Office 1982). It was a significant step forward in the acceptance of risk management to see Risk Registers treated first as the basis of contractual documents, then as the basis for a facilitated decision-making session by the project management team of which risks to transfer and which to keep (i.e. categorisation of risks, as discussed in Chapter 5). However, even at a simple level, risks cannot be treated individually and independently in the contract—it is reasonable to agree contractually that the client must pay X if risk A occurs and Y if risk B occurs; however, we have seen that in many cases the cost to the contractor will be greater than X + Y if both risks occur, and this is difficult to specify in a contract. Indeed, where there are many risks, it would be ludicrous to specify all possible combinations. Furthermore, Chapter 5 showed that taking a holistic view of the project, in particular looking at the inter-relationship between risks, is essential to understand how a number of risks combine and compound. Here, the types of systemic model in the previous chapters can be useful, but there is clearly more research to be done in this area.

Some work has been done, notably by Chapman and Ward (1994), in trying to optimise the choice or definition of contract type. They describe a mathematical treatment of allocating risk in contracts, with varying degrees of controllability (although note that this looks at the overall price of a contract, rather than at individual risks). Ward and Chapman (1995) look at distributions of profit under incentive contracts, with different levels of risk-averseness, assuming a triangular distribution for the total project cost. These techniques use a lot of calculations, but they are tractable calculations which a modeller could carry out. Similar calculations could also be carried out to see whether it is worth a client paying a risk premium—in other words, if a contractor asks for a higher payment in return for taking on more risk, the client needs to be satisfied that this option is preferable under his particular level of risk-averseness, by modelling the possible events and their outcomes.

All of these comments are confined to the modeller's work within the fundamental levels 2 and 3 we defined at the start of the project—the strategic and tactical levels. However, it is at this stage of the project, particularly, that the modeller can contribute to integrative level 1, as he is able to look at the project in its wider context. This has not been the focus of this book, as it goes beyond building models limited to the specific project, so we will not dwell on the subject here. However, there is an increasing emphasis on projects where the contractor takes on more than the responsibility for simply delivering a facility, and here the modeller has to look at level 1. In major infrastructure work, for example, BOO(T) (Build-Own-Operate-(Transfer)) projects require the contractor to fund and take on much of the risk of the project. Slightly differently, in the engineering domain, DBOM (Design-Build-Operate-Maintain) projects require the builder to take on the risk of operation and maintenance. In all of these cases, we are interested not simply in the cost of the project over the build phase but the (discounted) through-life cost (TLC) (or at least, cost over the fixed period). This means that we must build a model which includes at least (for DBOM and the simplest TLC models) the distribution of costs of maintenance and loss of availability through unreliability, discounted over time. (Models of BOO(T) projects must go even further, evaluating the expected costs of ownership and the expected income from the market.) Texts such as Blanchard (1998) describe how TLC (or LCC, Life-Cycle Cost) models can be built up; however, it is rare for analyses to be carried out that consider the optimum decisions accounting for both the dynamic impact on the design and build phase *and* the impact on TLC, so this is clearly another area needing substantial further empirical research.

2. At the start of the project

One of the most important stages in the project life-cycle is project start-up. This is a structured series of steps, including forming the team and getting it working together; creating a shared vision for the project, defining objectives, planning, organising and understanding constraints. A lot of effort is put into this process, during which many of the seeds of success and failure are sown. Fangel (1987) provides a useful handbook on the process.

Modelling underlies many of the actions in this process. At the highest level (which we called level 1 at the start of this chapter), a model needs to be specified for the project at the integrative level. The classic text (Turner 1993a, p. 282) calls this step "developing the project model". This will show the effects on the organisation beyond the project of, for example, later or earlier completion. But at the level at which we are normally working—levels 2 or 3—there are many more aspects requiring modelling, such as:

- exploring possible options for implementing the project; costing them and evaluating their multi-criteria benefits and disbenefits;
- analysis of the factors influencing success and their interrelationships;
- establishing the feasibility of resource-constrained plans (both budgetary and temporal);
- deepening the analysis of project risks and understanding the effects of planned actions to counter such risks if they arise—don't forget that many of the issues dealt with in Chapter 9 came from the (sometimes counter-intuitive) effects of management actions;
- identifying project-control metrics and understanding the meaning of those metrics.

Project start-up is most usually effected by a start-up workshop followed by the production of a project start-up report or manual (see Turner 1993a, Chapter 13). At the workshop stage, the modeller must be able to contribute to negotiations and discussions with support and advice; however, this requires the use of rapid-analysis high-level models. He must also be able to understand the implications and shortfalls of these models, so that caveats and warnings can be issued; this means that, where further analysis is necessary, the post-workshop negotiation stage can be used to ensure that the models are available to support the decisions. The key here is timeliness: a rough and ready, robust but requisite model which is available when decisions are being made is much better than a more "correct" model which is not available until irrevocable decisions have been taken.

Models developed in the pre-project stage are further developed and used in this stage, and form a useful link between the phases. Explanatory models that show the types of effects, albeit at a high level without all of the data in the models fully evaluated, are also used to give rapid support to team decisions. The project start-up phase is a rapid ramping up of the project, and this can be the time that the modeller is most in demand.

3. During the project

During the project, the modeller supports the team in two main tasks: *decision-taking/replanning* and *monitoring*. We'll look at these two in turn.

There are frequent points within a project where significant decisions have to be taken. At these points, the modeller's support is similar to that in stage 2, where he provides (a) increased understanding (e.g. why does the 90% syndrome happen? How does the $2000 hour occur? Both of these are shorthand for common effects seen in projects which we mentioned in Chapter 9), and (b) models of specific decision situations. Let's look at two examples.

A project will have a contractually agreed end-date. Generally there will be a mechanism for damages if the project is delivered late ("Liquidated Damages" or "LDs"), and frequently there will be bonuses if the project is delivered early. We discussed at length in Chapters 8–9 the chains of effects set up by management actions to accelerate a project, and tried to build these into our models. This means that, in a situation where events imply delay to a project, the modeller should therefore be able to advise on whether to simply accept LDs and not try to deliver on time, or to accelerate the project, or even decide if trying to gain bonuses is worthwhile. As an example, let's return to the naval ship life extension project example, which we followed through Chapters 7, 8 and 9. Chapter 9 arrived at a simple SD model of this project. Williams (1999b) takes this model and looks at the trade-off between increased time-extension and reduced man-hours—after this, finding the optimum is simple if the disbenefits of time delay (i.e. LDs plus any internal disbenefits such as the cost of occupying the dock, plus any further level 1 costs) are known. Of course, these require the acceleration rules to be specified and parameterised, but this simple example arrived at a single acceleration parameter and ran the model to show how total man-hours expended (M, normalised so that $M = 100$ represents the man-hours that would have been used had the disrupting event not occurred) and time-scale (T, similarly normalised) result from this parameter, giving the graph in Figure 11.1. From this the relative benefits and disbenefits of different levels of acceleration can be judged and balanced.

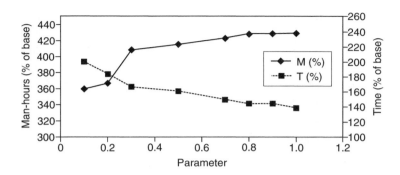

Figure 11.1—Relationship between spend and duration. From Williams, T.M. (1999b), "Seeking optimum project duration extensions", *Journal of the Operational Research Society* 50, 5, 460–467. Reproduced by permission of The OR Society Ltd, Palgrave Macmillan, on behalf of the Operational Research Society.

The second example is the attitude of the project team to change orders. Project management literature is full of sound advice on the need to evaluate the cost and time effects of proposed change orders. Barnes and Wearne (1993) say that "some crises and quick changes to plans are unavoidable, and drive in solving problems is very valuable, but failure to think through the decisions on problems can cause greater problems." However, in a complex project, the implications of change orders are impossible to evaluate without a project model. In Chapters 7, 8 and 9 we discussed in detail the chains of effects built up by change orders, especially continuous streams of change orders. This is discussed further in Eden *et al.* 2000. The types of model developed in Chapter 9's section on Scope change can be used to evaluate these rapidly. The implications are often greater than intuition would suggest, and these models can be very useful also in educating the customer as to the implications of a proposed change order, as well as being a useful negotiating tool (see Rodrigues and Williams 1998). In a complex, highly time-constrained project, this can be an area in which the modeller's contribution to the project team's decision-making is vital.

The second role for the modeller is in supporting project *monitoring*. There are standard metrics measured in every project, and the project management team monitors progress, and bases its control actions, on these measures. Some of these might be uncontroversial: for example, while digging a tunnel, if the team has completed 200 feet of tunnel, that might be a measurable fact (although even with this simple example there might be problems).

However, we discussed throughout Chapters 8 and 9 that some metrics might be uninformative or even misleading. The use of project models can suggest metrics to use (e.g. productivity overtime, engineering rework rate, and so on); can explain the implications of metrics (e.g. when work appears to be x% complete, then hidden rework implies that y% will need some reworking); and can explain how measures change over time if behaviour appears counter-intuitive (e.g. the 90% syndrome that we discussed a number of times). Some of these metrics might be subjective, but can be useful in showing at least how perceptions change over time. Again, more research is required to establish the "best" metrics to collect in project management when this more holistic view is being taken.

For project *monitoring*, there are two areas in which models are particularly useful. As discussed in Chapter 10, the metrics collected are particularly significant when it comes to Earned Value calculations. As we said there, if estimates of work completed are significantly overestimated, or if processes underlying the project are going to cause significant extra work or rework to happen downstream, then the Earned Value calculations will be misleading. So a project making significant use of Earned Value can be helped if a model describing the systemic effects within the project is available to explain and adjust the Earned Value results.

The second area is in risk monitoring. Major research projects such as Cooke-Davis (1996) shows that ongoing project-risk analysis and ongoing management is a major driver towards project success, and there are now many papers (e.g. Newland 1997) that extol the benefits of such work. Hillson (1997) provides a four-stage model of how "mature" an organisation is in this respect, and thus when to introduce which type of PRM within a company. In this model, at the second "novice" level, there should be at least one analyst able to understand and apply risk modelling techniques; but, moving to the higher "normalised" and "natural" levels, the project team needs to understand the impact of risks, and the meaning of collected metrics, and the likely effect of mitigation actions. In a complex project, these all require the project team to have the support of a modeller, with models to explain, analyse and estimate.

A final comment about the role of the modeller during his project concerns his organisational position. This will depend upon the type and size of the project—sometimes he will report directly to the project manager, sometimes to a risk manager, and so on. But an increasingly popular structure, particularly for larger projects, is the project support office (PSO). This is a group that administers the project management function, including maintaining the project plan, issuing progress reports, establishing configuration management, issuing production part-lists and so on. Given that this group maintains the plan and provides advice on proposals for change or implications of events, this can be a natural place for the modeller to ensure that models inform and advise this work. As a unified office, the PSO also enables the modeller to influence, where appropriate, the whole spread of the project management function, from planning and cost-control through to contract administration, purchasing and material management.

4. After the project

The role of the modeller is not complete after the project has finished. One essential and often neglected task is supporting post-project reviews and feeding this into the ongoing learning of the organisation. And—a closely related but subtly different task—there might be post-project claims, which also involve reviewing the project post-mortem but in a more detailed and sustainable way. We'll look at post-project reviews first, and the need for ongoing education past the immediate project, then turn to claims work.

The need for organisations to be "learning organisations" (Senge *et al.* 1994) is rightly emphasised these days, and there is a particular need for project-based organisations, if they are to flourish, to learn from one project to the next. But in individual companies in practice, project review processes are rarely in place, project failure and success are rarely analysed, and learning doesn't just happen. Frequently this is because the next bid and the next project are pressing and too urgent to leave time to reflect. Often it is because there are no standard methods in place for analysing projects. And when post-project reviews have been performed in the past, if companies have not found them to be helpful or useful, then there is no motivation to carry them out for currently completing projects. Barnes and Wearne (1993) say that "failure to analyse experience and compare conclusions [is] perhaps the most frequent shortcoming of project management." Similarly, Cooke-Davies (2002) in his large study of project practice, reports that:

> . . . the current state of practice in large organisations is showing three areas of practice in which it is difficult to make significant progress, and which appear to be critical to consistent corporate success", one of which is "an effective means of 'learning from experience' on projects, that combines explicit knowledge with tacit knowledge in a way that encourages people to learn, and to embed that learning into continuous improvement of project management processes and practices. Indeed, for Kerzner (2000), continuous improvement represents the fifth and highest stage of project management maturity in an organisation.

Even when post-project reviews are performed, there are no standard, structured, routine ways of analysing projects to ensure that the organ-isation can learn lessons and use them in future projects. For simple, clear-cut projects, the few words of advice in PMBOK may suffice: "The causes of variances, the reasoning behind the corrective action chosen, and other types of lessons learned should be documented so that they become part of the historical database . . ." (Project Management Institute 2000, section 4.3.3.3). But for more complex projects, how do we learn these lessons? Collecting data on what happened isn't the main problem (although it can be sometimes); it is gaining understanding about what went wrong (or right), and why. Gordon MacMaster (2000) wrote "It's not that there is a lack of data. The entire data warehousing industry is booming because of data's abundance. Are repositories of data also meaningful historical information? The answer is obviously no." He goes on to say that, "data repositories reflect the objective parameters of a project and the facts, figures, and approved documents . . . It takes a significant effort to sort through the official history . . . The effort involved is a significant deterrent to using historical data in project planning, regardless of the quality of the data repositories." And this is assuming that the official history is correct and fully documented—how much more difficult this is in real situations when data is contradictory or ambiguous.

Furthermore, the causal chains that led to the results are often not obvious. As Wheelwright and Clark (1992) note:

> . . . the performance that matters is often a result of complex interactions within the overall development system. Moreover, the connection between cause and effect may be separated significantly in time and place. In some instances, for example, the outcomes of interest are only evident at the conclusion of the project. Thus, while symptoms and potential causes may be observed along the development path, systematic investigation requires observation of the outcomes, followed by any analysis that looks back to find the underlying causes.

Thus we need to be able to trace complex sets of causal links from actions taken by the parties through the dynamic behaviours set up within the project, and to understand and quantify the resulting effects. It is only in this way that the effects of actions taken by the client (and/or contractor) can be tracked through all the complex interacting parts of the project and thus the outcome of the project explained. As we said in Chapter 3, projects are frequently characterised by "messiness": root causes of problems are often unclear, causality is unclear, and many of the effects observed are counter-intuitive—all features we have cited in this book to justify the need for modelling, and features which have prompted the use of mapping and modelling tools such as System Dynamics.

This use of non-trivial models is important but often neglected. Pitagorsky (2000) draws lessons from recording at the event-level and the project-level, then says:

> Once recorded, the project-level record . . . can be viewed along with other projects. If there are patterns—such as chronic lateness, chronic disputes regarding quality—the causes of the patterns can be analysed using the event-level record (change requests and resolutions, status reports) within the projects. . . . Learning from experience begins with recording each relevant event.

But this simply isn't realistic with complex projects, nor will it give the understanding that we require. Complex projects, as we discussed in Chapter 4, by their very nature, exhibit behaviours whose causality is not clear-cut—indeed, is often counter-intuitive. So for complex projects, simply listing what happened is not sufficient and we need the types of model that we have described in this book, which can capture the complexity of the events and their causality, and models that can explain why the outputs were as they occurred.

As well as capturing the facts and the causality underlying the facts, interviews and workshops can enable the stories of the project to be captured. MacMaster (2000) says that "the most valuable learning about past projects often comes from listening to those few individuals that assume the role of storyteller. One absorbs the context, nuances, and rationale (or lack thereof) behind the project documentation from them . . . Combining objective project documentation with subjective perceptions about a project is the leap between historical data and historical information." The use of cause-mapping helps to capture just these perceptions. But, much more than that, it captures the perceptions in a structured format, to ensure coherence and triangulation of data, and to allow a holistic perspective—a systemic view—to be taken. Furthermore, the natural transition into quantitative simulation (i.e. System Dynamics) allows those lessons to be established quantitatively, and alternative scenarios explored (what if we'd done this? What if the client had done that?).

In conclusion to our comments on reviews, five additional comments need to be made.

- Data doesn't always give understanding. In particular, counter-intuitive effects such as feedback and the compounding of individual effects are difficult to comprehend, let alone predict, intuitively. It is necessary to take a systems perspective of the project and what happened, and systems modelling can help to demonstrate such effects.
- We need to learn not only the easy lessons ("we neglected configuration control and that got us into a mess, costing $x to resolve") but also the lessons that derive from the more complex non-intuitive behaviours of our projects, discussed over the last few chapters ("we doubled our workforce on this project but it only yielded 5% extra output").

- We need project models to derive and then to explain these lessons. Cooper *et al.* (2002) call for "model(s) of the process that allow: comparison of 'unique' projects, and the sifting of the unique from the common; a search for patterns and commonalities between the projects; and an understanding of the causes of project performance differences, including the ability to do analyses and what-ifs." Such models are not commonly developed, and open a new field of contribution to the modeller that has only recently been explored by the likes of Cooper and his associates.

- Developing models post-mortem from nothing is a very time-consuming task. The modeller should aim to have his models operational during the project, so that post-project work is simply a continuation of the use of his models from stage (3) above. The project support office is a particular help here, with Turner (1993) pointing to its role as the project "conscience" (keeping project monitoring and control documentation up to date) as one of its most valuable features.

- There is a natural role for project post-mortems to play in the pre-project risk analysis of succeeding projects—and this is one way that project-oriented organisations can become learning organisations. We need to structure our post-mortems so that we can learn lessons from them to take into future projects. And as well as the specific circumstances of the individual project, running the final models can help to develop generic rules which can contribute towards understanding risks, particularly the likely impacts of risks upon the project that may contribute to later risk analyses—which takes us back to (1) and the cycle starts again!

One further way in which the modeller can help in the ongoing education of management is by supplying generic project management "games" or "management laboratories". It has been argued that the use of a simulation methodology such as System Dynamics can help overcome problems in perceiving feedback and offer a framework for conceptualising complex business issues (Graham *et al.* 1992). Thus the use of a project model generalised to avoid the specifics of the project can be a valuable tool by which managers experience the underlying positive feedback loops in time-constrained complex projects, thus developing their understanding of self-sustaining escalation and the significance of learning, design changes, client delays etc. (Williams *et al.* 1996).

This brings us on to post-project claims. Davidson and Huot (1991) state that:

such projects are apt to be litigated. It is difficult or even impossible, relying solely on traditional PERT/CPM system approaches, to find out who will be responsible for the impact cost; that is, the indirect cost caused by the ripple effect, by the delay and disruption of the original schedule, by the undiscovered rework when the construction is completed in the field . . . In a major fast-track project, it is almost impossible, with the traditional operational methodological approaches, to establish claims based on direct changes of original scope from the impact of the consequent rework. Too often we face a severe overlapping of design, procurement and construction.

Traditionally, claims, particularly Extension of Time (EOT) claims, have been based on a simple network methods. Since this is such a specific topic, the standard methods used are described in the appendix, which also describes some of the problems, which are those we have encountered in trying to model projects and describe their behaviour using linear disaggregation methods over the last few chapters. As described in the appendix, these problems and issues give rise to the suggestion of using causal mapping (to answer the question "why?") combined with System Dynamics (to answer the question "how much?") to answer questions about the effect of a delay, or a set of delays, upon a project, for example, as described in Chapters 8 and 9 and our discussion about "reviews" above. If the causal map and SD model are developed in parallel during the process of analysis (Ackermann *et al.* 1997), such a process can:

- show causality: the systemic interrelationships which caused the various ramifications of the delays to build up;
- show responsibility: show the party causing the initial causes of the delays (as opposed to the immediate causes, which might simply be reactions to previous effects);
- calculate the quantum of the effects—in other words, show the size of cost- and time-overrun resulting from a particular delay or set of delays;
- do all of these *transparently*.

However, as we discussed in Chapter 9, System Dynamics models do have problems, and the appendix describes procedures for:

- using simple Gantt or time-profile charts to find out the actual out-turn in a project;
- using standard network-based methods if there are a limited number of delays or disruptive events;
- understanding why the out-turn occurred, and to trace the causality from the triggering effects, using causal maps and System Dynamics;
- using a combination of methods for different parts of the project.

These models, then, show both time-effects and the reasons for cost-overruns; clearly, in a complex project which has been disrupted and thus accelerated, time and cost are closely related, and an analysis must be done of the two together.

Again, models should be developed *during* the project so they are available for claims—in practice, Alkass *et al.* (1995) said that 70% of the effort in a claim is spent on searching for and organizing information, much of which, had there been ongoing modelling work, should have been available.

Chapter summary

To summarise, then, the modeller has an important role throughout the project life-cycle, and we have looked at his contribution before the project starts, at its start, during it and after it has ended. In recent years, it has been the first and last of these where the modeller's role has been most visible. Before the project, modellers have been called upon when management needs to understand the issues behind fundamental questions such as whether to bid, how much to bid, the consequences of different technical or contractual decisions, and so on. And at the end of the project, modellers have sometimes been called upon to explain why the project turned out as it did, since counter-intuitive effects such as feedback and the compounding of individual effects are difficult to comprehend, let alone predict, intuitively, and systems modelling can help to demonstrate such effects.

However, it is becoming increasingly recognised that modelling is also important in the middle two stages. In order for a project team to carry out rational, coherent decision-making, a modeller is important to enable the consequences of decisions to be understood, the current status of the project to be comprehended, and sensible forecasting to be carried out. The difference between the second and third stages is often speed—in the start-up phase, important decisions are taken rapidly, so answers are also required rapidly. It is also in the start-up phase when relationships between the project team are developed, and this is where it is essential for the modeller to become an accepted part of the team. The modeller's personal qualities are important for his role to become established and for him to operate usefully.

This ongoing work throughout the project emphasises the advantages of having consistent models through the project life-cycle. Coming in mid-project or even post-mortem, and setting up detailed models from scratch, give the impression that modelling is a complex, expensive business. However, taking the simpler models built at the start of the feasibility stage, and populating and developing them, allows sophisticated, detailed models to be developed as the project develops, with models being appropriate to the project's stage in its life-cycle.

We haven't answered all of the possible questions in this chapter. There are issues about metrics collection that require more research so that project teams do collect metrics that usefully describe the progress of the project. And we haven't said a lot about project organisation, apart from highlighting the current vogue for Project Support Offices; and there is more useful work that could be done to establish the best way for a modeller to operate within the PSO. However, I hope that this chapter has given a taste of how the modeller operates over the course of a project and turned some of the ideas in Chapters 5–10, which can appear rather theoretical, into something that is immediately applicable and useful.

12   Conclusion

Projects are fascinating things. Each is unique, and each is special. But every project has resonances that remind us of other projects, and we can bring our experience of past projects to the next. Each project has its own particular thrill as it starts up, and as the team starts to come together. But as projects have become more complex and timescales have become tighter, some projects have started to go out of control, or have acted unexpectedly—complexity is coming into play, and even the experienced "gut-feeling" project manager needs some help to understand what is happening (or what might happen). So the modeller has found a role—perhaps as important within project management as any domain in which management science (or its alter ego, operational research) works.

Hence the reasons for writing this book, which is about how to model the behaviour of complex projects. It was written for analysts and workers in project management who find themselves needing to model how a project behaves. The modeller has a role throughout the project life-cycle—from feasibility studies before the project proper begins (when the modeller might be helping to advise and inform senior management about project strategies and risks) to project post-mortems after the project is completed (when the modeller might be helping a project team understand what happened in the project, to learn lessons for the next project, or be involved in preparing legal claims)—and all points in between.

This isn't a recipe book, telling you exactly what to do, or even a book espousing one particular point of view or technique. Much of the book has been about what complexity is, how complex behaviour is generated in projects, and why projects behave as they do—particularly why they sometimes behave disappointingly, unexpectedly or even counter-intuitively. But we have also discussed some techniques for modelling this behaviour. To keep this book a reasonable size, all of the examples we looked at were small, and lost some of their complexity as they were reduced down. But all of these techniques I, as a practising analyst, have used and found useful at the coal face in various different roles. Some of the techniques I hope you will go out and try straight away. Some you may want to find out more about, but I hope that this book has given you an idea of what's "out there". You will need to mix and match all the techniques and adapt them to your own circumstances and your own requirements. Above all, this book has been written to be useful to the practising modeller, and, through the individual modeller, to be useful to the successful management of projects. I trust that you will find it so.

Appendix: Extension of time claims

This appendix outlines some of the standard methods for preparing post-project Extension Of Time (EOT) claims, some of the problems associated with these methods, and some suggestions for using our systemic modelling methods, together with more traditional methods, to gain the advantages of each type of method. A longer version of this appendix appears in Williams (2003).

It is becoming all the more important for a contractor, when faced with delays caused by the client, to ensure he claims for a suitable Extension Of Time to his contractual finish date, otherwise he will find himself subject to Liquidated Damages (LDs) for reasons within the client's control, not within the contractor's own control. Cushman *et al.* (1996) say that (referring to US case law), "it is well established that in a construction contract, time is *not* generally of the essence unless it is expressly provided, and a contractor's failure to complete its work in accordance with the time requirements of the contract does not entitle the owner to terminate the contract or excuse nonpayment, *but* it may expose the contractor to liability for delay damages" (my emphasis).

EOT claims are often very difficult to prepare, both conceptually and practically. Scott (1993) describes a (UK) survey, and say that, "Claims for EOT appear on the majority of major civil engineering contracts, although acceleration claims occur much less frequently." Arditi and Patel (1989) say that "any time-related claim situation needs to be resolved with regard to three basic elements of time impact: causation, liability and damages." Cushman *et al.* (1996), quoted above, go on to say (still referring to US case law) that the "proof of delay has evolved dramatically in the last decade as a result of sophisticated owner requirements, evidential case law as described . . . , and advances in computer technology . . . The contractor bears the burden of proving the extent of the delays for which it seeks compensation and, in addition, the burden of proving the damages it incurred as a result of such delays." They assume that there is a fixed unambiguous entity known as "Time Impact Analysis" which can be used on each occasion an EOT claim arises—but this is over-optimistic, and there are a number of issues involved in even simple cases, and critical problems in complex projects. Alkass *et al.* (1995) identify three problem issues: the proper classification of delay types (so that the right party is credited), concurrent delays (which can have an effect on the overstatement of compensation), and real-time CPM analysis (so you use the CPM in effect at the correct time).

CPM, or the Critical Path Method, is the standard approach for considering the effects of delays on a project (Wickwire and Smith 1974), and forms the basis for discussion of EOT claims (a standard text, for example, being Rubin 1983). There has been a great deal of consideration of the issues involved in CPM analysis—let's divide this discussion into the four different questions asked:

- What is the effect of client-induced delays on a project?
- Which CPM should be used?
- What is the effect of many non-concurrent delays (excusable and non-excusable) on a project?
- What is the effect of many delays (excusable and non-excusable), some of which are concurrent, on a project?

Then we'll see when and whether the various CPM-based methods work, and which additional methods are needed, if any.

Before we start, we should mention the different categories of delay and entitlement. Various references define very similar categories, again mostly referring to US cases. Reams (1990) defines

Excusable/compensable	The client's fault, so the contractor gets extension of time and delay damages
Excusable/non-compensable	Neither the client's nor the contractor's fault, so the contractor gets an extension of time but no delay damages
Non-excusable/non-compensable	The contractor's fault, so he gets no extension of time, and indeed the client can claim damages

King and Brooks (1996) define (with US legal cases to illustrate each case):

- delays that are not excusable, when the contractor may be liable to pay damages to the owner, computed either based on actual damages suffered, or as contractually delineated liquidated damages.
- excusable delays, which are not the fault of the contractor, and may extend the time for contract performance; these can be compensable or non-compensable (note that "when each party has contributed to a delay, each party then bears its own costs of the delay").

Note also that Cushman *et al.* (1996) report that, in defining excusable delay in *J.D. Hedin Construction Co.* v. *United States,* the Court of Claims said that the contractor was not required to "have prophetic insight and take extra-ordinary preventative action which is simply not reasonable to ask of the normal contractor."

What is the effect of client-induced delays on a project?

If the contractor is claiming for an Extension Of Time on a contract due to a delay caused by the client, and there is just one delaying event at issue, how is the liability calculated—that is, how much (if any) time extension should be allowed?

McCullough (1989) gives the obvious answer to this question but points out the difficulties involved:

> The basis of most construction claims is a delay. CPM schedules are used to evaluate the delay caused by specific impacts. This process is quite simple in theory but extremely difficult in practice. In theory, a baseline schedule is developed based upon the best estimates of achievable production and sequence of activities at the time. As job conditions change, this baseline will be updated. To determine if a delay has occurred, the baseline at the time of the impact is used, and the actual impact is inserted into the schedule as a new activity or as a change to the existing one. The schedule is then recalculated, and the change to the end date of the schedule is the delay attributable to the impact being evaluated.

He then goes on to identify some of the problems with this—for example, schedules are not updated in practice, so you have to recreate the as-built schedule at the time of the impact from current diaries; quantifying the effect of the impact is not obvious, and so on. (Reams (1990) makes similar comments.) But these are practical problems—the essential technique of inserting an activity into the CPM seems, in theory, clear.

There is a generally accepted rule that delays to non-critical activities don't matter (unless the delay makes them critical). For example, Kraiem and Diekmann (1987) state that "concurrent delays on non-critical paths are not considered, because a delay that occurred on a non-critical activity does not participate in delaying the completion of the project." Yogeswaran *et al.* (1998) look at EOT claims under excusable delays, analysing 67 civil engineering projects in Hong Kong; looking at non-critical activities, they say that "an excusable delay to a non-critical activity does not give rise to an extension of time to the date for completion unless the delayed period exceeds the float available to the non-critical activity." Similarly, Cushman *et al.* (1996) say that "For purposes of determining whether the project has been delayed and for purposes of apportioning delays, only delays on the critical path of the project figure in the analysis because, by definition, delays not on the critical path will not delay the completion of the project [referring to *G.M. Shupe Inc.* v. *United States*]". However, we will go on to discuss below that this is a simplistic and over-discrete understanding of CPM. Indeed, it is worth noting here that Cushman *et al.* go on to say "there are many possible critical path schedules for any particular project, depending on variables such as projected or actual material, labor and equipment resources, and depending on the sequence of construction preferred by the superintendent in charge. In addition, the as-planned schedule almost always differs from the as-built schedule, because as the project moves forward contingencies arise that delay some activities and accelerate others so that the critical path changes."

Which CPM should be used?

This last quote takes us to a question which constantly recurs in such cases: which version of the CPM network should be used? A CPM can be drawn up representing the original plan for the project (we would hope that a network formed part of the original planning!). Similarly, a CPM could be drawn up representing how the project actually turned out; and in a well-managed project there will be CPMs representing various intermediate stages. So if a conventional EOT method analyses the effect of a delay on "the" CPM—which CPM does this refer to?

Reams (1990) says that classical methods (e.g. Rubin 1983) use the as-planned schedule. He discusses all the work involved in preparing an as-planned schedule for court, either when an as-planned schedule already exists (drawing on the then standard book, Hohns *et al.* (1981)—which says that the schedule must be complete, and error-free, and also points to cases where the use of the schedule for a claim was rejected because it did not reflect the sequence of work as actually intended and performed) or where it must be developed as a good guess of what should have happened. But then he points out that the schedule will have changed before the delay (due to errors, contractor's changes, changes in "client's scope, etc. etc.), so it isn't correct as it stands but must be modified—"a contractor may be held to have not acted prudently if it fails to reflect this new knowledge in subsequent project plans."

Scott (1993) says that, in the USA, the general approach is as described in Wickwire and Smith (1974), using an as-built schedule and then removing all of the delays due to the owner, whereas under the UK Institution of Civil Engineers Conditions of Contract (Institution of Civil Engineers 1995), the supervising engineer uses his best judgement to decide EOT claims ("the established procedure in the USA [of using as-built CPM schedules for claims] is almost unheard of in the UK"). He uses some extremely simplistic examples (based on two-activity networks), but even for these there wasn't agreement between practitioners on where liability lay or what should be claimed—so clearly the issues are non-trivial. (There was also no agreement about critical path issues, so clearly the difficulties here are recognised.)

In fact, to explain the complete course of events in a project, a number of CPMs are required. Arditi and Patel (1989) use five:

- the as-planned schedule;
- the as-built schedule;
- the owner-accountable schedule, which is essentially the as-planned schedule plus delays that can be attributed to the client;
- adjusted schedules—a series of schedules to explain how the as-planned turned into the as-built—so, first as-planned, then as-planned plus the first delay, used to quantify the effect of the second delay, then as-planned plus the first two delays and so on;
- as-projected schedule—used mid-project, which is as-built up to now and as-projected for the remainder of the project.

What is the effect of many non-concurrent delays (excusable and non-excusable) on a project?

Where there are many delays to a project, some of which can be blamed on the client and some on the contractor, it is necessary to identify the effect of what can be blamed on the client. To simplify things initially, let us assume that all of the delays considered in this section are *non-concurrent*.

Bordoli and Baldwin (1998) summarise methods to look into this situation, starting at the level of bar charts and scatter diagrams which, although simple, can still have a high visual impact. They look at the "as-built" network, showing the story of what happened; then at the "as-built subtracting impacts" network, which subtracts the impacts to give a "non-disrupted" programme; then the "baseline adding impacts" adds the impacts to a baseline; and finally a "window analysis" is carried out, referring to Galloway and Nielsen (1990)—since the as-planned network is updated throughout the project (and thus the critical path), the delay-impact assessment is only carried out within each window between major updates. However, since they felt there were clear flaws with these steps, they developed a multi-step methodology for assessing the events in all their implications. Based on the as-planned network, for each event the methodology:

- identifies progress at event date and updates the network using the progress data;
- simulates the event in the updated network; and
- considers mitigating actions (which we will discuss further below);

then the final analysis shows the extension of time increasing event-by-event, and these extensions can be summed for excusable and non-excusable events.

This is clearly a good method, which seems to get around a lot of problems. However, it does not cope with concurrent delays, and also (and crucially, as we shall see later), mitigation actions are not as simple as those modelled by Bordoli and Baldwin, and indeed can often have non-intuitive effects. Let us look at the first problem, then move on to the second.

What is the effect of many delays (excusable and non-excusable), some of which are concurrent on a project?

When both client and contractor delay the project concurrently, the legal position, at least in the USA, is essentially that the client is not eligible for extension of time or damages. Cushman *et al* (1996), for example, say that, "If the contractor would have been delayed in any event by causes within its control, that is, if there was a concurrent nonexcusable delay, the general rule is that it would be inequitable to grant the contractor either an extension of time or additional compensation [with rule stated in *Klingen-*

smith Inc. v. *United States*]. On the other hand, when the owner and contractor concurrently delay the work, and responsibility for the delay cannot be apportioned, the contractor is generally not liable for liquidated damages."

Kraiem and Diekmann (1988) give the equation:

New contract duration = as-planned duration + excusable delays + compensable delays + concurrent delays

So how are the delays combined? A well-known paper here is by Alkass *et al.* (1996), who define the combination of delays (quoting Rubin 1983) thus:

- if excusable and non-excusable delays occur concurrently only an EOT is granted;
- if excusable compensable and excusable non-compensable delays occur concurrently only an EOT is granted, but no damages;
- if two excusable compensable delays occur concurrently, an EOT and damages are granted.

They then describe the use of four types of schedule:

- as-planned;
- adjusted (as-planned adjusted for change orders, construction changes, delays, acceleration);
- as-built;
- entitlement schedules show the original construction completion dates, how these dates have been impacted by excusable delays, and the projected completion dates given the remaining work. Final entitlement schedules reflect the original, adjusted and actual completion dates used to establish the total time that the contractor or the owner is entitled for compensation.

And they describe six methods—all tested on a common simple test case (consisting of 10 activities, adapted from Kraiem and Diekmann (1987)):

1. The global impact technique—adds together all delays; this clearly overestimates the total delay.
2. The net impact technique—shows all the delays on a bar chart, then calculates the net delay (i.e. taking into account concurrency); this doesn't take into account delay types.

3. The adjusted as-built CPM technique—this takes the as-planned and puts into it the delays as activities to end up with the as-built. Alkass *et al.* discuss problems again by not taking into account delay types (and a discussion of the problem of claimants tying their delays to non-critical parts of the network).
4. The "but for" or collapsing technique—this takes the as-planned CPM and adds the delays that one party is willing to accept, to give an acceptable total delay. However, this doesn't take into account changes in CPM during the course of the project—so a delay might be on the as-planned critical path, but not on the as-built critical path.
5. The snapshot technique—this looks at the period between two "snapshots"—from a snapshot time, it takes actuality (durations and relationships) up to a second snapshot time and applies that to the as-planned, then compares the two end-dates; but this doesn't consider delays prior to the first snapshot.
6. The time impact technique—similar to the snapshot technique, this looks at just one delay or delaying event.

The authors concludes that (1)–(3) are very simplistic; (4) is better but is only done once; and (5) and (6) are good but don't classify delays by fault, implying that more analysis is needed. They then go on to describe a new, seventh, method

7. The "isolated delay" type—the authors say that this tries to combine the approach of (5) and (6) with the scrutinising approach of (4). The method looks at time periods, then applies only relevant portions of delays—so looking at project completion dates before or after shows change, and the discrepancy is attributed to the delays that were incorporated.

Problems with current CPM methods

The material covered in Chapters 5–9 of this book have thrown up a number of problems with current CPM methods when dealing with certain projects, particularly complex projects. There are three critical issues, and two additional problems.

1. The first, and perhaps most obvious, issue is that many delays or disruptive effects impact many activities simultaneously, as discussed in Chapter 5.

2. Where there are a significant number of delays, rather than simply assessing the effect of a single event, methods like those of Bordoli and Baldwin (1998) become impractical. But more than this, the delays will usually lead to effects which would not be obvious from simply looking at the network. In particular, they lead to the "softer" effects and then the feedback effects discussed in Chapter 6–9.

3. Most of the methods outlined above essentially assume an inactive management. That is, the effects of events are modelled but it is assumed that the network stays the same and management take no actions in response, which is clearly wrong, as discussed in Chapter 9 (see also Jorgensen and Wallace 2000). Some authors in these areas do allow some management reaction. For example, King and Brooks (1996) define excusable delays, as above, and say that they can lead to constructive acceleration (when a contractor is forced to increase the pace of work to meet a project schedule that has not been extended because of excusable delays); they also list typical cost categories (e.g. job site support, escalation labour, unabsorbed home office delay). Arditi and Patel (1989) assume simple acceleration rules, such as Unit Acceleration Cost and so on. And these ideas can go straightforwardly into Bordoli types of simulation.

   But even individual actions are not this simple—and of course combinations of actions have consequences that these methods cannot model, as discussed at length in Chapters 8 and 9. This last point leads on to a difficult issue when claiming. If management have taken some action in response to the claim, was the action optimum—or even reasonable? Indeed, if management action in accelerating projects is often counter-productive (Cooper 1994, Howick and Eden 2001), should management take action at all?

There are two additional problems.

1. Most of the authors above distinguish between delays to activities on the critical path (which are deemed to be important) and delays to other activities (which are deemed to be unimportant). However, as we've seen in Chapter 5, with resource-constrained networks, the idea of "criticality" is undefined. And, practically, even where specific resource types are not defined, often there will be implicit resource constraints (e.g. a senior engineer can only look after so many tasks at one time). This means that standard analyses can become meaningless as soon as there are significant resource constraints.

2. The effect of delays is not a simple function of their duration. We should remember that sometimes an apparently small and unimportant delay can lead to significant costs. For example, a three-month delay in a North Sea project which causes a weather-window to be missed could lead to a one-year delay to the overall project, as the project has to wait, idle, for the following summer. In the case of *Murphey* v. *US Fidelity*, reported by Arditi and Patel (1989), a contractor sued a supplier for losses due to a delay in delivery; here, despite efforts to expedite, the work ran into the winter and hence costs overran. The court found in favour of the contractor.

Using SD for EOT claims

These problems and issues have given rise to the use of causal-mapping (to answer the question "why?") combined with System Dynamics (SD) (to answer the question "how much?") to answer questions such as the effect of a delay, or a set of delays, upon a project, as described in Chapters 8 and 9. Such a process can (Williams *et al.* 2002):

- show causality: the systemic inter-relationships which caused the various ramifications of the delays to build up;
- show responsibility: show the party causing the initial causes of the delays (as opposed to the immediate causes, which might simply be reactions to previous effects);
- calculate the quantum of the effects: in other words, show the size of cost- and time-overrun resulting from a particular delay or set of delays.

One of the key aims of developments in this area is to provide *transparency* in the claims process. For some examples, we could look at Zack (1993)'s paper on "claimsmanship". He lists 11 "claims games" commonly played by contractors on public projects (note that some of these are not relevant to private projects), some of which could be validated (or not) or quantified by the types of mapping/SD techniques described in the previous paragraph. These include:

- loss of productivity claims: Zack questions the basis of numbers conventionally used to calculate productivity losses claimed—but this of course forms an important part of SD models, which seek to explicate the chains of causality and explicitly quantify the different elements of productivity losses, and an SD model could be a useful tool in explaining and supporting a loss of productivity claim.

- cardinal changes: this is an American concept, in which a change to a public contract which substantially changes the nature of the agreement is called a "cardinal change" and should have a separate procurement activity; but contractors can say the accumulation of many small changes eventually led to a cardinal change, effectively giving a cost-plus situation; again, in Eden *et al.* (2000) the cumulative effect of many small change orders is singled out as one of the modelling effects for which SD models are particularly appropriate.

- project float claims: Rubin (1983) include the (American) principle that float belongs to the contractor—so you can claim a compensable delay even when the project isn't delayed. Zack disgrees with this. SD models allow a transparent analysis of the effect of using up float (which of course is not a zero effect, as assumed in simple network models).

Other "games" include reservation of rights (when agreeing change orders), delayed early completion claims, accelerated delay claims (merging delay and acceleration claims) and "Hail Mary" change orders (throwing everything into one change order at the end of the contract). (By the way, Zack also lists 11 "claims games" starting to be played by public owners, some of them simply opposites of the contractors' "games".)

However, SD is not a panacea for all problems. SD models will not normally be at the operational level of a network, and will in practice need to consolidate activities into a smaller number of units. In Chapter 10, we also identified issues around SD's assumptions of continuity and homogeneity. However, it has been found to be a very powerful technique for capturing the counter-intuitive temporal effects that are seen in projects—and in particular which form an essential part of most EOT claims—where small causes compound to give significant delays, or where management actions have reduced or even had the opposite effect to that expected.

Combined procedure and conclusion

So, given that conventional network-based techniques have some disadvantages, but SD also has some disadvantages, as well as lacking the courtroom credibility of network-based techniques, what should we do?

The first step is to find out what was the out-turn in the project. To do this, Gantt charts or some sort of time-profile showing key dates (planned and actual) and the dates of key disruptive events is vital to illustrate the overall project time-performance. This doesn't explain why the out-turn was as it was, or whose fault it was, but it does give an overview of what happened—and, surprisingly, management within projects managed in a distributed way with no project manager (e.g. under a coordination-matrix management approach) can have only a hazy view of how late key interim dates were.

Then, if there are a limited number of delays or disruptive events (and, if change orders are an issue, the number of change orders is not sufficient to constitute a "cardinal change"), then the standard network-based methods are applicable and can be used.

Otherwise, if there are many effects on the project, or the project was so complex that the out-turn cannot be intuitively expected from the effects known to have triggered the behaviour, it is necessary to seek to understand why the out-turn occurred and to trace the causality from the triggering effects. For this, causal maps (to understand the causality) and System Dynamics (to quantify these effects) are necessary, as described in the section entitled Problems with current CPM methods, above. (Networks can give an answer to "what would have happened . . ." (had these effects not compounded together; had there not been systemicity within the effects; in particular, had management not acted in response to the triggering events and, for example, accelerated the project). But even an analysis that says, "this project would have been one year late due to the actions of the client—but in fact was only three months late because the contractor accelerated", while being useful (it can be a defence against a claim for Liquidated Damages if the contractor is completely blameless and caused no parallel delays), in general does not help to credibly explain delays and replicate what actually happened in the project.)

In practice, a combination of methods for different parts of the project has often been found to be most appropriate, as the effects on different phases of the project may be different. For example, it may be that design and manufacturing were heavily accelerated in the face of a high level of disruption (which would imply a very high level of overspend); in this case, a causal map/SD analysis would be needed to explicate the factors and effects and replicate the out-turn, showing why this limited overrun (and high overspend) occurred; but it may be that the commissioning phase was delayed as discrete events affected discrete activities (albeit the causes of those events might have arisen from complex interactions of triggers which can be shown by the causal map analysis), which can be modelled using networks.

Work underway, as described in Chapter 10, is looking at closer combination of these methods—bringing the benefits of systemic model-ling to the operational models provided by networks—but this is still under development. For now, we must use our judgement to apply the appropriate method to the appropriate project phase to provide effective understanding of the effect of delays and their claimability; other further work will formalise and systemise such judgements.

References

Abdel-Hamid T and Madnick SE (1991) *Software Project Dynamics: An Integrated Approach.* Prentice-Hall: Englewood Cliffs, NJ.

Ackermann F, Eden C and Williams TM (1997) A persuasive approach to Delay and Disruption—using "mixed methods". *Interfaces* **27**: 48–65.

Ackoff RL (1974) Redesigning the Future: a Systems Approach to Societal Planning. John Wiley: New York.

Ackoff RL (1979) The future of operational research is past. *Journal of the Operational Research Society* **30**: 93–104.

Alkass S, Mazerolle M and Harris F (1996) Construction delay analysis techniques. *Construction Management and Economics* **14**: 375–394.

Alkass S, Mazerolle M, Tribaldos E and Harris F (1995) Computer-aided construction delay analysis and claims preparation. *Construction Management and Economics* **13**: 335–352.

Amateur Athletic Federation of Los Angeles (1985) Official Report of the 1984 Los Angeles Olympic Games www.aafla.org

Andersen ES, Grude KV and Haug T (1987) *Goal Directed Project Management.* Kogan Page: London.

Ansell J and Wharton F (1992) (eds) *Risk: Analysis, Assessment and Management.* John Wiley: Chichester.

Arbogast GW and Womer NK (1988) An error components model of cost overruns and schedule slip on army R&D programs. *Naval Research Logistics* **35**: 367–382.

Arditi D and Patel BK (1989) Impact analysis of owner-directed acceleration. *Journal of Construction Engineering and Management* **115**: 144–157.

Ashby R (1956) *An Introduction to Cybernetics.* Chapman and Hall: London.

Ashley DB (1987) Knowledge-based approaches to construction project planning. In Proc. 11th International Expert Seminar, *New Trends in Project Management*, April 1987, International Project Management Association Zurich, p. 163–188.

Avots, I (1984) Information systems for matrix organisations. In *Matrix Management Systems Handbook*, DI Cleland (Ed), Van Nostrand Reinhold: New York.

Baber RL (1982) *Software Reflected.* North Holland: New York.

Baccarini D (1996) The concept of project complexity—a review. *International Journal of Project Management* **14**: 201–204.

Baker, BN, Fisher, D and Murphy DC (1988) Project management in the public sector: success and failure patterns compared to private sector projects. In DI Cleland & WR King (Eds) *Project Management Handbook*, 2nd edition. Van Nostrand Reinhold: New York, pp. 920–934.

Banxia (1999) Decision Explorer software is supplied by Banxia Software, 141 St James Road, Glasgow G4 0LT. It runs in the Windows environment.

Barlas Y (1996) Formal aspects of model validity and validation in System Dynamics. *System Dynamics Review* **12**(3): 183–210.

Barnes M (1988) Construction project management. *Project Management* **6**: 69–79.

Barnes NML and Wearne SH (1993) The future for major project management. *International Journal of Project Management* **11**(3): 135–242.

Bernstein PL (1996) *Against the Gods*. John Wiley: New York.

Berny J (1989) A new distribution function for risk analysis. *Journal of the Operational Research Society* **40**: 1121–1127.

Blanchard BS (1998) *Logistics engineering and management*, 5th edition. Prentice-Hall: Englewood Cliffs, NJ.

Boehm BW (1981a) An experiment in small-scale application software engineering. *IEEE Transactions in Software Engineering* **SE-7**(5): 482–493.

Boehm BW (1981b) *Software Engineering Economics*. Prentice-Hall: Englewood Cliffs, NJ.

Boehm BW and Papaccio PN (1988) Understanding and controlling software costs. *IEEE Transactions in Software Engineering* **14**: 1462–1477.

Bordoli DW and Baldwin AN (1998) A methodology for assessing construction project delays. *Construction Management and Economics* **16**: 327–337.

Bowers JA (1994) Data for project risk analyses. *International Journal of Project Management* **12**(1): 9–16.

Bowers JA (1996) Identifying critical activities in stochastic resource constrained networks. *Omega* **24**: 37–46.

Bowers JA (2000) Multiple schedules and measures of resource constrained float. *Journal of the Operational Research Society* **51**(7): 855–862.

Brooks FP Jr. (1978) *The Mythical Man-month*. Addison-Wesley: Reading, MA.

Bryson, L (Admiral) (1982) Large-scale project management. Proceedings of the IEE. Part A 129, 625–633.

Bryson, L (Admiral) (1986) "All at sea" Inaugural address as President IEE Proceedings A 133, 1–15.

Buchanan DA and Boddy D (1992) *The Expertise of the Change Agent: Public Performance and Backstage Activity*. Prentice-Hall: London.

Bureau of Labor Statistics (USA) (1947) US Department of Labor, Bulletin No. 917: Hours of Work and Output.

Burke CM and Ward SC (1988) Project appraisal—finance approaches to risk. In *Developments in Operational Research* (eds NB Cook and AM Johnson) Birmingham: Operational Research Society pp. 45–70.

Bushuyev SD and Sochnev SV (1994) Synergetic intelligence methods for risk management by projects. *Proceedings of the INTERNET 12th World Congress on*

Project Management, Oslo, June, 230–241.

Canaday HT (1980) Construction costs overruns in electric utilities: some trends and implications. Occasional Paper No. 3, National Regulatory Research Institute, Ohio State University, Ohio, November.

Canal C (1996) CMT (Critical Management of Projects)—an innovative system for project risk management. IPMA '96 World Congress on Project Management, Paris, June, Vol. 2.

Chan DWM and Kumaraswamy MM (1997) A comparative study of causes of time overruns in Hong Kong construction projects. *International Journal of Project Management* **15**: 55–64.

Chapman CB (1995) On the minimum cost project schedule—some comments. OMEGA **23**(4): 467–468.

Chapman CB and Ward SC (1994) The efficient allocation of risk in contracts. *Omega* **22**: 537–552.

Chapman CB and Ward SC (1997) *Project Risk Management: Processes, Techniques and Insights.* John Wiley: Chichester.

Charette R (1989) *Software Engineering: Risk Analysis and Management.* McGraw-Hill: New York.

Chatfield C (1970) *Statistics for Technology.* Penguin: Maryland.

Checkland PB (1981) *Systems Thinking, Systems Practice.* John Wiley: Chichester.

Chief Scientific Advisor (undated) CSA Guidelines for Technical Scrutiny, Ministry of Defence.

Churchman CW and Wagner HM (1972) (compilers) Discussion of the ORSA Guidelines. *Management Science* **18**: B608–B629.

Churchman CW, Ackoff RL and Arnoff EL (1957) *Introduction to Operations Research.* John Wiley: New York.

Clark P and Chapman CB (1987) The development of computer software for risk analysis: a decision support system development study. *European Journal of Operational Research* **29**: 252–261.

Clarke L (1994) *The Essence of Change.* Prentice-Hall: Hemel Hempstead, UK.

Cleland DI (1984) *Matrix Management Systems Handbook.* Van Nostrand Reinhold: New York.

Cleland DI and King WR (1988a) *Project Management Handbook*, 2nd edition. Van Nostrand Reinhold: New York.

Cleland DI and King WR (1988b) Project owner strategic management of projects. In *Project Management Handbook*, 2nd edition (eds DI Cleland and WR King) Van Nostrand Reinhold: New York, pp. 165–188.

Cleland DI, Bursic KM, Puerzer R and Vlasak AY (1998) *Project Management Casebook.* Project Management Institute, Upper Darby, PA.

Coats PK and Chesser DC (1982) Coping with business risk through probabilistic financial statements. *Simulation* **44**: 111–121.

Collins English Dictionary (1986) Second edition, William Collins: London.

Cooke-Davis T (1996) Learning in a project-based organisation. *IPMA '96 World Congress on Project Management*, Paris, June, pp. 421–430.

Cooke-Davies T (2002) The "real" success factors on projects. *International Journal of Project Management* **20**(3): 185–190.

Cooper DF and Chapman CB (1985) Risk analysis of a construction cost estimate. *Project Management* **3**:141–149.

Cooper DF and Chapman CB (1987) Risk analysis for large projects—models, methods and cases. John Wiley: Chichester.

Cooper KG (1993) The rework cycle: benchmarks for the project manager. *Project Management Journal* **24**: 1.

Cooper KG (1994) The $2000 hour: how managers influence project performance through the rework cycle. *Project Management Journal* **25**: 11–24.

Cooper KG (1997) System Dynamics methods in complex project management. In *Managing and Modelling Complex Projects* (ed. TM Williams), NATO ASI Series, Kluwer Academic Publishers: Dordrecht, the Netherlands.

Cooper KG and Mullen T (1993) Swords and plowshares: the rework cycles of defence and commercial software development projects. *American Programmer* **6**(5): 41–51.

Cooper KG, Lyneis JM and Bryant BJ (2002) Learning to learn, from past to future. *International Journal of Project Management* **20**(3): 213–220.

Coyle RG (1985) Representing discrete events in System Dynamics models: a theoretical application to modelling coal production. *Journal of the Operational Research Society* **36**(4): 307–318.

Cushman KM, Hoolyday JD, Coppi DF and Fertitta TD (1996) Delay claims. In Proving and Pricing Construction Claims (eds RF Cushman, CM Jacobsen and PJ Trimble) Aspen Law and Business: Frederick, MD.

Dalcher D (1993) The new project management mindset for the 21st century. *Proc. 1st British Project Management Colloquium*, Henley-on-Thames, UK, December.

Davidson FP and Huot J-C (1991) Large-scale projects: management trends for major projects. *Cost Engineering* **33**(2): 15–23.

Dawson CW and Dawson RJ (1994) Clarification of node representation in generalized activity networks for practical project management. *International Journal of Project Management* **12**(2): 81–88.

Dawson CW and Dawson RJ (1995) Generalised activity-on-the-node networks for managing uncertainty in projects. *International Journal of Project Management* **13**(6): 353–362.

De Marco T (1982) *Controlling Software Projects*. Yourdon Press: New York.

De Wit A (1986) Measuring project sucess: an illusion. In *Measuring Success: Proceedings of the 18th Annual Seminar/Symposium of the Project Management Institute*. Montreal, Canada, September, pp. 13–21.

Department of Energy, Peat Marwick Mitchell and Atkins Planning. (1975) North Sea Costs Escalation Study. HMSO: London.

Diehl E and Sterman JD (1995) Effects of feedback complexity on dynamic decision making. *Organizational Behaviour and Human Decision Processes* **2**: 198–215.

Dillon RL and Pate-Cornell ME (2001) APRAM: an advanced programmatic risk analysis method. *International Journal of Technology, Policy and Management* **1**(1): 47–65.

Dinsmore PC (ed.) (1993) *The AMA Handbook of Project Management*. AMACOM: New York.

Dodin BM and Elmaghraby SE (1985) Approximating the criticality indices of the activities in PERT networks. *Management Science* **31**: 207–223.

Eden C (1982) Problem construction and the influence of O.R. *Interfaces* **12**: 50–60.

Eden C (1987) Problem-solving or problem-finishing? In *New Directions in Management Science* (eds MC Jackson and P Keys) Gower: Aldershot.

Eden C (1988) Cognitive mapping: a review. *European Journal of Operational Research* **36**: 1–13.

Eden C and Sims D (1979) On the nature of problems in consulting practice. *Omega* **7**: 119–127.

Eden C and Huxham C (1996) Action research for the study of organizations. In *Handbook of Organization Studies* (eds S Clegg, C Hardy and W Nord) Sage: Beverly Hills, CA.

Eden C and Ackermann F (1999) *The Journey of Strategic Change*. Sage: Chichester.

Eden C, Ackermann F and Cropper S (1992) The analysis of cause maps. *Journal of Management Studies* **29**: 309–324.

Eden C, Williams TM and Ackermann F (1997) Dismantling the learning curve: the role of disruptions in the planning of development projects. *International Journal of Project Management* **16**: 131–138.

Eden CE, Williams TM, Ackermann FA and Howick S (2000) On the nature of disruption and delay (D & D) in major projects. *Journal of the Operational Research Society* **51**(3): 291–300.

Elmaghraby SE (1990) Project bidding under deterministic and probabibilistic activity durations. *European Journal of Operational Research* **49**:14–34.

Elmaghraby SE (1995) Activity nets: a guided tour through some recent developments. *European Journal of Operational Research* **82**: 383–408.

Fangel M (1987) (ed.) *Handbook of Project Start-up: How to Launch Projects Effectively*. INTERNET (now International Project Management Association): Zurich, Switzerland.

Farld F and Karshenas S (1986) C/SCS criteria for measuring progress under inflation. In *Measuring Success: Proceedings of the 18th Annual Seminar/Symposium of the Project Management Institute*. Montreal, Canada, September, pp. 139–144.

Farnum NR and Stanton LW (1987) Some results concerning the estimation of beta distribution parameters in PERT. *Journal of the Operational Research Society* **38**: 287–290.

Fayol H (1949) *General and Industrial Management*. Pitman: London.

Fishburn PC (1984) Foundations of risk measurement. I: Risk as probable loss. *Management Science* **30**: 396–406.

Ford DN and Sterman JD (1998) Dynamics modelling of product development processes. *System Dynamics Review* **14**(1): 31–68.

Forrester JW (1961) *Industrial Dynamics*. MIT Press: Cambridge, MA.

Forrester J and Senge P (1980) Tests for building confidence in System Dynamics models. *TIMS Studies in the Management Sciences* **14**: 209–228.

Franke A (1987) Risk analysis in project management. *International Journal of Project Management* **5**(1): 29–34.

Fraser DC (1984) *An Approach to Major Projects*. Major Projects Association: Templeton College, Oxford.

Gallagher C (1987) A note on PERT assumptions. *Management Science* **33**: 1360.

Galloway PD and Nielsen KR (1990) Concurrent schedule delay in international contracts. *International Construction Law Review*, 7 October.

Gass SI (1987) Managing the modelling process: a personal reflection. *European Journal of Operational Research* **31**: 1–8.

Gass SI (1990) Model world: danger, beware the user as modeler. *Interfaces* **20**: 60–64.

Golenko-Ginzburg D (1988a) On the distribution of activity time in PERT. *Journal of the Operational Research Society* **39**: 767–771.

Golenko-Ginzburg D (1988b) Controlled alternative activity networks for project management. *European Journal of Operational Research* **37**: 336–346.

Golenko-Ginzburg D (1989) PERT assumptions revisited. Omega **17**: 393–396.

Golenko-Ginzburg D and Gonik A (1996) Online control model for cost-simulation network models. *Journal of the Operational Research Society* **47**: 266–283.

Grady RB and Caswell DL (1987) *Software Metrics: Establishing a Company-wide Program*. Prentice-Hall: Englewood Cliffs, NJ.

Graham AK, Morecroft JDW, Senge PM and Sterman JD (1992) Model-supported case studies for management education. *European Journal of Operational Research* **59**: 151–166.

Gray C, Dworatschek S, Gobeli D, Knoepfel H and Larson EW (1990) International comparison of project organization structures: use and effectiveness. *International Journal of Project Management* **8**: 26–32.

Gutierrez GJ and Kouvelis P (1991) Parkinson's law and its implications for project management. *Management Science* **37**: 990–1001 and *Erratum in Management Science* **37**: 1507.

Haimes YY (1993) Risk of extreme events and the fallacy of the expected value. *Control and Cybernetics* **22**: 7–31.

Hall JN (1986) Use of risk analysis in North Sea projects. *International Journal of Project Management* **4**(4): 217–222.

Hartman F (1999) The role of trust in project management. In *Managing Business by Projects* (eds KA Artto, K Kahkonen and K Koskinen) Project Management Association Finland: Helsinki, pp. 417–438.

Hazelrigg GA and Husband FL (1985) RADSIM—a methodology for large-scale R&D program assessment. *IEEE Transactions of Engineering Management* **32**: 106–115.

Helbrough B (1995) Computer assisted collaboration—the fourth dimension of project management? *International Journal of Project Management* **13**: 329–333.

Hertz DB and Thomas H (1983) Decisions and risk analysis in new products and facilities planning problems. *Sloan Management Review* **Winter**: 17–31.

Hetland PW and Fevang HJ (1997) Exploring the value of project complexity—

beyond lump sum contracting. In *Managing Risks in Projects* (eds K Kahkonen and KA Artto) E & FN Spon: London, pp. 149–158.

High Performance Systems Inc. (1996) Stella is a registered trademark of High Performance Systems Inc., Hanover, NH, USA.

Hillson DA (1997) Towards a risk maturity model. *International Journal of Project and Business Risk Management* **1**(1): 35–46.

Hiltz (1999) *Project Management Handbook of Checklists*. Markcheck Publishing: Ottawa, Canada.

Hirzel M (1986) Holistic decision-making organizations in project management. *International Journal of Project Management* **4**: 14–16.

HMSO (1993) Report of the Investigation of the London Ambulance Service. HMSO: London.

Ho SSM and Pike RH (1992) The use of risk analysis techniques in capital investment appraisal. In *Risk: Analysis Assessment and Management* (eds J Ansell and F Wharton), John Wiley: Chichester, pp. 71–94.

Hohns HM *et al.* (1981) *The Law behind Construction Schedules: Deskbook of Construction Contract Law*. Prentice-Hall: Englewood Cliffs, NJ.

House of Commons (1988) The procurement of major defence equipment. House of Commons Defence Committee, 5th Report of Session 1987–8. HMSO: London.

Howick S and Eden C (2001) The impact of disruption and delay when compressing large projects: going for incentives? *Journal of the Operational Research Society* **52**(1): 26–34.

Humphries DE (1989a) Project risk analysis in the aerospace industry. In *Proc. Royal Aeronautical Society Conference: Project Risk Analysis in the Aerospace Industry*, Royal Aeronautical Society: London, 8 March.

Humphries DE (1989b) Risk Management in MOD. *Proc. Conf. Project Risk Analysis in the Aerospace Industry*, Royal Aeronautical Society: London, 8 March.

Institution of Civil Engineers (1995) The engineering and construction contract. Part of the New Engineering Contract System series, Thomas Telford Services Ltd: London, UK.

In't Veld J and Peeters J (1989) Keeping large projects under control: the importance of contract type selection. *Project management* **7**(3): 155–162.

Ireland LR and Shirley VD (1986) Measuring risk in the project environment. In *Measuring Success*: Proceedings of the 18th Annual Seminar/Symposium of the Project Management Institute, Montreal, Canada, September, pp. 150–156.

Jobling PE (1994) Probablistic or "possiblistic": is numerical risk analysis a benefit? *Proceedings of the INTERNET 12th World Congress on Project Management*, Oslo, June, Vol. 2, 79–85.

Jones RE and Deckro RF (1993) The social psychology of project management conflict. *European Journal of Operational Research* **64**: 216–228.

Jordan G, Lee I and Cawsey G (1988) Learning from experience: a report on the arrangements for managing major projects in the Procurement Executive. Report to the Ministry of State for Defence Procurement, Ministry of Defence: London.

Jorgensen T and Wallace SW (2000) Improving project cost estimation by taking into account managerial flexibility. *European Journal of Operational Research* **127**: 239–251.

Kahneman D, Slovic P and Tversky A (1986) *Judgement under Uncertainty: Heuristics and Biases.* Cambridge University Press: Cambridge, UK.

Kamburowski J (1995) On the minimum cost project schedule. Omega **23**(4): 463–465.

Kaming PF, Holt GD, Kometa ST and Olomolaiye PO (1998) Severity diagnosis of productivity problems—a reliability analysis. *International Journal of Project Management* **16**: 107–113.

Keefer DL and Verdini WA (1993) Better estimation of PERT activity time parameters. *Management Science* **39**: 1086–1091.

Keeney RL and Winterfeldt DV (1989) On the uses of expert judgement on complex technical problems. *IEEE Transactions of Engineering Management* **36**(2): 83–86.

Kerzner H (2000) *Applied Project Management. Best Practices On Implementation.* John Wiley: New York.

Kharbanda OP and Pinto JK (1996) *What made Gertie Gallop? Learning from Project Failures.* Van Nostrand Reinhold: New York.

Kidd JB (1990) Project management software—are we being over-persuaded? *International Journal of Project Management* **8**: 109–115.

King RA and Brooks PL (1996) Types of claim. In *Proving And Pricing Construction Claims* (eds RF Cushman, CM Jacobsen and PJ Trimble) Aspen Law and Business: Frederick, MD.

Klein J (1993) Modelling risk trade-off. *Journal of the Operational Research Society* **44**: 445–460.

Knoepfel H (1990) Cost and quality control in the project cycle. *International Journal of Project Management* **7**: 229–235.

Kohrs RH and Welngarten GC (1986) Measuring successful technical performance—a cost/schedule/technical control system. In *Measuring Success: Proceedings of the 18th Annual Seminar/Symposium of the Project Management Institute.* Montreal, Canada, September, pp. 158–164.

Kraiem ZM and Diekmann JE (1987) Concurrent delays in construction projects. *Journal of Construction Engineering and Management* **113**: 4.

Kraiem ZM and Diekmann JE (1988) Discussion of Kraiem and Diekmann (1987) *Journal of Construction Engineering and Management* **114**: 337–338.

Larson, EW and Gobeli DH (1989) Significance of project management structure on development success. *IEEE Transactions of Engineering Management* **36**: 119–125.

Laufer A, Denker GR and Shenhar AJ (1996) Simultaneous management: the key to excellence in capital projects. *International Journal of Project Management* **14**: 189–199.

Lichtenberg S and Moller LB (1979) Three types of biases in scheduling—and solutions applicable in practice. *Proc. of Internet World Congress*, VDI-Verlag, Dusseldorf, Vol. 1, pp. 247–262.

Littlefield TK and Randolph PH (1987) Reply: an answer to Sasieni's question on PERT times. *Management Science* **33**: 1357–1359.

Lock D (1994) (ed.) *Gower Handbook of Project Management*, 2nd edition Gower Publishing: Aldershot, UK.

Lockyer D and Gordon J (1991) *Critical Path Analysis*. Pitman: London.

Machol RE (1982) The ORSA guideline report—a retrospective. *Interfaces* **12**: 20–28.

MacMaster G (2000) Can we learn from project histories? *PM Network* **14** (July): 66–67.

Major Projects Association (1992) *Beyond 2000: A Source Book for Major Projects*. Major Projects Association: Templeton College, Oxford, UK.

Malcolm DG, Rosenbloom JH, Clark CE and Fazar W (1959) Application of a technique for research and development program evaluation. *Operational Research* **12**: 646–669.

Marshall AW and Meckling WH (1959) Predictability of the costs, time and success of development. Rand Corporation Report P–1821.

McComb D and Smith JY (1991) System project failure: the heuristics of risk. *Journal of Information Systems Management* **Winter**: 25–34.

McCullough RB (1989) CPM schedules in construction claims. *Cost Engineering* **31**(5): 18–21.

Merkhover MW (1987) Quantifying judgemental uncertainty: methodology, experiences and insights. *IEEE Transactions in Systems, Management and Cybernetics* **17**: 741–752.

Merrow EW (1988) Understanding the outcomes of megaprojects. Report: RAND/R-3560-PSSP Rand, Santa Monica, CA.

Ministry of Defence DPP(PM) (1992) Risk Management in Defence Procurement. Ref. D/DPP(PM)/2/1/12.

Ministry of Technology (1969) Report of the Steering Group on Development Cost Estimating (The Downey Report). HMSO: London.

Mitchell GH (1993) *The Practice of Operational Research*. John Wiley: Chichester.

Morgan MG and Henrion M (1990) *Uncertainty: A Guide to Dealing with Uncertainty in Quantitative Risk and Policy Analysis*. Cambridge University Press: Cambridge UK.

Morris PWG (1979) Interface management: an organisational theory approach to project management. *Project Management Quarterly* **10**.

Morris PWG (1988) Managing project interfaces—key points for project success. In *Project Management Handbook*, 2nd edition (eds DI Cleland and WR King) Van Nostrand Reinhold: New York, pp. 16–55.

Morris PWG (1989) Initiating major projects: the unperceived role of project management. *International Journal of Project Management* **7**: 180–185.

Morris PWG and Hough GH (1987) *The Anatomy of Major Projects: A Study of the Reality of Project Management*. John Wiley: Chichester.

National Audit Office (1986) Ministry of Defence: Control and Management of the Development of Major Equipments. Report by the Comptroller and Auditor General, No. 568. HMSO: London.

National Economic Development Office (1982) Target cost contracts: a worthwhile alternative. HMSO: London.

Neil JM (1986) *Construction Cost Estimating for Project Control.* Chapter 1: Estimating case study: the Montreal Olympics complex. Prentice-Hall: Englewood Cliffs, NJ.

Newland KE (1997) Benefits of project risk management to an organisation. *International Journal of Project and Business Risk Management* **1**: 5–14.

Niwa K and Okuma M (1982) Know-how transfer method and its application to risk management for large construction projects. *IEEE Transactions of Engineering Management* **29**(4): 146–153.

Oakes M (1986) *Statistical Inference: A Commentary for the Social and Behavioural Sciences.* John Wiley: New York.

Omsen AH (1992) Improving the management of development projects. *Proceedings of the 11th INTERNET World Congress: Project Management without Boundaries,* Florence, Italy, June INTERNET, Zurich, Vol. 2, 259–268.

Padman R and Smith-Daniels DE (1993) Early-tardy cost trade-offs in resource constrained projects with cash flows: an optimisation-guided heuristic. *European Journal of Operational Research* **64**: 295–311.

Palisade Corp. (1997) *@RISK and @RISK for Projects* are produced by Palisade Corporation, Newfield, New York.

Parkinson CN (1957) *Parkinson's Law and Other Studies in Administration.* Random House: New York.

Payne S (1994) Tightening the grip on passenger ship safety—the evolution of SOLAS. *Naval Architect* E.482.

Pearson A and Brochhoff K (1994) The uncertainty map and project management. *Project Appraisal.* **9**: 211–215.

Perry JG and Hayes RW (1985) Risk and its management in construction projects. *Proceedings of the Institute of Civil Engineers* **78**(1): 499–521.

Pidd M (1996) *Tools for Thinking: Modelling in Management Science.* John Wiley: Chichester.

Pike RH and Ho SSM (1991) Risk analysis in capital budgeting: barriers and benefits. Omega **19**: 235–245.

Pitagorsky G (2000) Lessons learned through process thinking and review. *PM Network* **14**(March): 35–40.

Powersim AS (1993 and later) Powersim software. From Powersim AS, PO Box 206, N-5100 Isdalsato, Norway.

Primavera (1995) Monte Carlo 3.0 is produced by Primavera, Bala Cynwyd, PA 19004-1586, USA.

Project Management Institute (1986) *Measuring Success: Proceedings of the 18th Annual Seminar/Symposium of the Project Management Institute.* Montreal, Canada, September.

Project Management Institute (1987, 2000) *Project Management Book of Knowledge* (PMBOK). Project Management Institute: Upper Darby, PA.

Pugh P (1987) Where does the time go? A review of development time scales for aircraft and guided weapons. Paper given at Development Time Scales: their estimation and control, Royal Aeronautical Society Symposium, February.

Ragsdale C (1989) The current state of network simulation in project management theory and practice. Omega **17**: 21–25.

Reams JR (1990) Substantiation and use of the planned schedule in a delay analysis. *Cost Engineering* **32**(2): 12–16.

Richardson G (1996) Problems for the future of System Dynamics. *System Dynamics Review* (Summer) **12**(2): 141–157.

Riggs JL, Brown SB and Trueblood RP (1994) Integration of technical, cost and schedule risks in project management. *Computers and Operations Research* **21**: 521–533.

Robinson J (1987) Comparison of tendering procedures and contractual arrangements. *International Journal of Project Management* **5**(1): 19–24.

Rodrigues A (2001) The application of System Dynamics to project management—an integrated methodology (SYDPIM). Unpublished PhD thesis, University of Strathclyde, Glasgow, UK.

Rodrigues A and Bowers JA (1996a) System Dynamics in project management: a comparative analysis with traditional methods. *System Dynamics Review* **12**(2): 121–139.

Rodrigues A and Bowers JA (1996b) The role of System Dynamics in project management. *International Journal of Project Management* **14**(4): 213–220.

Rodrigues A and Williams TM (1997) System Dynamics in software project management: towards the development of a formal integrated framework. *European Journal of Information Systems* **6**: 51–66.

Rodrigues A and Williams TM (1998) System Dynamics in project management: assessing the impacts of client behaviour in project performance. *Journal of the Operational Research Society* **49**: 2–15.

Rouse WB (1982) On models and modellers: N cultures. *IEEE Transactions on Systems, Man and Cybernetics* **13**: 257–267.

Rubin RA (1983) *Construction Claims: Analysis, Presentation, Defense.* Van Nostrand Reinhold: New York.

Russell RA (1986) A comparison of heuristics for scheduling projects with cash flows and resource restrictions. *Management Science* **32**: 1291–1300.

Russell C.S Elmaghraby ES and Graham JH (1992) An investigation of a standard simulation-knowledge interface. *Proceedings of the 1992 Winter Simulation Conference*, 807–815.

Saaty TL (1998) Reflections and projections on creativity in operations research and management science: a pressing need for a shift in paradigm. *Operations Research* **46**(1): 9–16.

Salapatas JN and Sawle WS (1986) Measuring success of utility projects: past, present and future. In *Measuring Success: Proceedings of the 18th Annual Seminar/Symposium of the Project Management Institute.* Montreal, Canada, September, 67–76.

Sasieni MW (1986) A note on PERT times. *Management Science* **32**: 1652–1653.

Schtub A (1986) The trade-off between the net present cost of a project and the probability to complete it on schedule. *Journal of Operations Management* **6**: 461–470.

Schultz RL and Sullivan EM (1972) Developments in simulation in social and administrative science. In *Simulation in social and administrative science: overviews and case examples* (ed. HK Guetzkow) Prentice-Hall: Englewood Cliff, NJ.

Schwartzkopf W (1995) *Calculating Lost Labor Productivity in Construction Claims*. Apsen Law & Business: Gaithersburgh, New York.

Scott RF and Simmons DB (1975) Predicting programmer group productivity—a communications model. *IEEE Transactions on Software Engineering* **SE-1**: 4.

Scott S (1993) Dealing with delay claims: a survey. *International Journal of Project Management* **11**: 143–154.

Senge P, Kleiner A, Roberts C, Ross R and Smith B (1994) *The Fifth Discipline Fieldbook: Strategies and Tools for Building a Learning Organization*. Doubleday: New York.

Shafer G (1976) *A Mathematical Theory of Evidence*. Princeton University Press: Princeton, NJ.

Shenhar AJ and Dvir D (1995) Managing technology projects: a contingent exploratory approach. *Proceedings of the 28th Annual Hawaii International Conference on Systems Sciences*, IEEE, 494–503.

Shooman ML (1983) *Software Engineering—Design Reliability and Management*. McGraw-Hill: New York.

Sietsman K (1994) The project cube: a three-dimensional approach to project classification. *Proceedings of the INTERNET 12th World Congress on Project Management*. Oslo, June 284–289.

Simon HA (1982) *Sciences of the Artificial*, 2nd edn. MIT Press: Cambridge, MA.

Simon P, Hillson D and Newland K (1997) *PRAM: Project Risk Analysis and Management Guide*. APM Group Ltd: Norwich, UK.

Skogen S and Huseby AB (1992) Dynamic risk analysis—theDynRisk concept. *Proceedings of the 11th INTERNET World Congress: Project management without boundaries*, Florence, Italy, June INTERNET', Zurich, Vol 2, pp. 511–520.

Smith RP and Eppinger SD (1997) A predictive model of sequential iteration in engineering design. *Management Science* **43**: 1104–1120.

Soroush HM (1993) Risk-taking in stochastic PERT networks. *European Journal of Operational Research* **67**: 221–241.

Soroush HM (1994) The most critical path in a PERT network. *Journal of the Operational Research Society* **45**(3): 287–300.

Statman M and Tyebjee TT (1984) The risk of investment in technological innovation. *IEEE Transactions in Engineering Management* **31**: 165–171.

Steiner GA (1969) *Top Management Planning*. Macmillan: New York. Quoted on p. 481 of DI Cleland and WR King (eds) *Project Management Handbook*, 2nd edition. Van Nostrand Reinhold: New York.

Sterman JD (2000) *Business Dynamics: Systems Thinking and Modeling for a Complex World*. Irwin McGraw-Hill: Chicago.

Stjern M (1994) TIDUS—a practical approach to risk-oriented network scheduling. *Proceedings of the INTERNET 12th World Congress on Project Management*. Oslo, June, Vol. 2, pp. 629–634.

Stringer J (1992) Risk in large projects. Tutorial papers from Operation Research Conference 1992. Operational Research Society: Birmingham, pp. 29–46.

Syan CS and Menon U (eds) (1994) *Concurrent Engineering: Concepts, Implementation and Practice*. Chapman and Hall: London.

Tampoe M (1989) Project managers do not deliver projects, teams do. *International Journal of Project Management* **7**(1): 12–17.

Taylor A (1991) Article, The *Financial Times*, 9 April 1991, pp. 1, 8.

Thompson JD (1967) *Organizations in Action*. McGraw-Hill: New York.

Toffler A (1971) *Future Shock*. Bodley Head: London.

Tuman J (1986) Success modeling: a technique for building a winning project team. In *Measuring Success: Proceedings of the 18th Annual Seminar/Symposium of the Project Management Institute*. Montreal, Canada, September, pp. 94–108.

Turner JR (1993a) *The Handbook of Project-Based Management*. McGraw-Hill: Maidenhead, UK.

Turner JR (1995) The commercial project manager: managing owners, sponsors, partners, supporters, stakeholders, contractors and consultants. McGraw-Hill: Maidenhead, UK.

Turner JR and Cochrane RA (1993) Goals-and-methods matrix: coping with projects with ill-defined goals and/or methods of achieving them. *International Journal of Project Management* **11**: 93–102.

Turner JR, Grude KV, Haug T and Andersen ES (1988) Corporate development: balancing changes to people, systems and organizations. *International Journal of Project Management* **6**: 27–32.

Tverksy A and Kahneman D (1974) Judgement under uncertainty: heuristics and biases. *Science* **185**: 1124–1131.

US Army Corps of Engineers (1979) Modification Impact Evaluation Guide.

Ventane Systems Inc. (1988 and later) Vensim software. From Ventane Systems Inc., 60 Jacob Gates Road, Harvard, MA 01451, USA.

Wahlstrom B (1994) Models, modelling and modellers: an application to risk analysis. *European Journal of Operational Research* **75**: 477–487.

Ward SC and Chapman CB (1995) Evaluating fixed price incentive contracts. *Omega* **23**: 49–62.

Wheelwright SC and Clark KB (1992) *Revolutionizing Product Development: Quantum Leaps in Speed, Efficiency, and Quality*. The Free Press: New York.

White W (1982) A risk/action model for the differentiations of R and D profiles. *IEEE Transactions of Engineering Management* **29**(3): 88–93.

Wickwire JM and Smith RF (1974) The use of critical path method techniques in contract claims. *Public Contract Law Journal* (USA) **7**(1): 1–45.

Willcocks L and Margetts H (1993) Risk assessment and information systems. *European Journal of Information Systems* **3**: 127–138.

Williams TM (1990) Risk analysis using an embedded CPA package. *International Journal of Project Management* **8**: 84–88.

Williams TM (1992a) Criticality in probabilistic network analysis. *Journal of the Operational Research Society* **43**: 353–357.

Williams TM (1992b) Practical use of distributions in network analysis. *Journal of the Operational Research Society* **43**: 265–270.

Williams TM (1993a) Risk management infrastructures. *International Journal of Project Management* **11**: 5–10.

Williams TM (1993b) What is critical? *International Journal of Project Management* **11**: 197—200.

Williams TM (1993c) Taking the risk manager to 2020. *Proceedings of the 1st British Project Management Colloquium*, Henley-on-Thames, UK, December. Association of Project Managers: High Wycombe, UK.

Williams TM (1994) Using the risk register to integrate risk management in project definition. *International Journal of Project Management* **12**: 17–22.

Williams TM (1995a) A classified bibliography of research relating to project risk. *European Journal of Operational Research* **85**: 18–38.

Williams TM (1995b) What are PERT estimates? *Journal of the Operational Research Society* **46**: 1498–1504.

Williams TM (1995c) Holistic methods in project management. *Proceedings of the INTERNET Symposium*, St. Petersburg, Russia, 14-16 September, pp. 332–336.

Williams TM (1996a) The two-dimensionality of project risk. *International Journal of Project Management* **14**: 185–186.

Williams TM (1996b) Simulating the man-in-the-loop: a proposed way ahead for simulating systems under human control. *Insight* **9**(4): 17–21.

Williams TM (1997a) (ed.) *Managing and modelling complex projects.* Proceedings NATO ASI Series. Kluwer Academic Publishers: Dordrecht, the Netherlands.

Williams TM (1997b) The need for new paradigms for complex projects. In *Managing and Modelling Complex Projects* (ed. TM Williams). Proceedings NATO ASI Series, Kluwer Academic Publishers: Dordrecht, the Netherlands.

Williams TM (1997c) The risk of safety regulation changes in transport development projects. In *Managing Risks in Projects.* (eds K Kahkonen and KA Artto) E & FN Spon: London, pp. 284–293.

Williams TM (1999a) Towards realism in network simulation. *Omega* **27**(3): 305–314.

Williams TM (1999b) Seeking optimum project duration extensions. *Journal of the Operational Research Society* **50**(5): 460–467.

Williams TM (1999c) The need for new paradigms for complex projects. *International Journal of Project Management* **17**(5): 269—273.

Williams TM (1999d) Allocation of contingency in activity duration networks. *Construction Management and Economics* **17**(4): 441–447.

Williams TM (2003) Assessing extension of time delays on major projects. To appear in *International Journal of Project Management* in 2003. Also in Working Paper 2001/11 University of Strathclyde, Glasgow, Dept. of Management Science.

Williams TM, Ackermann FR and Eden CL (1997) Project risk: systemicity, cause mapping and a scenario approach. In *Managing Risks in Projects* (eds K Kahkonen and KA Artto) E & FN Spon: London, pp. 343–352.

Williams TM, Ackermann FR and Eden CL (2002) Structuring a disruption and delay claim. To appear in the *European Journal of Operational Research*.

Williams TM, Eden CL, Ackermann FR and Tait A (1995) The effects of design changes and delays on project costs. *Journal of the Operational Research Society* **46**: 809–818.

Williams TM, Goodwillie SM, Eden CL and Ackermann FR (1996) Modelling the management of complex projects: industry/university collaboration. UNESCO International Conference on Technology Management, (UnIG '96), Istanbul, June.

Wolff JG (1989) The management of risk in system development: Project SP and the New Spiral Model. *Software Engineering Journal* 481–491.

Wolstenholme EF (1990) *System Enquiry: A System Dynamics Approach*. John Wiley: Chichester.

Wolsteholme EF and Coyle RG (1980). Modelling discrete events in system dynamics models: a case study. *Dynamica* **6**(1): 21–27.

World Bank (1985) Tenth Annual Review of Project Performance Audit Results. World Bank: Washingon DC.

Wright G and Ayton P (Eds) (1994) *Subjective Probability*. John Wiley: Chichester.

Wynne B (1992) Science and social responsibility. In *Risk: Analysis, Assessment and Management* (eds J Ansell and F Wharton) John Wiley: Chichester, pp. 137–152.

Yang KK, Talbot FB and Patterson JH (1993) Scheduling a project to maximise its net present value: an integer programming approach. *European Journal of Operational Research* **64**: 188–198.

Yeo KT (1995) Strategy for risk management through problem framing in technology acquisition. *International Journal of Project Management* **13**: 219–224.

Yin RK (1994) *Case Study Research: Design and Methods*. Sage: Thousand Oaks, CA.

Yogeswaran K, Kumaraswamy MM and Miller DRA (1998) Claims for extensions of time in civil engineering projects. *Construction Management and Economics* **16**, 283–293.

Zack JG (1993) "Claimsmanship": current perspective. *Journal of Construction Engineering and Management* **119**(3): 480–49.

Zhi H (1995) Risk management for overseas construction projects. *International Journal of Project Management* **13**(4): 231–237.

Index